VIOLENCE A.
IN THE SC _ ... UF ITALY

Apulia, 1900–1922

Until Italian unification, vast areas of Apulia were an uninhabited sheep walk. In the late nineteenth century this frontier area was settled and agro-business established. In the quasi-colonial context of the South of Italy, the relations between landowners and farm workers were characterized by extreme forms of oppression and brutality.

This book is a study of the world the landlords made and of the harsh structures of profit, tenure, and climate they faced. It is also a powerful investigation of the appallingly grim conditions in the teeming agricultural centres of the region and a vivid history of the struggle by the farm workers to win the ordinary decencies of life – clothes, clean water, and bread. In the process, the labourers established one of the most potent revolutionary movements in modern Italian history. Since this movement was anarcho-syndicalist in orientation, the work seeks to explain the social bases of syndicalism in the period between the first general strikes in 1901 and the restoration of the landlords' power by fascist terror in 1922.

The book also confronts broader issues – the nature of the liberal state in Italy, the stunted development of the South, the weakness of the Catholic Church in the area, the working of latifundism as a labour repressive system of production, and the nature of fascism in general and in Apulia in particular.

*To the memory of my
friend Leo Leva*

VIOLENCE AND GREAT ESTATES IN THE SOUTH OF ITALY

Apulia, 1900–1922

FRANK M. SNOWDEN

*Lecturer in History, Royal Holloway and Bedford Colleges,
University of London*

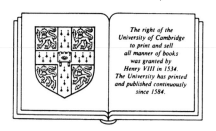

CAMBRIDGE UNIVERSITY PRESS

Cambridge

*London   New York   New Rochelle
Melbourne   Sydney*

PUBLISHED BY THE PRESS SYNDICATE OF THE UNIVERSITY OF CAMBRIDGE
The Pitt Building, Trumpington Street, Cambridge, United Kingdom

CAMBRIDGE UNIVERSITY PRESS
The Edinburgh Building, Cambridge CB2 2RU, UK
40 West 20th Street, New York NY 10011-4211, USA
477 Williamstown Road, Port Melbourne, VIC 3207, Australia
Ruiz de Alarcón 13, 28014 Madrid, Spain
Dock House, The Waterfront, Cape Town 8001, South Africa

http://www.cambridge.org

First published 1986
First paperback edition 2004

A catalogue record for this book is available from the British Library

Library of Congress Cataloguing in Publication data
Snowden, Frank M. (Frank Martin), 1946–
Violence and great estates in the South of Italy.
Bibliography: p.
Includes index.
1. Lane tenure – Italy – Puglia – History – 20th
century. 2. Peasant uprisings – Italy – Puglia – History –
20th century. 3. Facism – Italy – Puglia – History –
20th century. 4. Puglia (Italy) – Social conditions.
5. Puglia (Italy) – Economic conditions. I. Title.
HD679.P83S66 1986 322.4'4'094575 85-11675

ISBN 0 521 30731 7 hardback
ISBN 0 521 52710 4 paperback

CONTENTS

ILLUSTRATIONS

Note: Except for the map of Apulia, all these illustrations have
been reproduced from originals in the Archivio Privato Pavoncelli
at Cerignola by the courtesy of Count Pavoncelli.

PREFACE

The research for this book was made possible by the help of many people, and I am glad to have this opportunity to thank them. Dr De Lucia of the Soprintendenza Archivistica of Apulia was an invaluable source of information concerning the archives in the region. Franco De Felice and Luigi Massella also helped me to find source material. The staff of the Archivi di Stato at Bari and Foggia, and of the Archivio Comunale at Gravina, made every effort to assist me in locating documents. I am also grateful to Count Pavoncelli for his permission to consult the papers in the private Pavoncelli archive at Cerignola and for his generous hospitality. Family papers are all too rarely made available to scholars in Italy, and I have been very fortunate in being granted access to this extensive and valuable source.

Intellectual and moral support were also forthcoming from friends and colleagues. My thanks are extended especially to the following colleagues: Penelope Corfield, who read an early draft of the work and provided helpful suggestions; Francis Robinson and G.N. Sanderson, who gave enthusiasm and encouragement; and Jonathan Steinberg, at whose seminar the idea for this work began. The book was written with the constant interest and loving support of my wife, Smitty.

Finally, all research has financial foundations, and this project is no exception. Travel to archives in Italy was made possible by grants from the British Academy and the Central Research Fund of London University. My thanks to both of these institutions.

GLOSSARY OF ITALIAN TERMS

annarolo	A worker hired on a yearly basis by an estate.
carabinieri	Military police responsible for law and order.
curatolo	A hired estate manager.
demani	Common lands held in collective ownership.
fascio	A local branch of the fascist movement.
giornataro	Day labourer in agriculture.
latifondista	Proprietor of a great estate.
marina	The coastal zones of the region.
massaro	The commercial farmer leasing a large estate.
masseria	A farm. The term refers to the large units of cultivation into which a great estate is subdivided.
mazziere	Hired strike-breaker and hit man.
mezzadria	Sharecropping.
Mezzogiorno	The South of Italy.
opere pie	Catholic beneficent associations.
tratturo	A sheep highway across the Tavoliere.
ufficio di collocamento	Labour exchange and hiring hall.
usi civici	Collective rights of usage such as pasturage, tillage, fishing and gleaning.
versura	Neapolitan unit of measure roughly equal to 1.25 hectares.

INTRODUCTION

In the first quarter of the twentieth century, Apulia, with its population of 2,130,000 in 1911, was the only region in the South of Italy to produce an organized and powerful peasant movement. On the great latifundia that dominated the countryside of the Apulian interior, the farm workers launched a prolonged and combative campaign for the emancipation of labour. Consciously revolutionary in intent, the movement aimed at the institution of the right to work, the monopoly of the labour market, and the expropriation of the landlords in favour of producers' cooperatives. General strikes, land occupations, and local insurrections were the means of achieving this ambitious vision.

A major purpose of this work is to explain the rise of the farm workers' movement. During the period of great social and economic change marking the Italian industrial revolution and the commercialization of agriculture, peasants elsewhere in the South failed to create stable forms of political opposition to the power of the landlords. Despite appalling living conditions and brutal labour relations, they remained individualists. In Apulia, by contrast, the agricultural labourers exhibited a fierce determination to make their own history. The hypothesis is that their resistance was neither an irrational millenarianism nor a blind attempt to preserve antiquated social relationships. They attempted in a highly disciplined manner to experience economic development on their own terms rather than as its passive victims. An important problem is to explain the features of Apulian agricultural life which encouraged the emergence of a clear sense of class solidarity among those who worked the land.

1

To answer this question about a movement that has not yet found a historian, it is essential to reconstruct the texture of the labourers' lives in the teeming agricultural centres of the region. Wage scales, the work day, housing, rates of literacy, diet, gender roles, and causes of death are all important considerations. What were the relations among landlords, farmers, and labourers? How were the workers' lives affected by economic change, emigration, war, and the recurring crop failures of a backward and precarious agricultural system? Where possible, it is crucial to follow the descriptions the farm workers themselves provided of their experience in the direct testimony of proverbs, songs, and interviews. The aim is to undertake not the political history of the workers' movement but the social history of the society within which it emerged.

As the organization of the farm labourers in the region was anarcho-syndicalist in orientation, this work is also a study in the social bases of revolutionary syndicalism, which is still an under-developed area of Italian history. In the circumstances of early-twentieth-century Apulia, syndicalism was emphatically not a primitive protest marking a stage in the evolution towards a "mature" marxian socialist consciousness, nor was it a movement of uprooted petty bourgeois intellectuals. Syndicalism was instead a rational and disciplined response to the conditions the workers faced, and a denial of the bureaucratic reformism of the trade unions and the socialist party. The appeal of libertarian ideas, the effectiveness of direct action, organization by occupational grouping, and the general strike are all important considerations. Another purpose is to investigate the local issues raised, the sources of subversive ideas in a remote agricultural region, and the social groups most actively involved.

Since agrarian history cannot, however, be written exclusively "from the bottom up" by a one-sided attention to the agricultural labourers, it is essential also to consider the landed elite in equal detail. Only in this way is it possible to understand the logic of estate management and to explore the interface between landlord and field hand where politics had their origin. What were the profitability constraints within which farmers operated as Apulia was integrated into a national and international market? What was the movement of rents, prices, and costs? What were the mechanisms through which proprietors exercised their economic domination and their political control? What was their lifestyle, and how was it seen by the men and women they employed? What was the system of land tenure, and what were the methods of production? The impression is that it was not only poverty but also wealth that combined with the ubiquitous presence of hunger, debt, and early death to generate a sense of injustice and the idea of an alternative distribution.

Most of all, however, this book is a study of political violence. The reason is that violence was the essence of the relationship between landlords and farm workers in Apulia. The region earned a reputation as the "land of chronic massacres". Force was no accidental feature, but rather an integral part of labour discipline. Latifundism was fundamentally a labour repressive system of production. As political resistance to the system began increasingly to threaten the continuation of profit, deference, and hierarchy, violence escalated. As the unionization drive deepened and as massive strikes swept all before them, landlords turned from the individual violence of estate guards and overseers to the recruitment of gangs in the criminal underworld, the direct military occupation of cities, and the unleashing of a civil war to destroy the closed union shop. Here it is important to understand the uses of violence in the operation of Apulian latifundism. What were the instruments of violence and the changing forms that it took over time? It is hoped that such a study will have important implications for an understanding of latifundism and of the Italian Liberal state.

Since fascism was the final stage in the confrontation between proprietors and farm labour, the work is also, inevitably, a study in the social background to the rise of fascism. Fascism in Apulia had a long gestation period. Squadrist terror marked the end of the wave of strikes and demonstrations that began in 1901. The guns of Giuseppe Caradonna and Salvatore Addis drove subversion underground and reimposed the rule of property. Who supported this enterprise and how did it operate? What were the particular features of Apulian fascism?

1

WHEAT AND SHEEP

In 1900 the three provinces of Bari, Foggia, and Lecce were said to form "two Apulias". In a pattern common in southern Italy, coastal zones presented a sharp contrast with the interior. The coast, or *marina*, was an area of intensive cultivation of commercial crops (grapes, olives and almonds) grown largely by small peasant cultivators. Living standards were frequently low, but a number of factors inhibited political organization. These influences included a relatively stable social position for the peasants, steady employment for most of the year, long-term personal relations with the landlords, and the moderating role of the Church. In the *marina* a scattered pattern of settlement inhibited sociability, a complex system of stratification divided the peasants, and the dispersal of landownership blurred the lines of class cleavage. In such conditions the peasant remained an individualist. The *marina* was not an area of open class strife.

As a first approximation, one can define this zone as the southeast corner of Bari province – roughly the territory to the east of a line drawn from Bitonto to Alberobello – and most of Lecce province[1] except for: (1) the area of latifundia north of Taranto centred on the commune of Castellaneta and (2) scattered small wheat-producing enclaves, of which the most important was the zone surrounding Nardò. At the height of the rural agitation elsewhere in the region there was no organized peasant movement anywhere in this zone. The "father of Apulian socialism", Canio Musacchio, reported to the regional farm workers' congress in 1903, "Lecce province is unable to set up its own proletarian

5

1 Apulia at the period covered in this book.

organization."[2] In the local elections of 1920, when the left won
control of large areas of Apulia, not a single commune in Lecce
province returned a socialist majority. A recent study properly
refers to the "silence" of the peasants of Lecce.[3] When unionization did occur on a significant scale in the Salento after the
Great War, it took place only in such communes as Castellaneta
and Nardò, which were the southernmost extensions of the
latifundia rather than areas representative of the *marina*. The
marina, therefore, is marginal to our concerns.

The rest of the region – the "other Apulia" – was dominated by
great estates or latifundia. The heart of latifundism in Apulia was
the great plateau known as the Tavoliere, which was bounded on
the north and east by the Gargano Promontory and the Adriatic,
on the south by the Ofanto River, and on the west by the
Apennine Mountains. Covering 3,000 square kilometres in
Foggia province, the Tavoliere was a zone of highly concentrated
landownership. A representative case was that of Cerignola, the
storm centre of the peasant movement. Cerignola was among the
most extensive communes in Italy, with 61,000 hectares, two-
thirds of which were owned by just three families. Altogether the
landed interest comprised just 100 families. Similarly, in the commune of Foggia great estates covered 60 per cent of the 50,993
hectares of the territory, and 103 proprietors owned no less than
40,000 hectares.[4]

The holdings of such landlords were divided into smaller pro-
ductives units or *masserie*, which were typically 100–500 hectares
in size. The Apulian *masseria* was divided between extensive single
crop wheat cultivation and pasture through the regulating
mechanism of a backward and soil-depleting three-field rotation
(the *terziata*) consisting of two years of wheat followed by a year of
fallow. This antiquated cycle was common to the overwhelming
majority of farms. It was replaced occasionally by the still more
harmful *quartiata* – three consecutive years of wheat and one of
fallow.[5] The financial management of these estates was often
highly sophisticated, but the primitive methods of cultivation
were legendary – the absence of fertilization and irrigation; the

stunted development of animal husbandry; the use of archaic work tools such as the mattock, the sickle, the scythe, and a light and almost neolithic plough pulled by mules that literally scratched the surface of the soil; the year of fallow; the broadcasting of seed.[6] There were virtually no experimental farms or institutes of agronomy. The term latifundium and the antiquarian qualities of production are misleading, however, if they suggest that the estates were in any sense feudal survivals. On the contrary, the latifundia of the Tavoliere were a modern creation: they emerged in the second half of the nineteenth century on the crest of a speculative property boom.

Until unification, most of the plain had been an uninhabited sheep walk on which planting was forbidden by law.[7] The restrictive legislation was devised by Francesco Montaluber in the reign of Alfonso I of Aragon in the fifteenth century as an experimental fiscal measure designed to generate income for the crown through a levy on sheep brought to pasture from the Abruzzi. The sheep regime at the outset was a response to the demographic and social catastrophe of the fourteenth century, when famine, plague, the collapse of prices, and chronic insecurity had already led to mass flight from the land and the near destruction of Apulian agriculture. Cultivation, largely abandoned in practice, was formally restricted to a small number of authorized farmers – the *locati* – who planted fields of wheat in the midst of an immense permanent pasture. At its height, the Tavoliere accommodated 1,700,000 sheep. The very name Tavoliere originated with the Aragonese regulations. It was derived from the record books governing the tax on grazing – the *tavolae censurae*. Tavoliere originally, therefore, meant "customs zone".

The restrictive provisions, briefly interrupted during the Napoleonic era, were reaffirmed by the restored Bourbon regime in 1817. The Bourbons, fearful of change and opposed to modernization, sought to preserve the immobilism of the Kingdom of the Two Sicilies by sealing off the second largest plain in Italy from contamination by commercial and subversive influence. Identical provisions applied as well to the west of Bari province from

Spinazzola to Santeramo, where the social structures which emerged were identical to those of Capitanata. By the law of 26 February 1865, the Risorgimento, the Italian bourgeois revolution, abolished the four centuries of regulation and opened the Tavoliere to cultivation and the land to purchase. Foggia province in particular came to be known as the "Italian frontier", the "California of the South" and the "Texas of Apulia" as the scramble for land began.[8] A region of shepherds, commented a Bari newspaper, was transformed into a population of farmers.[9]

The process of deregulation had profound consequences for Apulian history. The Tavoliere provides a perfect illustration of Gramsci's analysis of the Risorgimento as a "passive revolution" imposed "from above" by the agrarian and commercial bourgeoisie of the North and Centre of the peninsula in alliance with the landed classes of the South without involving or benefiting the broad mass of the peasant population. Instead of attempting to use the disposal of the Tavoliere to create a broad base of popular support by creating a substantial class of peasant proprietors, Liberal Italy made its peace with the more backward propertied classes of the South. The Liberal common-land commissioner at Altamura in the 1860's, Vito Orofino, had hoped that the land settlement after unification would establish a democratic social system that would "demonstrate the advantages of the present free institutions to those citizens, now despised and ignorant, who will appreciate the difference between the old regime and the new".[10] Instead, Liberal Italy followed the course of least resistance by conciliating the powerful and wealthy notables eager to buy.

Financial exigency reinforced political expediency. After the burden of the wars of unification, the immediate priority of the new state with regard to the Tavoliere was to realize the maximum value from the sale of the land as rapidly as possible. The way to achieve this aim was to sell the property in large units to wealthy buyers with ready cash. Accordingly, disentailment was accomplished by legislation drafted hurriedly and rushed through parliament providing for the sale of large estates by public auction. The existing *latifondisti* – the former *locati* – were also confirmed in their holdings, which they were allowed to redeem from the state.

On the Tavoliere and in western Bari province, therefore, the early decades of unification concluded with the clear division of the population into two great unequal classes – the few landowners and the mass of the landless. In the observation of Orofino, Altamura was split between those with carriages and those without. Thereafter, there was little possibility, without active political intervention, of reversing the process. The sharp upward spiral in land values, the absence of agricultural credit, and a succession of crises in the last decades of the century placed landownership well beyond the reach of peasant proprietors. Virtually the entire plain was owned by just five hundred landlords.

By comparison with the North and Centre of the peninsula, there were severe limits to the productive potential of Apulia. The Tavoliere was far from expanding urban markets. The soil was hard and rocky, and the covering layer of topsoil was thin. The climate was forbidding: Apulia was notorious for its unreliable and badly distributed rainfall, violent storms, late spring frosts, and the strong prevailing wind from the south known as the Altina that swirled across the plain unbroken by any barrier of trees.[11] There was no supporting infrastructure of credit, marketing, and technical information facilities. The work force was unskilled, badly nourished, and illiterate. There was no dependable supply of water. The whole plain, moreover, was lethally infested with malaria. Most malarial of all was the zone between Foggia and the Ofanto River. As rivers dried up in the summer, they left stagnant ponds that were ideal breeding grounds for mosquitoes. The lack of drainage further encouraged the formation of deadly pools of water after the heavy rains that normally fell in late spring and in September.[12]

Thus the potential for modernization was hemmed in with constraints. The imitation of the fully rationalized northern farm was precluded. Within the more stunted context of the South, however, the Tavoliere stood apart because of the relative advantages that it afforded for the profitable cultivation of wheat. The virgin soil, for a start, promised high initial yields per acre. The terrain, furthermore, was flat and suitable for the introduction of machinery. Communications were easy, especially after the construction of the great Adriatic trunk-railway line. The rapid population growth in the region also created a new local market for grain. Finally, there was a substantial tax incentive. For the purposes of the land tax, holdings in the region were valued according to the cadastral survey of 1828 with no account taken of the economic transformation of the succeeding decades. As a result, estates in Foggia and Bari provinces were significantly under-assessed – to the benefit of landowners.[13]

In the circumstances, there was little room for the subsistence small producer, and the strategy adopted by the large landlords was passive. Their income was not a return on investment but an inflated rent earned by rack-renting. Such was the demand for land that there was often room for several layers of middlemen between the legal owner and the direct cultivator. Between unification and the agricultural crisis of the 1880's the movement of rent was steadily and dramatically upward. In Gravina, for instance, rent per hectare rose from 47 to 140 lire per year. During the crisis there was a sharp fall, followed by recovery at the turn of the century. In 1910 the annual lease for a hectare of land was about 100 lire – four times the land value in neighbouring Basilicata.[14] In Cerignola land sold in 1903 for 680 lire a hectare.

As a result, there developed at the top of the social pyramid a substantial class of *latifondisti*. The proprietors came from a variety of sources with previous interests in the region, as the leading families in the commune of Cerignola demonstrate. Some were ex-*locati*, like the Pignatelli. Others were sheep farmers from the Abruzzi such as the Zezza. There were also French notables involved in the wine trade, such as the Duke of Larochefoucauld and Léon Maury. Most of the new landlords were not notables, but "new men" from the world of trade and the professions.

2 Count Giuseppe Pavoncelli (1836–1910).

There is some evidence that banks were also involved in the purchase of land. Pointing above all to the Banco di Napoli, writers for the paper *Corriere della Puglie* reported that, by the new century, "Banks and agricultural credit institutions . . . have become the great *latifondisti*."[15]

The Pavoncelli family was the ideal type of the new proprietors. Giuseppe Pavoncelli was one of the most powerful of all Apulian landlords. Possessor of one of the great fortunes in the region with net assets worth 16,000,000 lire in 1903,[16] Count Giuseppe Pavoncelli was the deputy from the Cerignola constituency without interruption from 1874 until his death in 1910, and was briefly minister of public works.[17] Founder and president of the Cerignola Agrarian Association, he held the municipal council in his pocket, exercising a local rule known to his opponents as *Pavoncellismo*.

The family position was established by Giuseppe Pavoncelli's father Federico, the son of a silversmith at Foggia. Federico Pavoncelli moved to Cerignola in the 1830's, married the daughter of a local grain merchant, and took over the family business. He rapidly edged out rival Genoese merchants in Apulian markets and then made his fortune during the Crimean War, when he won the contract to supply the allied armies with wheat. He and his son used the proceeds to speculate in land on the Italian frontier. In a speech to his constituents, Giuseppe Pavoncelli later described himself as a "pioneer" who tamed the "wild", building cities and turning barren moors into farmland. "I administer eight hundred families", he announced in a letter. "They are poor people, as ignorant as the day is long, and they owe everything to me."[18] Federico and Giuseppe Pavoncelli, however, continued to manage every aspect of the family concerns personally. In this respect they were atypical. The Apulian landlord was normally an absentee speculator who performed no role in the agricultural cycle. Agriculture for him was not a vocation but a sideshow in a career in Rome, Naples, or Paris, where he took a degree in law or medicine. Instead of investing in Apulia, he mortgaged the land to finance other pursuits.[19] The landlords' bulletin *L'Agricoltore*

Pugliese itself painted an unflattering portrait of the typical *latifondista*:

> Under the present system a wealthy landowner always lives far from his holdings and knows nobody except his ignorant and unreliable administrator. In fact, almost all of our wealthy *latifondisti* do not know their properties, preferring the great cities where they enjoy their rents in idleness and pleasure.[20]

The landlords' interest in Apulia were normally left in the hands of an administrator, who was a lawyer, accountant or doctor charged with purely non-agricultural functions – negotiating leases, collecting rent, and paying taxes.[21]

So distant were the legal owners of the land that the local usage was to apply the term "landlord" (*proprietario*) to the leaseholding farmer – the *massaro*.

The *massaro* was an entrepreneur engaged in short-term financial speculation who assumed the management of the estate. The lease he held was normally for three to six years – the length of one or two crop cycles – and was not normally renewed. Even one-year contracts were common.[22] The result was "a rapid turnover, a game of musical chairs, a continuous change of characters on the rural scene who rise up and then disappear again".[23] The leaseholder was frequently a man with no experience of farming at all and no association with the community he entered. He was an outsider with savings or access to credit – a lawyer, doctor, or businessman who wanted to try his fortune in an Apulian gamble.[24]

As a temporary figure in the local economy, the *massaro* had no incentive to improve or even to preserve. His calculations of profit and loss stretched no further than a three-year period. Inevitably, therefore, he enjoyed no personal bonds with the community or with the men he employed. There was no reason for a long-term concern with productivity, stable labour relations, or the condition of the soil. Like the landlord, moreover, the leaseholder was crassly ignorant of the science of agriculture. He had no understanding of seeds and fertilizers, of the selection of animals, of the principles of land drainage, of the use of machines, of the techniques of crop rotation. In such circumstances, the *massaro* exercised an unhappy influence on Apulian farming. His entrepreneurial activity was purely speculative – the agricultural equivalent of strip-mining. He allowed buildings to deteriorate, spending only what was necessary to keep them standing, and ignored the maintenance of roads and the hygiene of wells. The leaseholder denuded the property of trees; overworked and underfed farm animals (mainly mules); neglected the draining of water; and failed to remove weeds and parasites. If the landowner was not vigilant, the *massaro*, in the local phrase, "cultivated in full",[25] omitting the fallow, and planting wheat or oats uninterruptedly throughout the years of his tenure. In this fashion the exhaustion of the soil proceeded systematically, and investment was reduced as far as possible to zero.[26]

So little attempt was made to apply a rational agricultural practice that the Tavoliere was frequently described as an automatic machine for the production of crops without human intervention.[27] The *massaro*, that is, ploughed the earth, scattered seed, and then entrusted the rest to nature. In local slang he was known as "the sower": he cast the seed, and did nothing more.[28] Success and failure depended on the elements. Farming was a game of chance, a throw on the roulette wheel. The effects of such neglect were dramatic. Describing the commune of Troia in the southern reaches of the Tavoliere, the newspaper *Il Foglietto* outlined a situation that was emblematic of wheat farming throughout Apulia. The paper commented,

> The condition of agriculture here is enough to make one cry. Technical training is non-existent and superstition rules. Yields are very low and of miserable quality . . . Wages are rock bottom and the peasants live in utter poverty. There is an absolute lack of capital, and mortgages and debts total four to five times the value of the property . . . Absenteeism is complete. Everything unites to make farming the permanent source of many evils.[29]

The short-term lease was the ruin of agriculture. Correspondingly, social relations were deeply embittered both up and down the social scale. The dealings between landlords and leaseholders were poisoned by conflicting interests over rent and the upkeep of the property. Their affairs were conducted in the midst of an unending stream of litigation. "Vampire" and "harpy" are the epithets used by owners to describe the entrepreneur.[30] It was standard practice for the landlords to regard the *massaro* as the villain of the countryside, responsible for the backwardness of cultivation and for the vulnerability of agriculture to the vagaries of the Apulian climate.

The relations between farmer and worker were still more impersonal and fraught with tension. There was no tradition of paternalism, no common stake in the future, no spirit of cooperation. Nor did the *massaro* enjoy the authority derived from the performance of a visibly useful entrepreneurial role. On the contrary, the *massaro* was actively engaged in destroying the soil and reducing the prospects of employment. Furthermore, pressed on all sides by a high rent, a less than buoyant market for wheat, and the acute uncertainties of the harvest, he engaged in extremely sharp practice with his men. Altogether, the *massaro* lived by the local proverb, "To farm is to die; to make deals is to live."[31] His greatest skill, that is, was not farming, but the management of men. Labour was the one variable in production over which he could exercise control.

2

DAY LABOUR

The work force was divided into two distinct and unequal categories. The distinction reflected the very uneven demand for labour under the prevailing system of backward single-crop dry farming. Percentage figures for land use in Foggia province (Capitanata) in 1913 reveal the overwhelming reliance on wheat, the "king of the fields"[1] (see Table 1)[2].

Table 1. *Percentages of land use in Foggia province, 1913*

Wheat	Pasture	Vineyards, olive groves	Woodland	Other
51.6	30.2	6.3	6.7	5.2

Table 2. *Land use in five communes in Bari province, 1929 (in hectares)*

Commune	Total area	Area under wheat	Pasture
Altamura	41,686	17,828	21,800
Gravina	41,701	22,765	15,012
Minervino	25,137	15,189	6,970
Santeramo	13,984	9,365	2,575
Spinazzola	17,810	10.390	6,093

17

3 View of the Tavoliere, 1903.

The absolute domination of the wheat/sheep alternation emerges clearly also from the pattern of land use in 1929 in five communes in Bari province where latifundism prevailed (see Table 2).[3]

Under this single-crop system the demand for labour at peak periods in the cycle of cultivation was intense. At harvest time the need for hands far outstripped the capacity of the resident population, and it was necessary to import thousands of workers from other provinces. Conversely, in the off season for wheat the labour market totally collapsed. The normal calendar for wheat production in Apulia was the following:

August/early September	ploughing
October	sowing
December	turning over the soil
March	weeding
late June/July	harvesting
July	threshing

In this cycle, even if one allows for the additional tasks performed on the fallow, which was ploughed three or four times during the year, the period from December to March constituted the slack season when the estates provided employment for only a skeletal labour force for the few jobs that continued year-round. A nucleus of fixed workers, or *annaroli*, was therefore hired on an annual basis. The *annaroli* were stable hands, warehousemen, shepherds, ploughmen, and carters. These men were an elite separated entirely from the mass of casual hands. Since the roads became impassable for weeks at a time during the rainy winter, it was essential that the *annaroli* be resident on the land. They lived in barracks on the property, returning to town only once a fortnight to purchase supplies.

Since it was in the growers' interest to secure the loyalty of the year men and to create a barrier between the contract workers and the rest, farmers normally recruited the fixed personnel from the *marina* rather than from the local population. The *annaroli* were normally of skilled peasant origin. They enjoyed a variety of privileges. They alone had steady employment for relatively high wages, plus rewards for good performance. The *massari* also granted the *annaroli* small plots of land on the estate – classically a *versura* (1.25 hectares) of eroded soil – on which to plant vegetables to supplement their income. Frequently farmers provided the contract workers with medical attention at their own expense and furnished them with meat when work animals died. *Annaroli*, furthermore, could reserve work for their own relations at harvest time, and after the harvest their wives and daughters were permitted to return to the fields to collect any stalks of wheat that had not been gathered in. Finally, the *annaroli* exercised supervisory functions over the day labourers. The ploughmen and carters served as overseers and recruiters for the work gangs, and were widely known as the "corporals" because of their task of enforcing discipline. To the casual hand, the corporal was "a little tyrant" charged with ensuring the observance of an oppressive social system.[4] To complete the military terminology, the work gangs were known as "companies" (*compagnie*).[5]

In this fashion a definite hierarchy was established on the *masserie*. The *annaroli* were the NCO's of the estates. Above them were the stewards, who guaranteed that the operational decisions of the *massaro* were carried out. The chief manager was the *curatolo*, the highest salaried official. His duties were to give the orders of the day to the work gangs, to keep accounts for pay day, to enforce discipline, and to prevent theft. In these tasks he was assisted by his deputies, the *sotto-curatoli*, and by the private estate guards. Both guards and *curatoli* were mounted and armed with whips and rifles.

Beneath the "corporals" clustered the much more numerous category of day labourers or *giornatari*. To understand the tensions of the Apulian countryside, one should note that the massive dependence on casual day labour set Apulia apart from the rest of the South of Italy. Nowhere else in the Mezzogiorno was the work force so homogeneous or so comprehensively proletarianized. By the turn of the century the vast majority of the agricultural population consisted of casual hands hired in the piazzas at dawn.

Census figures for 1901 illustrate this point abundantly, even if it is necessary to treat statistics in this period with reservation. The techniques for gathering information were poorly developed, especially south of Rome. The respondents' capacity to understand questions asked in the foreign language of Italian and the bureaucratic patois of the census takers is suspect. The categories and terms changed from one census to the next, so that the assessment of trends over time is often impossible. The results frequently conflicted with more specialized and sophisticated local investigations. The returns, therefore, must be approached with caution. In the absence of more reliable data, however, they provide suggestive indications, if not conclusive evidence. After these warnings, one finds valuable clues in the 1901 statistics which are supported by other sources. In the agricultural centres of Foggia and Bari provinces – Foggia, San Severo, Cerignola, Andria, Ruvo, Santeramo, Minervino Murge, Gravina, Canosa – between 70 and 85 per cent of those engaged in agriculture were landless day labourers. In Cerignola, "the citadel of subversion in Apulia", figures for the adult male agricultural population of 9,476 were the following:

peasant proprietors	301
leaseholders	185
sharecroppers	24
salaried yearly workers	399
day labourers	7,947
shepherds	427
other	193

Such a radical simplification of the social structure had important political implications. Only by recalling the importance of *giornatari* in Apulia – a feature noted by all observers – can one explain the success of revolutionary class-based political movements in establishing their presence. On the Apulian latifundia there was a sociological foundation for a strong horizontal sense of collective unity. Elsewhere, divisions of bewildering complexity were built into social relations. Workers in other regions of the South were not proletarians but poor peasants: they sold their labour, but also worked as sharecroppers, leased tiny plots, or even owned a postage stamp of land.[6] This was the phenomenon some historians of the Mezzogiorno term "role fragmentation". As a result, it was difficult for peasants in most of southern Italy to establish class solidarity. Marx's often misleading observation that the peasantry stands united "like a sack of potatoes" had a clear social foundation.

The absence of substantial intermediate strata of peasant proprietors, leaseholders and sharecroppers also closed the political safety valve of upward social mobility. There were few examples of men who by toil, initiative, and good fortune were able to gain land of their own. Between the narrow circle of proprietors and the mass of the landless there was an unbridgeable void.

The Apulian *giornatari* were not peasants but genuine agricultural proletarians. Their separation from the land was total and permanent. They subsisted entirely by selling their labour by the day. They worked one day for one employer and the next day for another.[7] Although employed as farm hands, they lived not on the land but in large agro-cities. In 1901 Bari and Foggia provinces had ten cities with populations of over 30,000 inhabitants. Adria and Cerignola – with populations respectively of 50,000 and 34,000 at that date – were classic examples of such cities populated almost exclusively by farm workers.

In those communes literally no one except for the fixed personnel of the *masserie* lived outside the city limits. The census of 1901 revealed this striking feature of the Apulian countryside. In Italy as a whole, 37.9 per cent of the population resided either scattered across the land or settled in bourgs and hamlets of fewer than 500 people. In the Po Valley and in central Italy the majority of people lived in this fashion – 57.7 per cent in Ferrara province and 62.5 per cent in Siena. The contrast in Apulia was dramatic. Foggia province provided the lowest percentage of dispersed inhabitants in Italy – 5.5 per cent. In the commune of Cerignola, one of the most extensive in the nation, with an area of 61,889 hectares, there was not a single village or settlement apart from the city itself. In the commune of Andria in 1911, only 2,693 people in a total population of 53,284 lived outside the city limits.[8] In the zones of latifundism in Apulia, the countryside presented a vista of utter and unbroken desolation in which a traveller could journey for miles without encountering a house, a tree, or a living soul. The Tavoliere plain was "so uninhabited as to resemble a deserted moor".[9]

Concentrated in towns in such an uncompromising manner, the farm workers were further proletarianized in owning no work animals and few tools, in working as individuals rather than as members of a family unit, and in having lost the traditional skills of a peasant. Most, for instance, no longer knew how to plough or to tend vineyards. They were unable to spin or to weave. They performed only unskilled heavy manual labour and so earned the epithet of *zappatori* – the "diggers". In the words of the unemployment commissioner for Bari province, the Apulian farm worker "merely carries out the physical tasks that he is ordered. He is a manual labourer in the literal sense of the word, and has no understanding of agriculture."[10]

Skilled jobs in the crop cycle were reserved for migrants from the *marina*, who were authentic and knowledgeable peasant cultivators. At Cerignola in 1907, for instance, the Agrarian Association explained to representatives of the local workers that the resident population was unfit for such tasks as grape-picking, grape-pressing, pruning, and the transporting of goods. For these chores the landlords required "workers from other towns, who are more handy". Furthermore, every traditional source of subsistence outside the market place was abolished through the enclosure by the great estates of common lands formerly belonging to the communes. Such traditional rights as gleaning, gathering wood, and fishing were extinguished. The Apulian *giornatari* lived entirely by joining the work gangs recruited before dawn in the piazzas.

The gang system itself favoured the development of class solidarity. Large groups of men working together for weeks at a time shared ideas, experiences, and information. Furthermore, there was no divisive job stratification. Wage differentials applied only to tasks performed at different seasons of the year. Harvesting in the summer, for instance, commanded a higher pay than weeding in the spring. Within the gang assigned to a particular job there was no internal hierarchy according to skill, diligence, or seniority. All were treated as unskilled and sometimes anonymous field hands working at the same task for the same money. There was no prospect of reward or promotion. The bonus given by the management for conscientious effort in the commune of Cerignola was described by the day labourer Giuseppe Angione. On Saturday, which was pay day, the men claimed their wage packet from the overseer and the landlord's bailiff, who handled the money. As Angione pictured the scene,

The overseer knew all the workers. Next to him was the bailiff, and both of them were illiterate. Every now and again the overseer nudged the bailiff with his elbow and said "This one's a good worker", and as a reward they let him put one finger into a tin of grease known as serbum so that he could take a fingerful to put on his shoes. Since our shoes were a thick leather, and we worked in the fields in the open, in the damp, the leather got hard, and we needed that grease. That was the bonus for good performance. But heaven help the man who asked for two finger-fuls: he was sacked.[11]

Under such conditions, it was a small step for the labourers to view their plight as a collective one. In this sense, the work experience was a social leveller. The organization of work helped to form a common bond in the fields.

If the facts of sociology created a potential for organization, the conditions of life provided ample motive for political militancy. In the speculative gamble that was the essence of farming on the Tavoliere, the *massaro* had sufficient means to ensure that the risks were borne almost exclusively by the labourers while the profits were entirely his. The economic means were several: the prevailing crop system; the growing disproportion between an expanding population and the relatively inelastic demand for labour; the utter lack of resources of the *giornatari*; and the absence of any economic activity apart from agriculture. For the labourers, access to the land was on the basis of radically unfavourable terms. With a sole crop determining the pattern of employment, the winter months were a period of universal hunger and unemployment in the towns of the Tavoliere, where the workers took to their beds for days at a time. The winter months, in the words of the parliamentary enquiry, were a "period of painful suffering".[12] A man who ate every day was reckoned to be wealthy, and his sons were "catches" in the local marriage market. In an average year an able-bodied farm worker could expect employment for a maximum of 280 days a year, with 250 normally considered the minimum for subsistence. In a year of failed harvest, there was famine in the towns.[13]

In theory, the winter trough in the demand for labour was balanced by the high season when the Tavoliere enjoyed the reputation of being the "El Dorado of the South" with wages that reached the dizzying heights of 2½ or 3 lire a day. Even if every worker were inclined to the necessary far-sighted frugality to save for the off-season, such wages were illusory. In practice the *massari* used the unevenness of the agricultural cycle as a form of wage control. The techniques were simplicity itself. One was the debt mechanism. During the winter and throughout the years of drought, the farm workers regularly ran up massive debts in order to survive. The phenomenon, as a parliamentary enquiry revealed in 1909, was universal: "The Apulian peasant is born in debt, and lives and dies the same."[14] With interest rates of 60 per cent for five months in Andria or Cerignola, the only way to settle accounts was to work in the coming season at rates well below the market wage, or even for meals alone.[15] The latter practice was standard, and was known officially as "free contracting", and more colloquially as "catching the wolf by the belly". As early as 1876 the deputy prefect at San Severo explained the usefulness of the debt mechanism to the landlord. The *latifondista*, wrote the official, "does nothing to mitigate the harsh conditions of his unfortunate hands. On the contrary, he makes use of hard times to put the workers into debt in order to render them unable to demand a fair wage for their toil."[16] A specific instance was described by a lieutenant in the *carabinieri* in the same San Severo district:

Taking advantage of the general misery, the landlords speculate on the labour of the impoverished workers. The farm hands are driven by hunger to go to work for nothing but their meals. And even these are inadequate, consisting of about 850 grams of bread a day, plus a jug of olive oil and a kilo of salt a month.[17]

In any event, the confrontation in the labour market between the "corporals" and the *giornatari* was fundamentally unequal. The workers were hungry, indebted, and in competition both among themselves and with a flood of migrants. In 1905, for example, 104,000 migrant workers arrived in Capitanata at harvest time from Basilicata, the Abruzzi, and the *marina* to profit from the seasonal El Dorado.[18] Having arrived in such force in the agricultural centres of the Tavoliere, they slept rough in the streets, on church steps, at the entrances to public buildings and private palaces. There they waited for the labour market to form in the central square.[19]

The resulting intense competition was revealed in the ritualized discipline of the piazza in the small hours of the morning. There were no bargaining and no discussion. Terms were offered, and those willing to accept them simply stepped forward to join the teams. Agreements, in any case, were invariably oral, and this fact too allowed scope for abuse. Often the men set off with a contract to work but no predetermined wage rate. The employer undertook only to pay what he could afford when the job was done.[20] In the course of negotiations with local workers, for example, the Cerignola Agrarian Federation stressed the point that "In agriculture it is not generally possible to fix wage levels in advance."[21] Furthermore, the corporal required a tip – the infamous "deposit" (*caparra*) that alone ensured a place in the gang.[22]

Since payment was by the day, the work itself was stretched to its natural maximum – from sunrise to sunset or, in the Apulian expression, "from sun to sun".[23] Regardless of the distance of the fields from town, the work teams were expected universally to begin their chores at dawn. To arrive punctually at daybreak, the workers left town at three or four in the morning, making the long trek to the fields with their work tools on their backs. It was the job of the women to keep vigil by turns throughout the night to keep their sons, brothers, and husbands from oversleeping. Thus roused, the men and boys departed into the darkness to travel distances of as much as ten or twelve kilometres on foot.

On a normal day, the initial work stint began at first light and lasted until nine o'clock. There was then a break of half an hour for breakfast. Work resumed at nine-thirty and continued until noon.[24] The teams were allowed two hours for lunch. For the rest of the day the corporals were expected to enforce a steady work rate under the baking Mediterranean sun, where temperatures regularly climbed above forty degrees centigrade at harvest time. Only at sunset was it permissible to down tools, and even then the men could not depart until they had knelt in compulsory prayer.[25]

Having said their prayers, the men were free to set off on the return journey back to town. By the time they reached home they had worked for twelve hours and walked up to twenty kilometres. The *giornataro* Giuseppe Angione from Cerignola recalled,

When you got home you were too tired even to unlace your shoes. Your wife undid them and took off your socks while you started to eat. You fell asleep over your food and tumbled into bed. Then your wife would be there, saying "Get up there! You're due on the job!"[26]

For good reason the Apulian lullaby "Child, Child" that mothers sang to their daughters painted this picture of daily life:

> Child, child,
> Don't marry a digging man.
> It's you for sure
> Who's up first in the morning.
> You put on your dress
> And put out the beast of burden.
> When your man comes home
> He finds his beans
> And he leaves them.
> He falls on the bed,
> His mouth twisted to snore
> And his legs spread apart.[27]

In this fashion the work day was fully filled throughout the crop cycle. During the harvest season in late June and early July, when the task was most pressing and the daylight hours longest, similar thought was given to the work week. Then the contract normally ran for two or three weeks during which the labourers were forbidden to return to town or to observe Sunday or other holidays. During this period the estates provided no transport and frequently no accommodation. Workers slept rough in the fields or found shelter in the stables with the work animals or in filthy barrack rooms. If bad weather or the breakdown of machinery stopped work, there was no compensation for the time lost in the field. If a worker fell ill, he found his own way home.

Furthermore, wages were invariably partly in kind – in the form of three meals a day. The meals consisted of bread and water twice daily in the fields, plus wine at harvest time when the work was most intense. In the evening there was *acquasale* – a soup consisting of hot water flavoured with salt, a few drops of olive oil, and – sometimes – vegetables. The workers drank this gruel with their bread. If one is to judge by the insistent demand of the labourers that the bread be of "good quality" and that the wine be "drinkable", the adulteration of food was a handy means to devalue wages.[28] Such was the inadequacy of the provisions that workers regularly ate wild plants and weeds, especially the weed native to southern Italy known as *ruca* ("rocket salad"). Agreed pay-scales in any event were nominal, and account should be taken of the system of fines used to guarantee productivity. Minor infractions were punishable by pay deductions and the withholding of rations. More serious offences led to instant dismissal and blacklisting. In the words of the mayor of Altamura, "relations cease with a stubborn and ungrateful worker".

The inadequacy of the labourers' real wages was recognized by all concerned. The landlord and deputy Antonio Jatta wrote in 1901:

To stress the insufficiency of wages is like pushing on an open door. No one any longer doubts the necessity and the justice of the demand for an increase. But whose fault is it if we are all bound to a poor and ailing industry that does not leave the margins we would wish to pay the workers?[29]

"Mean and derisory" was the description given by the Barletta landlord Carlo Romussi.[30] At Foggia in 1906, the socialists calculated that the average year-round daily wage of a *giornataro* in the commune was 0.70 lire. The following were the daily pay-scales of other members of the community:

peasant	1.50 lire
cotton operative	1.50
primary-school teacher	2.50
bricklayer	2.50
blacksmith	3.00
doctor	6.00
magistrate	8.00

| infantry captain | 8.00 |
| public prosecutor | 33.00[31] |

The average pay for the farm labourers was based on a combination of the various seasonal rates and the months of idleness. Daily wages for adult men for various particular tasks, agreed after the 1901 strike, were:

sowing	2.25 lire
tending fallow	1.50
spreading fertilizer	2.00
killing mice	2.00
mattocking	
January to March	1.50
March and April	1.70
May	2.00
winter work	1.50
summer work	2.00[32]

In terms of purchasing power, the pay scales must be related to the major expenditures in the labourers' budget. Bread, the only regular item in the diet, cost from 0.35 to 0.45 lire a kilo on the Bari market in 1907, with 330 grams per person per day estimated as the minimum survival ration. Flour cost 0.34–0.35 lire per kilo for third quality and 0.38–0.40 lire for the best.[33] Other food stuffs, based on the market at S. Paolo di Civitata in northern Foggia province in 1908, were:

pork	1.80 lire per kilo
lamb	1.30
goat's meat	1.40
beans	0.35
pasta	0.60
olive oil	2.00 lire per litre
wine	0.10[34]

Rent at Foggia ran at approximately 0.35 lire a day per room. Clearly the prevailing levels of pay were wages of hunger. It is important, furthermore, to remember that Foggia was privileged in comparison with many of the smaller and more remote communes of the province. There were places where adult men worked for 0.40 and even 0.30 lire a day.[35] Celenza Malfortore was such a place. Even in the boom year of 1904 the normal wage for a day in the fields did not rise above 1.29 lire. In the terse comment of the mayor, such pay was "inadequate for the necessities of life".[36]

The workers' diet at home, scarcely better than the regimen they received in the fields, demonstrated the general impoverishment. For three-quarters of the year meals consisted of grain products – poor-quality pasta and bread – supplemented with broad beans cooked without salt, fruit and wild plants gathered in the countryside. Holidays were marked by the luxury of good flour, and by the appearance of chick-peas and green beans mixed with the pasta. Only on Christmas and at Easter – and not always then – was there meat. Eggs, milk, coffee and sugar were unknown luxuries. In the slack season there was frequently nothing. "Here", commented the socialist paper *Avanti!*, "there is real, authentic, permanent hunger".[37]

The worst effects of all, however, were produced by child labour, which was universal. Boys normally went to work from the age of eight or nine, when they left home and school for weeks at a time to join the work gangs for half the pay of adult men. It was the boys who received the most brutal treatment. The *curatoli* managed adults mainly by means of economic sanctions and the threat of sacking. Children, too, were afraid of dismissal. They were afraid of being sent back to town across unknown fields in the dark, afraid of encountering the watch dogs employed to deter vandals and thieves, afraid of confronting their families empty-handed. Children were less able, however, to remember the economic imperative throughout a twelve-hour day. Their attention drifted and – especially in the afternoons – they left clods of earth unbroken and weeds unpulled.

The corporals established a regime of terror to keep their minds focused. The boys were sworn at throughout the day. They were beaten or threatened with cudgels, and unfortunate lads were made to run the gauntlet between lines of foremen who lashed their backs with their belts. The latter technique was known as the "blood line". More ingenious overseers devised special systems of public humiliation and intimidation, such as making a careless boy who had missed weeds pull out the offending plants with a string tied one end to the stalks and the other to his penis while the work gangs looked on at the spectacle.

Such treatment had profound consequences for the physical welfare of the juvenile labourers, and still more far-reaching influences on family life, religion, and morals. Removed from friends and family to be entrusted to the care of the rustic Fagins who recruited the work teams, the boys learned little except to steal, to carry knives and to hate their employers. Writing about child labour in an article entitled "Sad Capitanata", the agricultural authority Antonio Lo Re commented, "The poor boy lives several long months away from his family and has about him not a single friendly person to help him and to give him a cheering word. Almost invariably maltreated, he grows up like a weed and turns out devious, ignorant, and wicked."[38]

Poverty was especially harsh for all because there was no regularized system of social security or poor relief.[39] The existing measures of social welfare, which provided accident, disability, and old-age compensation, applied only to industrial workers. Peasants and farm workers were specifically excluded. Unemployed or disabled farm labourers could expect no assistance. The lack was all the more acutely felt because of the early age of superannuation. Only young people could perform the back-breaking toil with the short-handled mattock. By the age of fifty, those *giornatari* still alive were regarded as already unemployable. The fortunate few found light work in the stables, where they earned the same half pay as eight-year-old boys.

Occasionally municipal governments intervened. Town hall records reveal that small sums were sporadically granted to provide food or medical attention to individual citizens. Such payments, however, were on a purely *ad hoc* basis, and were insignificant in relation to the needs of the population. They established no right to assistance, and should be seen as political patronage rather than welfare. In years of drought and mass unemployment some communes also set up soup kitchens and launched public works projects with emergency funds supplied by parliament. Again, however, such relief was limited and occasional. There was no ongoing provision for the chronic needs of a permanently impoverished population.

The only other system of relief was the network of Catholic beneficent organizations – the *opere pie*. Through the *opere pie* some attempt was made to provide a variety of services for the indigent – orphanages, shelters for the blind, medical care, and asylums. Such services, however, were painfully insufficient. The *opere pie* were unequally and irregularly distributed and communes in possession of a beneficent association were the exception rather than the rule.[40] Furthermore, the income of the Catholic charities, based on revenue from estates they owned and sporadic grants from local government, was notoriously inadequate, particularly since the beneficent associations allocated most of their available resources for devotional functions rather than material aid. Feast-day celebrations, funeral services, dowries for orphan girls, masses – all had first call on the available money.[41] Often, too, as the deputy prefect at San Severo noted, the bureaucratic processes involved in the actual distribution of aid were painfully slow. All too commonly, according to the official, "Assistance (in itself inadequate) arrives too late and is therefore useless."[42]

In many cases the standard of care provided was severely deficient. An example was the Russo Hospital at Cerignola. There free medical attention for a population of 35,000 depended entirely on the services of a single elderly surgeon, Dr Casale. Casale had been hired on the strength of the qualification that, of the applicants for the post, he alone had been willing to accept the salary of 900 lire a year that the charity was prepared to pay. The attentions of this septuagenarian surgeon were such that the Russo Hospital was the terror of the populace. Anyone with money travelled to Naples for treatment, and most of the poor preferred to suffer untreated at home. Casale was said to regard his scalpel as a scourge to punish the godless and the subversive.[43]

At Gravina, too, the mayor complained that the services provided by the local charities were scandalous. The bulk of the funds of the beneficent associations was absorbed in "labyrinthine bureaucratic procedures". What little remained was spent on a shelter for handicapped paupers and an orphanage. The orphanage had a wholly insufficient number of places and operated as a recruiting ground for the brothels of the city. The shelter presented "an inhuman and horrible state of affairs" in which ill men slept in foul cellars and attempted to subsist on starvation rations.[44]

A further difficulty was that the charities were often seen by farm labourers as an instrument of the employers. The *opere pie* were legally accountable to the local authorities, and their boards of governors were invariably chosen from the ranks of the landed classes. A characteristic case was the San Severo orphanage, where the president of the board was the Marchioness Concertina Maselli, the wife of the largest landlord in the commune. Many men and women refused to deal with bodies so constituted. In the failed harvest of 1912 the soup kitchens at San Marco in Lamis remained empty. At Cerignola the poor refused bread, commenting with pride that they wanted work, not charity.[45]

Such misgivings on the part of the poor are better understood if one recalls that charity was sometimes used by employers and town hall as a weapon. In 1905 at San Marco, for instance, the town council refused to distribute emergency relief funds, even though they had been provided by central government. The reason was the desire to punish the local labourers, who had the temerity to demonstrate and to organize. Nothing in the way of assistance was done, the authorities informed Foggia, "because of the opposition of the leading families of the ruling class. They have taken up an attitude of resistance against the workers, whom they regard as unworthy of aid."[46]

For the vast majority of the population, the only available recourse was therefore self-help. The elderly, the blind, and the unemployed eked out their lives by depending on their families for support. Such support was not always forthcoming. To have an elderly parent was a calamity for the young. The alternative to the extended family was begging. There were reports of whole armies of mendicants who roamed from door to door.[47] Many people simply starved to death. Marasmus – sheer starvation – was the tenth leading cause of death in Apulia, and it claimed its victims disproportionately among the aged.[10]

3

GRAPES

The planting of wheat from the 1860's marked the great transformation of Foggia province and of the interior of Bari province.
Wheat remained the dominant and, in many zones, the only crop
wherever latifundia prevailed. In a more restricted area, however,
a second and later change took place. This was the establishment
of vineyards, which occurred in the late 1870's and the 1880's.
Grapes were cultivated at the southern extremity of the Tavoliere
and in the northeast of Bari province – from Cerignola to Bitonto
and from Canosa to Barletta. Grapes were also grown in the commune of San Severo in the far north of the Tavoliere.

In this grape belt, which was dominated by great estates run by
latifondisti and capitalist farmers, a combination of crisis and
opportunity led to the new departure. The crisis began with the
completion in the late 1870's of a single world market through the
development of modern transport and communications facilities.
The immediate consequence for Apulian farmers was the massive
importation of cheap wheat from America. The results were a
major decline in the price of wheat and a crisis of profitability. In
the long term, profits were to be maintained artificially by tariff
protection, culminating in the great tariff of 1887.

In a limited area, however, the combination of special opportunity and a favourable topography encouraged wheat growers to
respond to the crisis by converting a portion of their holdings to
vineyards. The opportunity was provided, firstly, by phylloxera,
which began to destroy the vineyards of France from 1875. The
prospect of capturing the rich French wine market opened vast

4 The Tavoliere, *ca.* 1900: Harvesters at work under the surveillance of mounted estate guards.

new possibilities for profit. A fortuitous topographical factor was the fact that the zone between Cerignola and Bitonto was one of the rockiest and most calcium-rich soils in Europe, ideally suited to vines, whose roots could go deep in search of water. Finally, the completion of the railroad link at the start of the 1870's was vital because grapes are a highly perishable crop that requires good transport facilities.

The obstacle to the conversion was financial. The planting of vineyards was an enormously labour-intensive process beyond the resources of landlords who had just sunk their available funds in the purchase of land and the planting of wheat. The problem was compounded by the circumstance that vineyards were a long-term investment which would yield no returns for an initial period of several years. Furthermore, there were substantial risks involved in the venture because of the uncertainties of the export trade in an era of rising protectionism and because of the danger of the spread of the vine lice to Italy.

The solution adopted was elegant in its simplicity. Landlords were able to afford the conversion from wheat to grapes by not paying for the process at all. The costs and risks were overwhelmingly transferred to the work force through the device of a harsh and ingenious leasing agreement known as an "improvement contract". Under the improvement scheme, an open competition for access to the land was first publicly announced by the estate owner. The landlord then chose at will among those who came forward, certain in the knowledge that the land hunger and lack of bargaining power of the workers would secure favourable terms.

The winners, known as *versurieri* (after the southern measure of the *versura* – 1.25 hectares) were day labourers promoted to peasant status with a poor man's imitation of proprietorship. The plots they were awarded were, as the name implied, dwarf holdings of one or two hectares that were inadequate to absorb the tenants' labour for a substantial portion of the year. Instead, the peasant continued to work as a day labourer for most of the year, devoting himself to his plot only during the off-season. During the slack period the *versurieri*, now possessing the incentive of a long-term interest in the land, undertook the prodigious labour of clearing the ground, digging trenches, and planting vines. Instead of receiving compensation, they paid rent.

The improvement contract was normally a lease for a period of twenty-five to twenty-nine years.[1] Even though the vineyards yielded a product only after an initial period of three to five years, payment of rent often began at the outset. Then, at the expiration of the lease, the vineyards – now fully productive – reverted to the landlord. The contract was never renewed. The landlord opted instead to continue cultivation with day labourers. The *versuriere* was evicted and thrown into the piazza to seek work from the corporals as a full-time proletarian. In Gaetano Pavoncelli's description of the system devised by his father, "At the end of the term [of the contract] the leaseholder is obliged to give up the land and all its improvements with no right to any compensation by the Estate."[2]

During the twenty-five-year period, the terms of the lease protected the long-term interests of the estate owners. The landlord was concerned that the vineyards consisting of many tiny individual plots would be of a uniform quality, and that their arrangement would eventually permit cultivation as a single large unit. He also looked to the profitability of the wine cellars that constituted his own major capital outlay. It was clearly important that the grapes supplied to the cellars should be furnished at low cost, in predictable quantities, and of a known quality. These interests were all safeguarded by the contract at the expense of the tenant. A variety of detailed provisions ensured a low level of remuneration – "derisory" is the description of the historian of this process – for the peasant, and vested control securely in the hands of the owner. For good reason Giuseppe Tammeo, a student of Apulian agricultural contracts in the late nineteenth century, wrote of the "iniquity of the improvement contracts", which transformed agriculture without investment – through the naked exploitation of the peasantry.[3]

The contract removed decision-making entirely from the *versuriere*. Every phase of improvement and cultivation was carried out under the strict supervision of an overseer appointed by the owner. The overseer gave instructions regarding the depth and site of trenches, the selection of plants, the spraying and pruning of vines, and the harvesting of grapes. If any aspect of cultivation departed from the landlord's specifications, the overseer reserved the right to have the work performed by men of his own choice at the tenant's expense. Furthermore, the peasant was required to sell his product exclusively to the cellars belonging to the estate owner, on the dates and in the quantities determined by the landlord.[4]

On this basis the most rationalized and intensively cultivated sector of Apulian agriculture was established. In the process the social structures but not the crop system of latifundism were instituted. Part of the grape zone (the communes of Cerignola, Trinitapoli, and S. Margherita) was located on the southern Tavoliere. Most of the area, however, was south of the Ofanto in

Bari province. Here the sheep-walk regulations were never applied. Nevertheless, many of the features which followed in the wake of the vineyards produced conditions closely resembling those in Capitanata. Landownership was highly concentrated just as it was on the Tavoliere. Here, too, there were such features as a sudden influx of population; a boom in land prices; the creation of such agro-cites as Barletta, Ruvo, and Andria; the formation of a wholly landless agricultural proletariat; and all of the social problems which resulted from the overwhelming of the urban environment. In the grape zone there was also a chronic problem of overpopulation and acute competition in the labour market, with the attending abuses of low wages, the corporal system, harsh conditions in the fields, and moneylending. Andria, in its own way, was a booming frontier settlement with an urban social structure and urban social problems identical to those of Cerignola. As Presutti remarked in drawing up the parliamentary report, there was a "resemblance in the material and moral conditions" between the Tavoliere and the grape belt. "It seems strange indeed", he wrote, "that . . . the condition of the peasants here should resemble those of the relatively distant towns of the Tavoliere plateau rather than those of the neighbouring towns of the coast."[5]

One feature which distinguished the grape-growing communes from the wheat-producing centres of the Tavoliere, however, was the existence of two major crops. Alongside the vineyards, extensive wheat cultivation on *masserie* continued in the now familiar manner. The establishment of vineyards north and south of the Ofanto in this fashion had consequences which made labour relations in this area particularly volatile. The coexistence of wheat and grapes in the communes between Cerignola and Bitonto provided the farm workers of the grape belt with a security and continuity of employment not present in the areas of single-crop wheat cultivation. The cycles of wheat and grape production were staggered, with the result that the period of employment during the year was extended. The calendar for grape growing was:

January/February	first digging
May	second digging, ensulpheration
August	third digging
September/early October	harvesting.

Vineyards, furthermore, required more continuous attention throughout the year than wheat. Thus at Cerignola the labourers found work for 290 days a year on average, as compared with the norm of 250 days in Foggia commune, where wheat was the only crop.[6] Finally, vineyards, unlike wheat fields, could not be readily mechanized. Therefore the workers had a greater capacity for resistance and control of their terms of employment.

As a result, the bargaining-power relations between capital and labour were different in the grape belt from those prevailing in the single-crop wheat communes. The day labourers in the grape-producing area had a larger measure of independence and larger reserves with which to support organizations of their own. They also had a higher level of skill than the workmen who cultivated only wheat. Furthermore, the political consciousness of workers in the zone was sharpened by the sudden expropriation en masse of the *versurieri* at the turn of the century when the improvement leases expired. It was no accident that the two greatest centres of subversion in Apulia – Cerignola and Andria – were both located in the grape belt.

4

THE COMPANY TOWN

Thus far we have considered only the relations between workers and employers in their official economic roles. To appreciate the depth of the feelings aroused, one has to remember that they met again in town. The Apulian *giornataro* had the double disadvantage of combining rural and urban poverty. The "agro-cities" were classic company towns. Landlords owned urban property as well as land, and they used the settlement boom to extract a sizeable unearned surplus. Towns like San Severo, Cerignola, Andria, and Spinazzola had expanded at breakneck speed. The urban infrastructures, however, had not kept pace. The social structure of the Apulian city – a "human beehive" in the words of the socialist Gaetano Salvemini – was highly abnormal. "Pathological" is the term used by one paper to describe Cerignola.[1]

The agro-town normally had an elegant high street lined with the palaces of the local *signori*, the theatre, the churches, and town hall. The Corso at Cerignola was typical. There stood the cathedral, built at the turn of the century to suggest the great Duomo in Florence; the Manfredi family home, which was finished in 1908 in imitation of the palaces along the Grand Canal in Venice; the grand Mercadante Theatre; and the Ducal Palace of the Larochefoucauld family with its elegant bell tower. These and other monumental buildings served as a "curtain of stone"[2] that hid the surrounding workers' quarters and gave an illusion of grace and elegance to the town.

Stretching out on all sides from the Corso, as from similar high streets throughout the zones of latifundism, was a network of

5 Cerignola, 1900: A team of workers spraying the vineyards.

narrow and unpaved mud tracks that, in the absence of a sewage system, served as communal cesspools. Such was the stench that it was reported to be impossible to cross the road without being overcome with nausea. On either side of such streets there crowded the rows of limestone workers' barracks that the press described as "rabbit hutches".[3] These dwellings were built and let by the same families who owned the land.[4] Here the labourers lived without light or water, squeezed at the rate of ten people to a single squalid, windowless room five metres square that served at once as living room, kitchen, bedroom and lavatory. A room normally, commented one landlord, was not even suitable for use as a stable.[5] The streets themselves, where the children spent their days, were said to be "like paradise in comparison with the inside of the dwellings".[6]

The fearful degree of overcrowding in the cities of the region is indicated by comparative figures for the number of dwellings occupied on average by every hundred families in the ninety-two

Italian cities with a population of more than 20,000 inhabitants.[7]
The national average was 96 dwellings per 100 families. Some
representative non-Apulian communes were:

Turin   100
Bologna   96
Pisa   101
Rome   84
Naples   100
Reggio Calabria 106
Catania   100

In Apulia the ratio reached its lowest levels, as the following sample
communes in the region suggest:

Andria   69 (lowest in Italy)
Foggia   79 (second lowest in Italy)
Cerignola   82
San Severo   83
Canosa   86
Barletta   89

Worst of all were the notorious subterranean dens known as
"grottoes", which were a peculiarly Apulian amenity. Nationally,
only eleven occupied dwellings per thousand were subterranean.
At Cerignola the figure was 95, at Foggia 98, at Andria 188.
Terlizzi established the national record with a proportion of 284
underground dwellings per thousand. Altogether 500,000 people
in the region lived in damp, filthy and airless cellars in 1911.[8] Of
all the evils of peasant life in Apulia the grottoes were regarded by
the commissioners carrying out the parliamentary enquiry in 1909
as the most unjustifiably inhumane.[9]

Rents for such accommodation reflected the alarming
imbalance between supply and demand. At a time when workers
earned 1½ lire a day for 250–280 days a year, the average annual
rent per room on the Tavoliere stood at over 100 lire, ranging
from 40 to 250 lire. It was standard practice, moreover, for property owners to demand a year's rent in advance.[10] Not surprisingly,

the occupants did without furniture, or a change of clothes, and slept on mats of straw – men, women, and children from more than one family together in utter disregard of privacy.[11] Since the workers possessed neither plots nor allotments, they also shared their rooms with any domestic animals it was their fortune to own – chickens, a pig, a donkey. The workers' quarters at Cerignola were commonly known as the "pigsty" because of the large numbers of pigs that lived with the tenants[12] and because of the ubiquitous filth and evil smell. In the working-class neighbourhoods of Bari the local press estimated that 90 per cent of the dwellings were unfit for habitation.[13]

Lucia Barbarossa, a day labourer at Cerignola, recalled the quality of the farm workers' lives in the town:

We endured a lot in our time. Life was tough, really tough. You didn't have a change of clothes. You'd come home from the fields with your clothes soaking and your shoes broken, and you stayed in them. You stayed just as you were. At home three or four families slept all together. I saw you, and you saw me, and you would cover yourself . . . And the poor kids, they didn't have bread, or anything.

When I went to the *masserie* in the country, I left my five children behind. Someone would give them a bite, and some else a bit of bread. And I went far away – to Manfredonia, where they worked with machines . . . We went to pick grapes and load them up. Oh, what a life, what an ugly life we led . . . In those days . . . husband, wife and all the children slept together. And they shared their beds with lice, fleas, and bed bugs. You could barely live – three, four families all squeezed together.

When you got home you ate an anchovy. We bought those, and put them on our bread. Then we sat by the door and ate, and that was what we had. What did we know of soup in those days? We didn't know about anything. Four, five children, the mother and the father all ate from the same plate, and sat on the floor because there weren't any chairs.[14]

The Lucera radical weekly *Il Foglietto* described the process which produced such severe housing conditions, with particular reference to San Severo:

Here, all at once, there was a flood of settlers from all the surrounding communes . . . In the meantime, no preparations had been made to house thousands of newcomers, with the result that any hovel, basement, or shed was turned into a dwelling. When these proved insufficient, poorly constructed houses and single-room shelters were built, giving offence not only aesthetically but even to common sense. These too were let for a king's ransom. Who cared about sturdiness or appearances, as long as the demand was met! And we can only wish that there had been enough of them.

Instead we find a new situation that is fatal to public health. Families of peasants are forced to live in homes even before they have been fully built . . . Accommodation here is let before the foundations have been laid! . . . But even then a man's pay is not enough to cover the rent.[15]

This account is comprehensible if one recalls the rush of settlement. The number of day labourers in the city of Foggia increased sixfold between 1881 and 1901, according to the estimate of the proprietor Angelo Fraccacreta.[16]

The absence of water was a further hardship. In most agricultural centres in Bari and Foggia provinces, water was brought to town in barrels for sale by merchants. In the summer and in years of drought the cost of water was a major item in the labourers' budget. The consequences for health were serious. The union organizer Giuseppe De Falco explained,

Cleanliness! Hygiene! Dreams, illusions! Cleanliness is impossible without its principal component – water.

Down here, remember, people die of thirst. Only those few who can afford water, which sometimes costs more than wine, ever wash their faces.[17]

Here were serious sources of misery. More importantly, for our purposes, urban poverty linked economic hardship with an explosive charge of resentment. It was not poverty alone that produced political subversion, but the juxtaposition of social extremes. Apulia was also a region of great wealth. One of the contradictions of Apulian society was that, with the exception of

6 Cerignola, *ca.* 1900: A street in the workers' quarters of the city.

Naples and Palermo, Foggia province had the highest per capita income in the South – 1,787 lire per annum in 1904.[18] The difficulty was the radical inequality of distribution.

The squalid life of the labourers was eked out in close proximity to the expensive amusements put on by men of substance to provide distraction from the tedium of provincial life. The *signori* entertained themselves by hunting, training horses for their car-

riages, racing thoroughbreds, and gambling. They imported the
finest English fabrics and competed to outshine one another in a
whirl of masked balls, cotillions, gala concerts, and – the last word
in fashionable society – the English garden party. Leaseholders
who had made their fortune vied with each other in ostentatious
display. From the point of view of social stability, wealth came too
quickly and too plentifully.[19]

The commune, too, obliged by putting on seasons of operas and
concerts at the local theatre, which "offered a marvellous sight
because of the rich luxurious dresses and hair styles of the
ladies".[20] There was no need to leave Trani, Molfetta or Taranto
in order to enjoy *La Bohème, Cavalleria Rusticana*, or *I Pagliacci*.[21]
Then there was the café world, where musicians brought from
Naples provided an evening out. Proprietors with more exotic tastes
travelled abroad – to Russia to buy furs or to Serbia to collect cats
with eyes of unusual colour.[22] A measure of the glamorous lifestyle of the wealthiest landlords is the fact that the family expenses
of the Pavoncellis in 1903 amounted to 38,000 lire. They lived in a
villa valued at 100,000 lire, although the official and still more
stately family residence was in Naples.[23]

The agro-city brought together not just two distinct and unequal social classes, but two entirely separate civilizations between
which there was no comprehension, no communication, and no
sympathy. The landlords represented the cultural universe of the
European city as they had imbibed it in the southern metropolis at
Naples. They were urbane, spoke Italian and often foreign
languages as well, travelled, possessed university degrees in law or
architecture and would have felt at home in Florence, Milan, or
Paris. They shared only physical proximity with the labourers,
who inhabited an entirely separate cultural and psychic space.

To gentlemen, the farm workers were utterly beyond the pale
of twentieth-century European society. They were wild,
unwashed people who lived underground with their animals, and
spoke an impenetrable dialect. The workers believed in magic and
committed savage crimes. Even northern socialists sympathetic to

their plight regarded the Apulian day labourers as primitive barbarians, as children to be taught and civilized. Southern landowners looked upon them with a mixture of fear and condescension. They referred to the farm hands pejoratively as *cafoni* and *terroni* – "kaffirs" and "clods". The Apulian landlords resembled European settlers in the colonies. They imagined themselves in the wilds of a dark and dangerous land. The pioneering, frontier ideology implied a civilizing mission not only to the land but also to its inhabitants. The colonial analogy alone conveys the cultural abyss that divided the classes.

For the labourers, in their turn, there was a deep resentment of the contempt and the airs of the proprietors, who adopted the deportment, and demanded the outwards signs of respect, that befitted their image of a traditional aristocracy. As a parvenu nobility with freshly acquired titles, the Apulian proprietors assumed the grand manner. On the rare inspection tours that owners made of their property, for instance, they insisted that the labourers should bow and kiss their hands. Everywhere proprietors displayed utter disdain for manual labour. Even the infamous *ius primae noctis*, the claim of a landlord upon the virginity of peasant women in his employ at their betrothal, was occasionally exacted.

In a more settled rural order, social inequalities of such proportions could be accepted as part of a seemingly eternal system. To the extent that they were resigned to their lot, peasants in such a stable world accepted their position because it was the society into which they were born. The established order rested upon the unspoken ideological force of tradition and the appearance of inevitability. In Apulia, however, the agricultural labours on the latifundia were new arrivals who saw all too clearly that a new society was in the process of being constructed *de novo*. In this environment the relations between farmers and workers had a deep potential for conflict. Incomprehension and fear on both sides led to antipathy, which was repaid with compound interest.

With virtually no middle strata, the class divide was sharply drawn, and was accentuated by the subsidiary ventures of the owners – moneylending, the truck system, urban property-letting, and organized prostitution. The lack of a substantial middle class was central to the social relations of the region. In the words of Giuseppe Pavoncelli, "Only shopkeepers, professionals, and a handful of workers manage to live any better than the generality of the population."[24] Indeed, this was the factor to which the deputy from Cerignola attributed the rise of subversive politics in the region.[25]

The explanation for this pronounced bipolarity of the social structure of the major centres was the absence of any major economic activity independent of agriculture. The 1936 census, which laid particular stress on occupational patterns, made this point clearly. In Foggia province at that date the active population over ten years of age was engaged in the following branches of activity:

Agriculture	119,434
Industry	36,557
Commerce	7,442
Transport	2,855.[26]

The preponderance of agriculture is evident at a glance. The figures for people involved in industry, trade and commerce, however, are misleading in the suggestion of independent sectors in the economy. The mass of the non-agricultural population consisted in fact of impoverished builders, petty producers, and vendors who provided the necessities of life for the farming population – food, clothing and housing. To them one needs only to add the narrow circle of professionals who tended to the needs of the farmers for legal, commercial, and medical services. There was no factory production whatever. In 1911 only 6,911 horse-power of machinery were employed in the whole of the province.[27] In Capitanata industry consisted of mills at Foggia and San Severo, wine cellars at Cerignola, and scattered saw mills, olive presses, brick works, and pasta plants employing, 4,827 people in 1912.[28] The "industrial workers" listed in the census were construction workers and artisans – tailors, cobblers, bakers, black-smiths, hatters, masons, and barbers. Similarly, those involved in commerce were precarious retailers, trading more often from market stalls or hawking their wares in the streets than operating from fixed shops.[29]

Gravina in 1908, therefore, was a typical Apulian agro-city. The mayor, Sergio Marcalli, described the economy of the commune as based exclusively on agriculture. Commerce and industry were "rudimental" concerns run on a family basis solely for the purpose of local consumption by the field hands and their employers. Every activity was directly linked to farming.[30]

The relationship of the sparse middle strata to the day labourers was not, however, without political consequence. The tradesmen and vendors added a bitter edge to urban poverty. The retailers were moneylenders to whom the workers' families were invariably indebted. Since a labourer was paid on a weekly or fortnightly basis, his family managed its daily needs on credit, especially during the slack season. Frequent sources of personal tragedy were the taverns – "always full and not only on holidays" – where farm workers lost their wages and ran up debts drinking and gambling at the card game of *zecchinetta*. Although their own living standards were far from luxurious, tradesmen and retailers were further separated from the labourers by the possession of a tiny garden plot where they grew vegetables for market, by a higher degree of literacy, and by a sense of relative social privilege. The narrow middle strata were also clients of the ruling political faction, which controlled the granting of licences and dispensed patronage. The petty bourgeoisie of the towns was the source of recruitment for the municipal police, the employees of urban contractors, and the excise men.

In addition, retailers profited at the expense of the labourers from the laissez-faire policy of local government. Since town hall made no effort to enforce health regulations or to protect the interests of consumers, the market was the scene of every form of abuse and negligence. There were normally no scales, so that 800 grams became a kilo. The bread was kneaded with unwashed feet, and the loaves were regularly filled with surprises. Flour was subject to every manner of chemical experiment. Wheat flour was augmented with less expensive varieties, such as rice, barley, and oats, and then stretched further by the addition of clay, sand, chalk, and pulverized marble. The resulting mixture was next bleached with copper sulphate and alum to make it appear white. It was then stored improperly in damp cellars, and was sold infested with mites and their excrement. When a single miller enjoyed the monopoly of a captive local market, even appearances were often neglected, as laboratory tests on produce sold in Gravina demonstrated. The flour there was described as reddish yellow in colour, coarse, heavy, sour tasting, and nauseating to smell.[31]

Meat at the market stalls was often beyond identification. The flesh of horses that had died of disease, of superannuated goats masquerading as lamb, and of fish in an advanced state of putrefaction was sold at exorbitant prices. The vegetables were sometimes lethal after being grown in untreated human waste used as fertilizer and after being sprinkled with night soil to freshen them up for market day. Everything was covered with flies, except the water. The water instead often originated in contaminated and uninspected wells. It was then transported in unwashed barrels, and arrived cloudy, foul-tasting, and teeming with life.[32]

A final corrosive of social relations was the conduct of local government. The commune was a family affair of the propertied classes, with the electorate restricted by a property-based franchise until 1912. A few hundred notables and their clients were the grand electors in cities with populations of tens of thousands. Local government in the company towns of the region became a national scandal. As the state authorities in the zone of San Severo reported, "Here politics, for the big landlords, is confused with private interest, with profit, with greed . . . Neglect, waste, and maladministration – these are the words that describe the practice of nearly every commune in the district."[33] "Acute municipalitis" is the description of the malady afflicting the region.[34]

To read the minutes of the meetings of the executive of the

town council of Cerignola is to appreciate the distance between the councillors and the populace.[35] 1912, for instance, was a year of drought and, therefore, of large-scale unemployment and suffering. The hardships of the citizens, however, found no echo in the deliberations of city hall. During the year no plans were drawn up to deal with the emergency, and no collective measures were taken to alleviate the human misery involved. Such matters as hunger, compulsory idleness, disease, and debt were never discussed.

The executive committee (the *giunta*) had other preoccupations. It considered personnel changes within the local administration, the appointment of new officials, and their salaries. Regular meetings discussed the granting of licences for shops and stalls in the market. The councillors arranged the terms for contractors engaged to pave the streets, construct new military barracks, repair public buildings, and collect refuse. They approved the per diem expenses of officials; established electoral lists; set the level of local taxes; granted subsidies to the local Mercadante Theatre for its season of concerts; and gave assistance to a handful of individual citizens in favour with the administration. Finally, the executive agreed, in view of the economic catastrophe, to intercede with the ministry of finance to obtain exemption from the land tax for local proprietors. The sordid affairs of thousands of farm hands out of work had no claim on their attention.

Where did the money to finance the commune come from, and how was it spent? The basis of local-government financing was utterly regressive and served the purposes of buttressing profitability by lightening the burden on property owners of transfer and welfare payments and of minimizing costs to the exchequer. The main prop of the local budget was a retail consumption tax, the *dazio consumo*, levied on flour, bread, pasta, and wine – the staples of the workers' diet. The total budget for the city of Andria in 1898, for example, was 687,733.60 lire, of which the octroi yielded 449,585.50 lire.[36] For farm labourers the levy was onerous. The inhabitants of Bari province in 1900 contributed an average of 6.61 lire a year per person.[37] A *giornataro* with a family of four, therefore, paid 26.4 lire, or roughly the wages of the entire harvest season. The *signori* avoided the excise entirely by purchasing wholesale. Now here was a major source of misery and inequality. Furthermore, such financing based on the contributions of the destitute made town halls permanently short of funds and unable to meet the requirements of poor relief, sanitation, or education.

Educational attainment is a well-documented measure of the failure of local government to meet public needs. At Andria and Cerignola statutory primary instruction took place in scattered and unheated rooms rented from the friends of city hall. Many classrooms were empty grain stores lacking facilities of any sort. As a measure of economy, moreover, student numbers were allowed to climb to the point where "it was impossible to conduct orderly lessons". Instruction was carried out by temporary teaching assistants possessing no formal qualifications and costing little.[38]

The quality of education in the city of Andria is suggested by the fact that at the end of every year two thirds of the pupils failed to achieve promotion to the next class. Of the total population in the town of 49,625 in 1902, 40,690 were illiterate. Such conditions were in no sense confined to Andria. Illiteracy in Apulia was as widespread as in any region in the South, just at a time when it was beginning to disappear in the cities of the North. In 1903, for instance, of those people who were married in Italy, 31 per cent of men and 44 per cent of women were unable to read. The corresponding illiteracy statistics for the three Apulian provinces are shown in Table 3.[39] Of the total population of the region of 2,130,151, in 1911, 65 per cent of females over the age of six and 54 per cent of males were illiterate.[40]

Health and hygiene fared no better. The communes economized by hiring far too few medical staff and by providing them with virtually no facilities. The Apulian physicians' journal noted in horror that it was standard practice for there to be no isolation ward, no disinfectants, no equipment, and no stocks of medicine.

Table 3. *Illiteracy percentages in three Apulian provinces*

Province	Men married in 1903	Women married in 1903
Foggia	52	69
Bari	61	73
Lecce	50	74

There was no attempt at all to apply government regulations concerning public health.[41] The cholera epidemic of 1910 revealed, for instance, that Trani, a city of 60,000 inhabitants, had no laboratory or diagnostic facilities. The doctors themselves showed their commitment by fleeing the region during the outbreak.[42] At San Marco, where the local cemetery had long been overcrowded, the dead were buried at a depth of 10–15 centimetres.[43] Even in the regional capital at Bari the medical situation was catastrophic. In 1920 in a population of 120,000 people, 6,000 inhabitants in the city were estimated to have tuberculosis. Of these only 180 had received medical attention of any kind.[44] In health matters throughout Apulia, the review established, the rule was "negligence and crass ignorance".[45]

The medical journal had no doubts concerning the causes of the problem:

The blame falls first of all on the local authorities, which spend public money badly and often dishonestly. It falls secondly on the national government, which makes laws but does not enforce them. The prefectures know that many, many towns violate the existing regulations, but they close their eyes. They know full well that otherwise the mayors will run to the deputy.[46]

This gloomy conclusion on the part of the medical profession was corroborated by the state authorities. The deputy prefect of San Severo was categorical. "I have noted", he wrote in 1890,

that everywhere hygiene is utterly forgotten, and that the relevant regulations are not invoked.

Every branch of public health I have found to be neglected and incomplete. Doctors, midwives, veterinary surgeons – all are incompetent or insufficient or non-existent.[47]

Other public services – street lighting, refuse collection, road building and maintenance – produced similar results, but by a different means. These services were not performed by employees of the commune. Instead, they were contracted out at extortionate rates to clients of the faction in power, which neither expected nor demanded performance. Sub-contracting was a means of patronage intended to serve political purposes rather than to satisfy public need. The only regularly visible effects of money budgeted by local authorities were those on which gentlemen counted – the police, the opera, and the salaries of local officials.

Such were the official results of municipal expenditure. Public funds were also diverted into irregular channels. The local treasurer's office served as a bank for local notables, lending funds to friends of the mayor, financing the electoral expenses of the party in power, and maintaining expense accounts enabling members of the town council to travel and to entertain. An official enquiry into the finances of the Andria town council concluded that the administration "made a joke of the municipal budget".[48] The police revealed "numerous administrative, financial, and moral irregularities" in the commune of Altamura.[49] So pervasive were such practices that among the most common chants in popular demonstrations were *"Abbasso la camorra!"* (Down with the gang of thieves!) and *"Fuori i camorristi!"* (Out with the criminals!).

The method of collection multiplied the occasions for friction caused by the excise. Communes were "closed", and their entrances were blocked by customs barriers where all goods entering the township were assessed for the consumption duty. The concession to man the barriers and collect the levy was sold at public auction to tax farmers who paid the town a fixed annual sum and profited from any extra money collected. As a result, the excise men squeezed the system for all it was worth. The customs barriers became notorious for abuses of every sort. At Andria twenty-four of the sixty-seven customs guards were ex-convicts. With ample justification the Apulian medical journal accused local government in the region of "moral nihilism".[50]

Furthermore, since both the landlords and the creditors to whom they mortgaged the land were absentee figures, there was a systematic exodus of capital from the region. A large proportion of the wealth of Apulia never entered the local economy, and never provided the basis for funding municipal services.

The extent of the resulting lack of confidence in the local authorities was poignantly demonstrated at Barletta during the cholera epidemic of 1910. In the city a violent uprising of thousands of labourers occurred in September when health officials attempted to launch a campaign of vaccination. The workers believed that the officials had been sent to spread the contagion with their syringes in order to kill them off in a final settling of scores. They also feared a new swindle when the authorities arrived, in the company of the hated municipal police, to confiscate the bedding and the clothes of families suspected of infection. The crowd, hoping to lynch the medics, raged through the centre of the town shouting and destroying everything in its path.[51]

Through a variety of circumstances then, the conditions of the labourers were desperately harsh. Contemporary observers across the political spectrum were unanimous on this point. The reforming republican paper *Il Foglietto* observed of Foggia, "Let us not mince words: everything contributes to make residence here odious."[52] The paper commented further that, "The ruin of society touches rock bottom here."[53] The Bari Liberal daily *Corriere delle Puglie* commented in a similar spirit in 1901 that the Apulian farm workers were "worse off, far worse, than any other peasants in Italy".[54] The *giornataro* Domenico La Barbutta, born at Minervino Murge in 1900, said to me in an interview, "What you have to remember is that Minervino was the poorest place, not just in Italy, but in the whole world!" La Barbutta described conditions as a form of slavery and "systematic abuse". The work animals, he remarked, received better treatment than the men.[55]

And, finally, Giuseppe Pavoncelli himself remarked in a speech at Cerignola, that

There is no part of Italy that provides such a sad spectacle of death as ours . . . There is no other town with so many widows and orphans. Whoever works in the fields . . . wears himself out and cannot fail to succumb to disease, leaving behind poor unfortunate creatures with no bread and no protection.[56]

The pattern of death in Apulia reveals the lethal social conditions prevailing in the agro-cities of the region. In Apulia the overwhelming majority of deaths was caused by intestinal and respiratory diseases, the inevitable by-products of malnutrition, overcrowding, pervasive filth, and substandard housing. Diarrhoeal illnesses, the greatest killers of all, were responsible for nearly a third of all fatalities in the three provinces. They decimated the population of children under five years of age, especially during the summer months. For adults, respiratory diseases – bronchitis, tuberculosis, and pneumonia – were the great scourge. They accounted for the large majority of adult deaths. Respiratory illnesses reached a high point of ferocity in the winter when workers skimped on food, heat, and clothing.[57] The working environment also contributed to the grim statistics – the practice of sleeping rough in the fields in all weather; the alternation of heavy labour and rest on open plains known for high winds and sharp variations in temperature; the inadequacy of rations. In June and July there were accounts in the press of waves of death from heat stroke among the harvesters.[58]

Mortality figures alone, however, conceal many of the major problems of public health in Apulia. A series of widespread and incapacitating illnesses debilitated more often than they killed. Malaria, syphilis, and tuberculosis were rampant, and leprosy was endemic. 100,000 Apulians were afflicted with trachoma, the great cause of blindness in the underdeveloped world, where the chlamydia parasite spreads among cramped and unwashed bodies.[59] Arthritis was universal among the inhabitants of the grottoes. Farm workers were also deformed by the use of a short-

7 Cerignola, *ca.* 1900: A street in the workers' quarters of the city.

handled mattock unique to the region that produced such curvature of the spine that by middle age most *giornatari* could no longer stand erect. "Already, in youth," observed Presutti, "work with the mattock so deforms their limbs that their bodies are bent in the shape of an ellipse."[60] Premature aging affected everyone. Finally, the Apulian medical journal disclosed a high but undocumented rate of industrial accidents leading to disability among a work force that was untrained and composed of large numbers of children.[61] It was hardly surprising that at Foggia at the turn of the century 60.6 per cent of conscripts were rejected by the army as physically unfit for military service.[62] For good reason one journalist described the workers' life as "short, weak, and barren – a galloping moral and physical decline".[63]

Mortality statistics support our sombre conclusions. In this period Apulia became the region of Italy with the highest death rate and the shortest life expectancy. Five times between 1895 and 1905 Apulia led the national list with death rates nearly double those of Liguria or Piedmont.[64] In 1903 the rate of death per thousand inhabitants was the following:[65]

England and Wales	15.46
Ireland	17.51
France	19.26
Italy	21.00
Treviso province	18.10 (lowest in Italy)
Pisa province	18.20
Foggia province	30.70 (highest in Italy)
Bari province	29.30 (second in Italy)
Lecce province	27.90 (third in Italy)

Apulia consistently set national records for death by the diseases of poverty, malnutrition, and poor sanitation – cholera, typhus, tuberculosis, typhoid, smallpox, and pneumonia.[66] Statistics for the causes of death at Cerignola in 1905 establish the point (see Table 4), even after one makes allowances for changes in diagnostic fashion and for the sometimes cavalier attitude of local authorities to the gathering of statistical information.[67]

The social pathology of the agricultural centres of the region was reflected in alarming rates of violent crime as well as disease. The murder rate at Foggia in 1900, for instance, was 26 per 100,000 inhabitants, as contrasted with 6 in Milan and Turin, while the rate of assault was 600 as compared with 131.[68] The public prosecutor at the Lucera tribunal, which had all of Foggia province for its catchment area, gave annual addresses to mark the

Table 4. *Causes of death at Cerignola, 1905*

Population of Cerignola	35,000
Total of deaths from all causes	1,075
Leading causes	No. of deaths
diarrhoea, enteritis, endemic cholera	335
acute and chronic bronchitis	140
tuberculosis	72
croup	58
immaturity, congenital weakness	57
eclampsia	59
cerebral congestion	46
heart disease	37
marasmus	35
acute bronchial pneumonia	31
gastritis	23
typhoid fever	18
malaria	16
meningitis	14
kidney disease	12
anaemia, leukemia	12
hepatitis, cyrrhosis	11
accidents	11
malignant tumours	10

opening of the judicial year. In these reports at the start of the century the prosecutors stressed that Capitanata was characterized by a "rising tide of delinquency".[69] Furthermore, Giovanni Giocone noted in his address in 1905, the province stood out for the prevalence, not only of crimes against property, but also for violence against the person. Foggia province was notable for "the frequency and the savagery of its crimes".[70] Some landlords went abroad accompanied by bodyguards and watchdogs.[71]

The pages of the major Apulian daily paper, the *Corriere delle Puglie*, confirm the observations of the Lucera prosecutors and explain the prudence of the proprietors. Its columns are filled with reports of chilling deeds that occurred with depressing regularity.[72] Infanticide, parricide, fratricide, and incest all abounded. There were notices of farm workers who stabbed estate guards to death in their sleep, of labourers who ambushed overseers in the dark and slashed their faces with razors. Debtors and creditors discharged revolvers at one another. Adultery often ended in murder as husbands defended their honour with knife in hand. "A husband if betrayed", commented Giuseppe De Falco, chairman of the Bari Chamber of Labour, "generally kills".[73] Sexual and family violence of other sorts were legion. Everywhere men beat their wives and children. Rape was widespread. In the Gargano the custom survived for men to choose their wives by first abducting them and then marrying them to right the wrong. The practice was known as la trasciuta.[74]

Such acts provide a suggestive indication of the quality of life in the agro-cities of Giolittian Apulia. Crime, like disease, thrived in the crowded urban slums. Poverty, hunger, unemployment, broken families, and overcrowding provided the natural conditions for its growth. The tensions of a deeply oppressive society found an outlet in aggression.

5

••

SEEDS OF REBELLION

The conditions of workers' lives in the region, and the social relations in which they were set, provided the necessary but not sufficient premises for organized resistance. In addition, it was essential that there should be potent sources of new ideas – catalysts that would transform discontent into a conscious sense of injustice. Such catalysts, too, were present in abundance in the period between 1900 and the Great War. Emigration, urban workers, enclosure, republicanism, and anti-clericalism particularly merit attention.

Emigration

The first of these powerful forces was emigration. Under the calamitous impact of agricultural crisis and the tariff war with France, peasants and labourers fled the South of Italy in massive numbers between the closing decades of the nineteenth century and the First World War. For the deputy prefect of San Severo in Foggia province, the cause of this vast movement of population to Argentina and the United States was no mystery: "Since the wages currently prevailing are almost insufficient to cover the essentials of life, many people go abroad."[1] The explanation advanced by the *Corriere delle Puglie* was identical: "People decide to emigrate only when their resources are exhausted, and they are unable to solve the problem of existence at home."[2]

Although poverty, despair, and a demand for cheap, unskilled labour in the New World provided the impetus for the great

8 Cerignola, *ca.* 1900: A family of farm workers in front of their dwelling.

transoceanic migration of Italians, peasants rather than day labourers played the dominant role. With more stable village communities, a more cohesive network of extended families, and often a bit of land with which to secure a loan, poor peasants were better able than farm workers to raise the 150 to 200 lire needed for a steerage passage to New York or Buenos Aires. As a region with a uniquely large proportion of rural proletarians, Apulia therefore contributed a smaller percentage of her population to the exodus than any region in the Mezzogiorno, with the exception of Sardinia.

Within the three provinces, furthermore, the movement began among the impoverished small proprietors and leaseholders of the *marina* rather than among the field workers of the Tavoliere and the interior of Bari province. With the unleashing of the tariff war with France in 1887, the market for Apulian wine suddenly collapsed and prices for grapes plunged precipitously. At the same time the phylloxera louse began its ravages, making its first appearance in Lecce province in 1889.[3] In 1892, moreover, a fungal infection seriously damaged olive trees in the region as well, increasing the general misery and resulting in the dispossession of many small cultivators. Large numbers of the peasants thus affected sought work overseas.[4]

The movement began as a trickle in the 1890's and broadened into an ever-widening stream until the war. Sample years between 1894, the first year that more than a thousand people departed from any of the three Apulian provinces, and 1913, the last year of unrestricted movement abroad, establish the point. The progress of emigration can be seen in Table 5.[5] As early as 1909, 10 per cent of the population of Bari province was estimated to be living abroad.[6]

The emigrants were overwhelmingly family men in their twenties and thirties who went overseas temporarily, incurring debts with the usurers known as "emigration agents".[7] After an absence of several years the majority returned to their homes, normally with considerable savings. The intention to return can be inferred from the exclusively male character of the emigration. Of 19,223 emigrants from the region in 1904, 17,022 were men.[8] The commune of Molfetta in Bari province is an illustrative example. Of the population of 45,525 in 1910, 4,773 resided across the Atlantic. Of these emigrants, 3,406 were men between the ages of twenty and forty, most of whom were married but who had departed

Table 5. *Transoceanic migrants from Apulia*

Province	1894	1900	1904	1913
Bari	1,234	2,321	10.931	22,380
Foggia	807	1,523	6,100	9,667
Lecce	none	86	2,192	4,305

alone. In the three years 1910–12, only 128 women left Molfetta to travel overseas. The emigrants departed for one reason – "to satisfy the needs of subsistence" – and returned to the commune after a median period of three years of absence.[9] Unfortunately, there are no regional records of the rate of repatriation, but it is indicative that in Italy as a whole 54 per cent of those who emigrated between 1880 and 1914 returned.[10]

As the movement broadened to a flood in the new century, it spread to encompass large numbers of day labourers from the zones of latifundism both in Apulia and elsewhere in the South. During the agricultural crisis the farm workers on the great estates had been too poor even to escape, and only the economic recovery of the Giolittian period permitted them to take part in the phenomenon. In the early twentieth century the great agro-cities of the Apulian interior witnessed the departure of hundreds of men every year. The emigration of 103 people in 1904 from Gravina, one of the smallest of the great centres, demonstrates this point. Thirty-three of these men were explicitly listed as farm workers, and they were further described as illiterate, poor, and "deficient in stature".[11]

The effects of this mass migration on Apulian politics were considerable, as contemporary observers stressed. The men who came back – the "Americans" – were difficult to re-absorb in the local labour market. In the United States they had benefited from a boom in the demand for unskilled labour in the urban centres of the northeast. There they worked on the roads, railways and trams; in the building trades; and in municipal sanitation crews. By American standards, the Italian labourers filled the bottom rung of unskilled, dead-end jobs. By comparison with what they could earn in the South of Italy, however, they made their fortune. Wages for such jobs during the Giolittian period ranged from 1.50 to 2.50 dollars a day.[12]

On their return to Andria, Spinazzola and Barletta, the wealthy Americans were reluctant to take up the mattock. After years in New York, New Haven or Boston they had acquired new notions of a minimal standard of living, and they expressed contempt for the wage scales prevailing in Apulian agriculture. As one landlord commented in distress, "The 'Americans' stroll cheekily through the streets, refusing offers to work and persuading their comrades to do the same."[13] New ideas of a living wage were being imported, together with the expectations and values of urban America.

Most striking of all was the fact that about 10 per cent of the returning Americans had sufficient savings to buy land.[14] Their purchases were normally tiny plots that were economically unviable and that they were eventually forced to sell. The immediate result, however, was to stimulate the land hunger of those who had been left behind, awakening feelings of envy, resentment and injustice.[15]

Furthermore, emigration upset the existing bargaining-power relations in the labour market. A major weapon in the hands of Apulian employers was overpopulation, which set workers in competition with one another and drove wages down. Mass emigration blunted this weapon, and this fact, too, promoted class solidarity. The large-scale departure of *marinesi* thinned the numbers of "foreigners" seeking work on the latifundia at harvest time. At Cerignola, for instance, the prefect of Foggia province attributed the success of the farm workers' strike in 1913 to "the reduced labour force caused by emigration abroad. The consequence of this migration is that the Pavoncelli house, during the recent strike, was unable to recruit in Bari province the workers it used to pay to replace local labourers."[16] In the same vein, the Bari Chamber of Commerce conducted an enquiry in 1907 into the effects of emigration on wages and conditions in the province. Its conclusion was that the direct result of emigration was a "considerable increase in the levels of pay", putting an end to the starvation wages of 0.80 lire a day that had been common at the turn of the century.[17]

The experience of Apulia thus belies any overly simple or mechanistic theory of the relationship between economic hardship and revolutionary politics. Although economic distress was crucial to the impetus behind the leagues, the movement did not develop in the worst decades of all – the decades of the agricultural crisis of the 1880's and 1890's. On the contrary, unionization began on a large scale only after emigration had already produced a significant amelioration in real wages. At the same time, remittances and savings increased the margins for resistance and the funds available to union organizers. According to the Bari Chamber of Labour, the average emigrant during the years 1904 to 1906 sent 700 lire per year back to Italy. The secretary of the Chamber, Giuseppe De Falco, even wrote of the "de-proletarianization" of the day labourers as a result.[18] One of the ironies of this period was that American money made a major contribution to the financing of syndicalism in Apulia.

Finally, emigration transformed gender roles. A rigid sexual division of labour was one of the props of the social order, isolating half of the population in the home and removing them from contact with nascent bonds of class solidarity. The degree of the exclusion of women from agricultural work varied from locality to locality. The prevailing practice on the latifundia, however, was simply stated by the mayor of Altamura in 1875, when he reported that "Women are not employed in the cultivation of the land, either as day labourers or as salaried personnel."[19] As emigration made the labour market less favourable for employers, they began increasingly to turn to women. In the short term, the result was to contain wages. From a longer time perspective, however, the effect was to transform the position of women in Apulian society. It was no accident that women were regularly among the most militant participants in every strike and demonstration, bringing to labour issues scores of their own to settle. On many occasions the women lay down with their babies in front of the horses of the cavalry, or conspicuously took their place in the front line of crowds besieging town hall. In 1908 the socialist paper *Avanti!* noted the transformation that had overtaken the women of Foggia:

In the present strike those who stand out most for their enthusiasm and pride are the women . . . They are genuine heroines!

They do not rest for even a minute. Their activity is phenomenal: they dash wherever there is a danger of strikebreaking; they urge their husbands on and call out for resistance.

The women strikers number more than a thousand, and they are all organized. Until three years ago the women were at the very depths of human exploitation, forced not only to undertake the most brutalizing work for shameful wages that never passed 0.60 lire a day, but also . . . to endure a condition of slavery in which the feudal right of the first night was still practised.

And now . . . these women . . . declare aloud that they would rather die of hunger on the spot than yield to the scheming demands of the Agrarian Association.[20]

Urban workers and intellectuals

Emigration, then, was a powerful influence. There were others. One was the effect of urban workers. Although Apulia was far from the national centres of union activism and political militancy, the integration of the region into the national and international markets and the construction of improved means of transport quickened the movement of goods, people, newspapers, pamphlets and ideas. The example of labour struggles in other regions of Italy was keenly felt in the three provinces. In the early 1890's Apulian labourers carefully followed the organization of unions and cooperatives in Sicily, known as the *fasci siciliani*. The repression of the movement by military force under Francesco Crispi led to a series of spontaneous protest demonstrations in Apulia in support of the workers in Sicily. The similarity between the two great regions of latifundism in the South gave the union drive on the island a particular resonance in Bari and Foggia provinces. When strikes were legalized by Giolitti in the new century, Apulians kept informed of the progress of socialism in the North, and especially the organization of day labourers on the commercial farms of the Po Valley. Apulians who had been to the North reported their observations; union leaders born in the North toured Apulia to spread the union gospel; and the socialist daily *Avanti!* circulated from hand to hand while local weekly papers informed their readers of major developments. Apulian politics did not operate in a vacuum.

Closer to hand, however, were the industrial workers of the region itself. Although Apulia was overwhelmingly agricultural, there were pockets of organized urban workers as well – dockers, railwaymen and builders. The peasant movement was influenced by their presence, as its leaders acknowledged. It was not by chance that the early centres of the farm workers' unionization drive were located on the railway line – Cerignola, Andria, Ruvo, Barletta, San Severo – and that the railroad workers were engaged in agitations at the same time.

The Bari Chamber of Labour, which acted as the organizing centre of the agrarian agitation throughout the province, owed its early dynamism and key position to the militancy and the financial contribution of the dockers of the city. The union paper noted that it was the example of the proletariat of the city that "galvanized the energy of our peasants".[21] Precisely the same argument would apply to the emergence of unions on the latifundia to the north of the port of Taranto.

More broadly in the agricultural centres themselves, artisans and skilled workers set an example of sociability and organization. As early as the 1860's and with an increasing tempo thereafter, cobblers, carpenters, tailors, and builders established a network of mutual-aid societies, workers' clubs, and consumers' cooperatives. From the standpoint of agricultural labourers, the significance of such initiatives was severalfold. The artisans experimented with forms of organization that farm labourers could imitate. They read newspapers aloud, discussed ideas, shared experiences, and circulated books. The workers' societies also often consciously undertook the task of politicizing the farm workers, some of whom were enrolled in the cooperatives or political circles.

An intensification of this process occurred in the last decade of the nineteenth century. In the 1890's a sector of the workers' movement joined the Socialist Party (PSI), which was launched nationally in 1892 and established in Apulia three years later.

Until the turn of the century and the emergence of the farm labourers' organizations, the PSI in Apulia remained a marginal political force confined to non-agricultural workers in an overwhelmingly agricultural society. The formation of the party did, however, lead to an accelerated and more systematic effort to extend socialist propaganda to the farm hands. Under socialist sponsorship members of the intelligentsia and skilled artisans also began to conduct electoral campaigns in the major Apulian agrocities. The aim of these early electoral tours was to spread propaganda rather than to secure election.

The narrow stratum of the intelligentsia was also an important source of subversive ideas. Members of the professions in the Apulian cities felt constrained by the shortage of economic opportunities in the region and by the quasi-absolutism of local government. Many had direct professional contact with the realities of the farm workers' lives, and some found what they witnessed abhorrent. The story of the revolutionary movement in the region cannot be understood without an appreciation of the role played in its development by teachers, doctors and lawyers. The founder of the unionization drive among the *giornatari*, and the first socialist mayor in Apulia, was Canio Musacchio, a school teacher at Gravina. Giuseppe Di Vittorio, the most famous of all Apulian syndicalist leaders, first encountered radical ideas in books lent to him by a school master at Cerignola.[22] Many of the leading union organizers – Domenico Fioritto, Giuseppe De Falco, and Giuseppe Di Vagno, for example – were lawyers.

Police reports on anarchist propaganda at San Severo in 1879 and 1893 confirm the role of artisans and professionals in attempting to spread libertarian ideas among the farm workers. The eighty-three active agitators kept under surveillance by the authorities included tailors, students, a watchmaker, telegraph operators, pharmacists, school masters, doctors, cobblers, barbers, lawyers, landlords, and an ex-priest.[23] The message they carried was direct – "Property is theft!" – and they gave particular attention to the problem of reaching the farm workers. Particularly ingenious was the ex-priest Ambrogio Ciminelli, who continued to wear his clerical robes "as a means of reaching even women with his ideas". Some of these men had been to the North of Italy, to Switzerland, to France, and even to America before settling in San Severo. It was such individual apostles who formed the first channels by which revolutionary doctrines and slogans penetrated San Severo and other centres. As the *carabinieri* observed as early as the 1870's, "Among the middle strata of our citizens, there is a small number of individuals who make a great display of their principles within the four walls of a pharmacy or a workshop. They are then left with the fear that they have been heard and reported."[24]

Disinheritance

Another powerful stimulus to a widespread sense of injustice was the process of expropriation, by which the Apulian peasantry lost former rights of access to common land. The commons (*demani*) in the former Neapolitan kingdom consisted of vast tracts of woodland and pasture belonging to the villages collectively at unification. On these lands the inhabitants exercised ancient rights of tillage, pasturage, fishing and gathering wood (*usi civici*). The *demani* and *usi civici* were authentic popular rights of astonishing antiquity. They were the vestiges of pre-Roman pastoral communities that practised collective ownership and appropriation. Their basis was local custom and usage.

The early history of the dissolution of collective property in the land is a multisecular process that lies beyond our concerns. The point that directly influenced the emergence of an Apulian labour movement is more immediate. Italian unification, as Paolo Grossi has demonstrated in a recent work,[25] brought to power a Liberal ruling class that was ideologically committed to the destruction of communal forms of ownership and to the triumph of possessive individualism based on the sole principle of individual proprietorship recognized in Roman law. For a parliament of landlords at Montecitorio, collective rights were at best aberrations, encumbrances on property that shackled progress and initiative.

At worst, they were a subversive challenge to the dominion of private property. Furthermore, with settlement and the upward spiral of ground rent in Apulia, the opportunity costs of leaving great areas of land in the hands of peasant users rose enormously. The existence of commons weakened the sway of employers in the labour market. Thus the result of a variety of pressures – doctrinal, financial and entrepreneurial – was the piecemeal but relentless extinction of rights of usage and the enclosure of *demani.*

The opportunities for the enclosure of commons were numerous. The legislation of the Liberal state was unbending in its aversion to any form of agrarian collectivism or consuetudinary right. Local proprietors, moreover, controlled communal government, which possessed the power of eminent domain. Armed with this right and backed by the authorities, proprietors possessed the juridical and administrative means to carry out disentailment. The users, by contrast, had no forum in which to defend their inheritance. The decades following unification, therefore, witnessed the systematic alienation of common land by local government at advantageous prices. In the tracts of once collective forest, field and pasture the latifundia discovered yet another frontier to colonize and plant.

The extent of the loss to local communities was substantial. *La Ragione*, the union paper in Bari province, estimated that, between 1806 and 1898, 170,000 hectares of commons in the province were alienated from collective ownership and enclosed. Only 3,000 hectares of *demani* remained to mark the meagre residue of primordial popular rights.[26] The result was a severe blow to living standards and to the last props of independence of the agricultural population, which henceforth subsisted exclusively through the labour market.

The burning question of *demani* and *usi civici* was common to the whole territory of the former Kingdom of the Two Sicilies. A further particular aspect of disinheritance was specific to Capitanata. The issue was the former royal sheep highways known as *tratturi*. To facilitate access to the Tavoliere and passage across it, the Aragonese had devised a system of broad swathes of public grazing land crossing the Foggia plain in several directions. Originally intended for shepherds, these *tratturi* had also furnished an important economic resource for the peasants, who enjoyed access to them. With the end of the sheep regime, however, the *tratturi* lost their official sanction. They were unceremoniously encroached upon and planted by the managers of the adjoining estates. A number of the smaller agricultural centres of the province – Ordona, Stornara, Ortanova, Carapelle, Trinitapoli – were built entirely upon the former public grazing land. Here entrepreneurs built dwellings to house their rapidly expanding work force.[27]

The passions aroused by commons and sheep highways were second to none in generating hostility to the latifundia, which were seen as the beneficiaries of legalized theft. Already in 1863 the common land commissioner Vito Orofino commented on the class antagonisms aroused by the question of common land in the commune of Altamura. "I have come to understand", he wrote, "that the proletarians are so distrustful that they no longer believe in the reality of government measures with regard to the problem. On the contrary, they openly display their hatred for landlords and officials."[28] The sheer complexity of the question exacerbated the social tensions and the suspicions involved. The legal resolution of the problem of ownership led to suits, appeals, and conflicts of jurisdiction. A final decision often involved years of legal conflict and reversals of decisions. Prolonged uncertainty, anxious expectation, and then disappointment heightened the bitterness of the issue.[29]

The terrain was thus cleared for union organizers and agitators to plant the seeds of subversion. In many places demonstrations for the re-appropriation of usurped commons by the people marked the beginning of political mobilization. At the second provincial congress of the Bari province union federation in 1903, Guglielmo Schiralli recognized the importance of the issue to the organization. The restoration of common land, he reported, was a "proletarian demand" that provided the foundation for the class struggle of the farm workers against a "systematic class theft".[30] The issue of *tratturi*, the press confirmed, was the great weapon of the left in their propaganda.[31]

Here was a paradox. The defence of *usi civici* was the attempt to protect archaic usage and antique social relationships. Nevertheless, the issue contributed powerfully to the emergence of a modern labour movement looking forward to modernization and social progress. The reason was that the loss of access to the *demani* and *tratturi* was a goad to protest. In the wake of enclosure, workers ate less and did without fuel and light. The struggle for the preservation of collective rights provided the otherwise disunited inhabitants of a commune with a common set of interests to protect and a common set of adversaries to attack. Horizontal bonds of solidarity and a consciousness of community identity were forged. Common rights in Apulia were a catalyst to the development of syndicalism in much the same way that struggles over forest rights in France in the first half of the nineteenth century prepared the way for a democratic socialist politics among peasants under the Second Republic. In Apulia the libertarian slogan "Property is theft!" linked past and future.

San Nicandro Garganico, one of the most combative centres of union activity in Foggia province, illustrates the stakes involved and the way in which conflict over common rights helped to forge a class identity.[32] At San Nicandro common land dated from antiquity, when vast areas of woodland, marsh, lake, and terrain too rocky for easy cultivation were regarded as the property of the villagers collectively. The flat, fertile territory of the commune became instead, the property of the barons. Even here, however, a compromise was reached. A portion of the arable land was designated as subject to *colonie perpetue*. These were permanent collective tenancies of the entire population of San Nicandro. The land was formally owned by the nobility, but the inhabitants as a community enjoyed the right to grow crops in exchange for the payment of a tenth of the harvest to the proprietors. A committee of residents met annually to determine which areas of the *colonie* were to be planted and which left fallow or given over to pasture.

The assault of the Roman-law principle of private property upon collective property at San Nicandro began during the Napoleonic era, when a Feudal Commission was set up in 1806 to disentangle the chaotic and untidy arrangements of the *colonie*. This land was divided into commons and private property, with a substantial loss of territory to the peasantry. The erosion of communal ownership thus began gathered momentum as the century progressed. In 1808, in 1853, at unification, and in the closing decades of the century, the local authorities, armed with the power of eminent domain, sold the commons to individual landlords. By 1900 collective rights of access to both the land and to Lake Lesina had been legally abolished.

The destruction of ancient rights did not go uncontested. On the contrary, from the Risorgimento onwards litigation, protests, and violent clashes increased in frequency and intensity. The first popular agitation dated from 1867, when "shouting, tumults and crowds" were reported and the popular chant of "*Reintegra!*" ("Re-appropriate the commons!") gained currency. Litigation aiming at the recovery of 2,000 hectares of commons began simultaneously, only to result in defeat for the populace in a decision of the prefect of Foggia in 1886, which was confirmed by the Appeal Court at Trani. Thus legally resolved, the issue remained a powerful source of tension. From the end of the 1880's poor harvests and the onset of the agricultural crisis led to invasions of the woodlands, sometimes by thousands of men and women at a time, to illegal fishing in the lake, and to violent confrontations with the rural police.

In the Giolittian era the league movement grafted itself onto the spontaneous tradition of popular protest, and provided it with a coherent political and organizational framework.

Republicans, radicals and democrats

Part of the impulse to challenge the legitimacy of the social order in Apulia came from the landlords themselves. If the dominant spokesmen for the proprietors and *massari* were uncompromisingly authoritarian in their political outlook, there was also

9 Cerignola, 1910: The central estate buildings of the *masseria* "I
Pavoni" of the Pavoncelli family.

a small but vocal current of reformers – republicans, radicals, and
democrats – who constituted the left wing of the agrarian bloc.
Like the landed class as a whole, the radical faction was dis-
organized and local in orientation. There was no organized radical
party at the provincial or regional levels. Radicalism consisted of
the local followers of important notables in particular communes,
such as Enrico Fraccacreta at San Severo, Pasquale Caso at
Altamura, Leandro La Porta at San Marco in Lamis, and Raffaele
Cotugno at Ruvo.

What made such landlords republican was partly simple political prudence. Some far-sighted employers held that the long-term interests of property required timely concessions to de-fuse the growing hostility between landlords and labourers. Reforms, they argued, could be a useful means to prevent social polarization.

Beyond prudence, radicalism defended the interests of exporting wine producers with a vested concern in free trade against the triumphant protectionism of the wheat growers. The attack on protection also formed part of a strategy of agricultural improvement through the removal of the tariff wall which sheltered antiquated methods of production and an excessive cultivation of wheat. The radicals condemned the reigning trinity of absenteeism, parasitism, and short-term contracts. Reform meant the adoption of a developmental strategy to rationalize the structures of the *masserie*. Here was the appeal of radicalism to Giuseppe Pavoncelli, who was both a wine producer and the leading Apulian practitioner of modern agricultural techniques.

Most simply, however, the radicals became critical because they were excluded from power. Republicanism developed as a political force among the disgruntled opposition factions in local politics, among notables who did not enjoy the benefits of running town hall. To secure election, they proposed an alternative political programme that would win the support of professionals, artisans, and even farm workers. They denounced favouritism, corruption, and electoral fraud. They proposed the abolition of the consumption levy, extension of the suffrage, and the municipalization of local services. They preached anti-clericalism and raised the thorny problem of the Southern Question. They promised school buildings, street lighting, the free distribution of quinine to combat malaria, the paving of streets, dormitories for paupers, the removal of sewage from the streets, and reform of the municipal guard. In some places they also called for the re-appropriation of common land by the community.[33] The 1890's and the early Giolittian years witnessed the formation of a series of local populist electoral alliances known variously as "the Reds", the Popular Party, "the Democrats", and the Republican Party. When these

parties were victorious in the battle for town hall, there was singing and dancing in the streets.

In practice the reforming commitment of such parties led by
landlords was limited. Where Reds and democrats gained election, the change of faction in town hall made little real difference
to the reality of social inequality and poverty. The success of
Pavoncelli at Cerignola was a disappointment to the labourers
who had initially welcomed his campaign. Caso abolished the
consumption levy at Altamura, but then settled into the familiar
pattern of repressive rule and peculation so familiar in the region.
Enrico Fraccacreta followed an identical trajectory. According to
the authorities, his "Red" administration at San Severo was no different in practice from its predecessors. After three years of
observing Fraccacreta since his election in 1902, the deputy prefect concluded that "For some time the administration of the
commune has fallen into a state of apathy and indifference. Local
affairs proceed by inertia and the momentum of bureaucracy
rather than by any direct and coherent action by the elected
officials."[34] Similarly, the "democrat" Leonardo La Porta, elected
mayor of San Marco in 1903 with the support of the unions, did
not fulfil a single commitment. On the contrary, he raised the
consumption levy, left public services in "complete neglect", and
sarcastically justified his policy with the comment that he did not
understand public health regulations. "Everything", the prefect
of Foggia learned from his depty at San Marco, "continued just as
before".[35] As a recent study of the left in Foggia province
generalized, "Despite its role in opposition, the Republican Party
in Capitanata stopped at a purely theoretical commitment to ideas
more advanced than those of the forces in power. In practice the
republicans never succeeded in developing a clear will to reform
or in carrying their reformism into practice."[36]

Although the direct impact of radical landlords as a vehicle for
reform was severely limited, their contribution to the emergence
of a new political awareness must not be overlooked. In many
communes it was the "Reds", the Popular Party, and the radicals
who first brought the mass of the population into political life.

Their electoral oratory spread the awareness of social injustice and raised many of the concrete issues that were later taken up by the unions. Their promises, lamented the deputy prefect in the district of San Severo, "stimulated the peasant's demands – demands that were strange and unfounded either in law or in common sense."[37] Worst of all from the standpoint of state officials, the republicans undermined the respect for authority. The San Severo "Reds", for instance, constantly accused the police and the *carabinieri* of "bullying, favouritism, and a lack of delicacy in the performance of their duties".[38] With such propaganda, the republicans subverted the working class.

Even the failure to carry out their promises of renewal by radicals elected to office had a strongly politicizing effect. Having experienced first the corruption and repression of the dominant local faction and then the disillusionment of betrayal by the dynastic opposition, workers were more vigilant and determined not to be deprived again of the fruits of victory. Republicans and "Reds" taught the bitter lesson of the need for independent organizations and for the election by workers of their own representatives.

In conclusion, however, one should mention the rare, and possibly unique, case of Pasquale Manfredi, an important landlord, the former mayor of Cerignola, and the owner of one of the prominent palaces of the high street of the town. In 1904 Manfredi experienced a crisis of conscience, renounced his past, and declared himself a socialist. Thereafter he became the honorary president of the Cerignola farm workers' league, which he supported by campaigning on its behalf, by volunteering as a speaker on public occasions, and by opening his purse.[39]

Anti-clericalism

Although positive catalysts were important, the success of the leagues also owed much to a powerful negative factor – the weakness of the Church. In those regions of Italy where Catholicism was a strong influence, the Church presented a formidable barrier to the penetration of subversive ideologies. In the Apulian interior, however, the hold of the clergy over the popular imagination was minimal. This important aspect of Apulian political life was noted by many contemporary observers. Drawing up the report of the parliamentary enquiry, E. Presutti described the farm workers as "irreligious" and noted that, in the areas of strongest union activity, the labourers no longer attended mass. Feast days continued to be observed, but more as quasi-pagan celebrations that the workers preferred "as noisy as possible". Popular belief took the form of superstition rather than of Catholicism.[40]

Presutti's view was confirmed by Salvemini, who even reproached the union leaders for their anti-clericalism. To attack the Church, he argued, was to tilt at windmills. Salvemini wrote, for instance, "If there is one danger that does not exist in the South and above all in Apulia, it is Clericalism."[41] In Apulia the parish churches already stood empty, and civil ceremonies took precedence over religious weddings. Socialism and anarchism, therefore, could take hold with relative ease in a region where the ideological terrain was free of competitors. Only in the *marina* was the Church a serious rival.[42]

A measure of the weakness of the Church is the feeble performance of the Catholic Popular Party in the centres of latifundism in 1919 and 1920. The parish clergy formed the backbone of the Popular Party (PPI), and inability of the priests to deliver the vote is an indication of their lack of influence. In the district of Barletta, which included both a substantial portion of the wheat-growing interior of Bari province and an area of coastal towns, the prefect of Bari instructed his deputy to report on the state of the political parties on the eve of the local-government elections in the autumn of 1920. The resulting report confirmed that the Catholic party was a marginal force among the farm workers in the agro-cities of Minervino, Canosa, Corato, Ruvo, Andria, Spinazzola, and Barletta. The extreme case was Minervino Murge, where the Chamber of Labour numbered 6,000 members and was affiliated with the Italian Syndicalist Union, while the *popolari*, in the words of the deputy prefect, were "non-existent".

In the other centres, the unions belonging to the Chamber of Labour had thousands of members, while the PPI counted only several hundred, most of whom were not day labourers. Only in the *marina* – at Molfetta, Bisceglie, and Trani – did the Catholic movement possess a mass following.[43] The accuracy of the deputy prefect's analysis was confirmed, moreover, by the electoral results. Of the eleven communes in the district, the PSI won five, the reformist socialists one, the parties of order three, and the PPI only one – Bisceglie, which was not a centre of latifundism. The reasons for the pervasive lack of religious feeling in the Apulian interior are many. The most obvious factor was the weakness of the parish network. In the mass settlement following unification, the church infrastructure had been swamped. Foggia and western Bari provinces in this respect resembled that other frontier region in modern Italy – the reclaimed land of the Po Valley, where socialism also profited from the absence of a powerful church presence. In Apulia there were simply too few parish priests per capita, as the 1901 census revealed. Nationally there was an average of 1,567 inhabitants per parish church, and in traditional centres of Catholic strength in north and central Italy the presence of the clergy was still more intense, as Table 6 demonstrates.

Table 6. *Inhabitants per parish in selected dioceses in the North and Centre of Italy*

Diocese	Inhabitants per parish
Lucca	889
Assisi	820
Perugia	617
Urbino	383
Fiesole	1,048
Cremona	1,186
Borgo San Sepolcro	357

Apulia, by contrast, was marked by the high ratio of population to parish with a national high of 15,084 in the diocese of Trani, Nazareth, Barletta, and Bisceglie in Bari province. (The statistics for the other fourteen dioceses of Bari and Foggia provinces appear in Table 7.)[44] In such circumstances, the priest was inevitably a distant figure, unable to exercise a constant spiritual and ideological guidance. The standard of pastoral care also suffered.

A further important but more imponderable factor was the quality of the Apulian clergy. This remote and malarial region was an undesirable and unprestigious assignment far from the main currents of Italian life. The most dedicated and committed priests were rarely to be found in Apulia. On the contrary, morale was perennially low, and a constant complaint of the press in the region was that the local clergy was illiterate, superstitious, and corrupt. The Lucera weekly *Il Foglietto*, for instance, commented:

Table 7. *Inhabitants per parish in Bari and Foggia provinces*

Diocese	Inhabitants per parish
Andria	7,853
Ascoli Santi and Cerignola	6,225
Bari	7,611
Bovino	3,121
Conversano	10,678
Foggia	7,829
Gravina and Irsina	4,377
Lucera	4,341
Manfredonia and Vieste	5,704
Molfetta, Terlizzi, and Giovinazzo	8,290
Monopoli	6,991
Ruvo and Bitonto	3,200
San Severo	6,454
Troia	2,791

"Our clergy is deeply ignorant, undisciplined, and mindless of their duties."[45]

A series of widely publicized scandals involving parish priests in major centres provoked popular outrage and seemed to confirm the point. The arrest of the priest Arcangelo Strippoli at Cerignola in 1904 for sexually assaulting two orphan girls set off an angry demonstration by hundreds of people, who chanted, "Give the coward to us! Lynch him!"[46] At San Severo the priest Vincenzo di Lembo shot and killed a peasant who owed him money and with whose wife he was having an affair.[47] At Vieste an uproar ensued when the priest Vincenzo Abbruzzini was found guilty of adultery with the wife of a labourer who had emigrated temporarily to America.[48] The view of the farm worker, in the words of Giuseppe De Falco, was that "The priest is his natural enemy."[49]

The impact of farm labour itself further undermined the workers' faith. Traditions rapidly collapsed in the frontier atmosphere of the region with large numbers of settlers from widely different regions and conditions. An environment in which parents were absent for weeks at a time, leaving their children to the care of the streets, seriously diminished the family as an institution for transmitting religious values. The prevalence of child labour further removed boys at an early age from the formative influence of family and school, and made regular church attendance impossible. Most profoundly of all, the workers' history of poverty and oppression produced an enduring hatred of authority in every form, whether religious or political. Giuseppe De Falco, secretary of the Bari Chamber of Labour, explained,

These people believe in nothing. Their long past of betrayal, domination, exploitation, and swindling makes them sceptical. They take justice into their own hands because they believe that justice is the servant of the powerful. They set fire to town hall because they know that the mayor plunders the municipal coffers. They have a deep and unquenchable hatred for authority in whatever shape, because they know that authority is the oppressor that drains their blood.[50]

With regard to religious authority in particular, it was a common perception that the Church was the ally of the employers. Symbolism here had a deep impact. The churches in the great agricultural centres were invariably located in the main street – the landlords' part of the town. In many communes, furthermore, the piazza in front of the Church was the local labour market. In Cerignola the workers negotiated with the corporals directly in front of the Chiesa del Carmine. The attempt made by many employers to enforce religious observance by compelling their hands to kneel in prayer at the end of the work day widely associated official religion with labour discipline, giving Catholicism overtones of oppression.

The clergy and the propertied classes were also organically linked. Part of the explanation was historical – the political legacy of the Bourbon regime, under which throne and altar were allied. In addition, the Church itself was an important landowner that hired labour and operated *masserie* – through the parishes and through the *opere pie*. Priests were also sometimes dependent on landowners for financial support. The Duomo at Cerignola, for instance, was built at the turn of the century with funds collected by the employers. Finally, priests occupied a position of privilege. From the vantage point of the urban "grottoes", even the humblest priest was still a *signore*. There was a widespread resentment that his services at marriage and funeral ceremonies could not be had without payments that the labouring poor could hardly afford. In the drought of 1908 the clergy announced from the pulpit that the failed harvest was God's punishment for the people's irreligiosity.[51] Most seriously of all, the parish priest was often a moneylender, and there was nothing better calculated than usury to arouse the enmity of the populace.[52]

The distance between farm workers and the clergy was rapidly transformed into active anti-clericalism when the Church took a stand against the workers' organizations. The intervention of the Apulian clergy in politics was clumsy and ineffectual. During open-air rallies held by the leagues the church bells rang to drown the voice of the speakers.[53] Bishops threatened anyone who joined a union with excommunication. Priests counselled resignation and prayer. They refused absolution to known subversives,[54] and denounced class antagonisms. The effects were counter-productive. At Andria, for example, the union organizers reported that the threat of excommunication was a powerful fillip to the leagues, which saw their numbers grow rapidly on the strength of popular resentment at the bishops' strictures.[55]

With the rise of the Italian Socialist Party as a mass force on the national level, the Vatican had revised its opposition to the Liberal state. In 1904 the Pope relaxed the stern *non expedit*, by which Pius IX at the time of Italian unification had forbidden Catholics to take part in the political life of the new state. In socialism the Church confronted an adversary more menacing than the Liberal regime. An important feature of the politics of Giolittian Italy was the entrance of Catholic voters into political life as a counterweight to subversion. In Apulia the clergy took advantage of the new dispensation to make common cause with the ruling parties of order, campaigning actively against the early candidates put forward by the leagues.[56] The result was to create widespread resentment, which erupted in angry outbursts of anti-clericalism. In Cerignola the crowds responded to the electoral intervention of the priests by a series of mass demonstrations, 5,000 strong, in front of the bishop's palace. Here the people assembled to chant "Long live Giordano Bruno!" in memory of the sixteenth-century philosopher burned at the stake for heresy, and "Down with Struffolini!", who was the bishop of the diocese.[57] Religious processions in the city were pelted with stones and broken up.[58]

Apart from such immediate circumstances, the opposition of the unions to the Catholic Church was perhaps inevitable. The leagues combatted a cosmology in which there was a place for saints, miracles, and divine intervention. They rejected the idea of a universe in which men and women could react to hardship and adversity by quietly praying or lighting votive candles. The leagues sought to propagate a purely secular world view in which people were responsible for their own history. They opposed an organization based on hierarchy and authority. They condemned

Catholic social doctrine, which justified property, encouraged quietism, and taught that inequality was an ineradicable part of God's will. Syndicalism, in the last analysis, was a secular faith incompatible with Catholicism.[59]

Under a variety of influences, then, opposition to the clergy became a leading theme of union propaganda. Speakers exposing the corruption of the Church toured the region and held open-air mass rallies devoted to the theme. The union press was filled with articles on the lax conduct of parish priests. Anti-clerical demonstrations became a regular part of popular protest. A measure of the importance of the issue in the eyes of the movement is provided by the founding congress of the provincial union federation of Bari in 1907. The opening address of the organization was devoted to a denunciation of the Church.[60]

6

••

REVOLUTIONARY SYNDICALISM

Not surprisingly, relations between the classes were strained to breaking point. There were many indications of deep and abiding social tensions. One measure of the enmity between workers and landlords was the stream of reports from the various Apulian communes to the prefects of Bari and Foggia provinces from the 1870's. Asked to describe labour relations in their communes, the mayors in the zone of latifundism often gave sobering replies. At Barletta the relations between workers and employers "are such as may exist between creditors and debtors."[1] In a similar spirit, the mayor of Spinazzola observed, "No love is lost."[2] At San Severo the deputy prefect wrote to Foggia, "Being generally oppressed by misery, the class of peasants does not look upon the landlord with much favour."[3] There was a "widespread general discontent",[4] a "feeling of resentment on the part of the poor". Indeed, by the turn of the century Apulian farm workers had acquired a reputation for being "turbulent, bad tempered, and insubordinate". Employers in neighbouring Basilicata refused to hire them.[5]

The gathering crisis in Apulian society found outlet in the closing decades of the nineteenth century in a variety of forms of open class warfare. One was an epidemic of poaching and theft from the *masserie*. These crimes spread and deepened to the degree that the authorities by the early years of the twentieth century considered them the major problem of public order. In two of the most crime-ridden provinces in Italy, poaching and rural theft were overwhelmingly the most frequent of all offences.

87

10 Cerignola, 1900: Sanctuary of the Madonna di Ripalta. The crowd accompanying the icon of the patron saint to the shrine.

More revealing than the extent of the phenomenon was the attitude of the labouring population, as the prefects described it. The normal view of the populace was that the holdings of the *latifondisti* were an illegitimate usurpation. Thieves were regarded as avengers. Thus, after describing the squalor of the farm workers' life in the 1870's and the advantage the landlords took of the workers' misery, the deputy prefect of San Severo concluded, "This is the reason that, when theft or incendiarism occurs on the estates, the peasant stands indifferently aside and watches, unless he actively lends a hand to the thieves, either sharing in the booty or refusing to name the guilty parties to the police."[6] The result, lamented the prefect of Foggia, was that, although both theft and arson were rampant, "the culprits are never discovered".[7] Incendiarism, even more than theft, was transparently a settling of scores and a warning. The social significance of such occurrences was that they revealed a widespread tacit disbelief in the legitimacy of the existing order. Theft, furthermore, was characterized by a fierce determination. The men who stole sheep and plundered stores went armed and opened fire on watchmen and rural police who attempted to forestall them. On the northern Tavoliere in the district of San Severo and San Nicandro, where the nearby mountains of the Gargano furnished a natural refuge, theft took the form of large-scale cattle stealing. Organized gangs of bandits laid siege to whole estates, setting fire to buildings and shooting the occupants.[8] Here the *masserie* had the appearance of armed fortresses in enemy territory.

So pervasive were crimes of this sort that they supported a sizeable class of men – known as *cicivuzzi* – who occupied no place in the census returns. According to the parliamentary enquiry, these were former independent peasants who had been expropriated and forced to settle on the Italian frontier.[9] They were ambitious and bitter, and found in crime an alternative to the life of the work gangs. Thanks to them, men of wealth in Andria lived in constant fear for their lives and property, despite the presence of four police forces.

If theft, rustling, and incendiarism were indicators of the stresses in the countryside, there were also spontaneous local demonstrations in times of acute hardship during the last quarter of the nineteenth century and the opening decade of the twentieth. The years between 1887 and the early 1890's were the blackest period in modern Apulian history. Preceded by the onset of the Great Depression and a fall in the world price of wheat, the hard years began in earnest with the tariff war with France, which closed the great export market of Apulian wine, and lasted until the conclusion of commercial agreements in the 1890's providing alternative outlets in central Europe. In this crisis employment in the grape zone collapsed, producing hunger on a horrific and unprecedented scale. Wages fell as low as 0.10 and 0.15 lire a day.[10] These were years when people died of starvation on the streets of Andria, Barletta, and Cerignola. A captain in the *carabinieri* at Andria wrote to his superiors, "The peasant Riccardo Ruberti collapsed on the public thoroughfare from starvation . . . There is now every sign of such cases occurring with some frequency."[11] In the same vein the captain's commanding officer, Colonel Caracciolo, observed, "Whole families have been without food for days. They move about the streets of the town and make a horrifying sight. Any description would seem exaggeration. Many people are so hungry that they are unable to stand upright, and they take to their beds in the worst possible misery."[12] The town council of Gravina in 1888 reported the "general pauperization of Apulia" and noted "the crudest and most squalid poverty".[13] The average per capita consumption of wheat, which had stood at 145 kilos a year in 1871–5 and at 132 in 1881–5, plunged to 119 in 1891–5.[14]

In this period of extreme hardship crowds gathered spontaneously and marched on town hall to the chant of "Work and Bread!". Bands of labourers also went from villa to villa demanding money. On such occasions, it required only a flashpoint to transform a desperate and angry demonstration into a riot. Apulian history in the closing decades of the century was punctuated by local risings when workmen turned on those they regarded as responsible for their misery – local authorities, the police, the clergy, excise men, retailers who suddenly raised the price of bread.

Economic recovery, when it came in the second half of the 1890's, produced only a relative amelioration for the farm workers. In 1900 workers experienced conditions which were no better than in the decades preceding the great crisis. As the new century began, wages in absolute terms were at the same level as they had been at the time of unification, while expenses in the new urban centres had increased. A single bad harvest, a rise in the price of bread remained sufficient to set off an explosion.

Ginosa in 1908 and Molfetta in 1902 illustrate the way in which such events occurred. At Ginosa in the drought of 1908 a procession of hungry children marched to beg the intercession of the priest to bring rain. Instead he mockingly threw buckets of water of them as they gathered on the church steps. In the resulting panic and flight two children were crushed to death. Within the hour a mob of 1,000 farm workers arrived, determined to lynch the priest and to burn down the town hall. Only the prompt arrival of the *carabinieri* saved him. Molfetta provides another example. There a shortage of flour brought thousands of angry men and women into the piazza. They looted the mills, besieged the police barracks, and tried to storm the offices of the municipal government.

Riots of this nature reveal the extent of popular disaffection. They were not, however, a serious challenge to the power of the landed classes. The riots had no organization or leadership, and they collapsed almost as quickly as they began. They sometimes achieved the immediate aim of frightening shopkeepers into lowering the price of flour or of exacting vengeance. They did not, however, produce lasting social change or an alteration of conditions. In 1889, for instance, Colonel Caracciolo described the political situation at Andria for the benefit of the prefect. "There are", he wrote, "no political sects in Andria. Any popular movement or disorder will be only a direct reaction to misery. It is a simple question of hunger."[15]

The beginning of the new century marked a turning point. Spontaneous local riots continued to occur. For the first time, however, popular protest began to assume organized political forms. Even the chants of demonstrators revealed a growing political awareness. The old slogans of "Work!" and "Bread!" gave way to much more combative imprecations, such as "Down with town hall!", "Down with the landlords!", and "Out with the thieves!". The Bari daily, *Corriere delle Puglie*, caught the essence of the change when it remarked of popular protest in 1904:

The discontent of the masses ... is by now the result of a persistent conviction.

It is not only hardship and low pay that engender this hatred. There is a factor more important than economic conditions. In the consciousness of the people there is a moral objective that in the course of years of experience urges people on to destroy traditions that the modern world does not accept.[16]

Landmarks in the history of the region were passed in 1901 with the proclamation of the first agricultural strikes in the history of the region, beginning at Foggia; the establishment of the first farm workers' unions, known as "peasant leagues"; and the setting up of the Bari Chamber of Labour. The Foggia Chamber of Labour followed in 1902. In the first week of April 1902, moreover, the first Regional Congress of Apulian Peasants met at Foggia to establish priorities and to determine the strategy of the new organizations. In this fashion the impulse to individual or spontaneous protest was slowly supplanted by conscious and disciplined political activity. Theft and rioting continued, but an interesting development which all observers acknowledged was that both crime and riot declined *pari passu* with the advance of the union movement, which was mainly anarcho-syndicalist in political orientation, under the influence of such leaders as Giuseppe De Falco, Raffaele Pastore, Giuseppe Di Vittorio, and Enrico Meledandri.

Since syndicalism at the national level first emerged within the socialist party and throughout the Giolittian era formed an organized revolutionary faction within it, there was no contradiction between being a socialist and being a syndicalist. Italian syndicalist intellectuals such as Arturo Labriola and Enrico Leone took the position that they were in fact the true socialists. Their mission was to win the party back to its proper course after the betrayal of Filippo Turati and the reformists. Considering themselves orthodox marxists, they had no intention of breaking their links with the organized working class. Instead of forming a movement outside and against the socialist party, the syndicalists sought to win the party over to a revolutionary strategy.[17] It is not surprising that the Apulian syndicalists followed in the same direction, although, as southerners, their commitment to the party was more tenuous. It was a clear indication of the political stance of the newly founded Apulian labour movement that the Apulian delegates to the national congresses of the PSI formed part of the syndicalist faction and voted overwhelmingly in favour of its resolutions.[18] It was common practice, furthermore, for the chambers of labour in both Foggia and Bari provinces to affiliate with the syndicalist union confederation, the USI, rather than the reformist CGL. In Capitanata all agitations under the aegis of the Foggia Chamber of Labour and its secretary Euclide Trematore were carried out in consultation with the USI.[19]

Revolutionary syndicalism flourished in Apulia for a number of reasons. Theory, however, was not one of them. Abstract political doctrine was of minimal influence, as one would expect in a movement whose membership was illiterate and undernourished. Apulian union members did not read Georges Sorel or Arturo Labriola. Indeed, there was a widespread hostility to abstraction as a luxury for which there was little place in the midst of more pressing political tasks. Leaders who attempted to theorize at union congresses were reminded that the movement had more urgent concerns. In more than two decades of intense political activity, the Apulian farm workers' movement did not produce a single major theorist - if one excludes Sergio Pannunzio from Molfetta. Pannuzio's ties with the left were fleeting, and he eventually found a different political career as a foremost apologist for fascism.

The very directness and clarity of the syndicalist message were part of the strength of the movement in Apulian conditions. Giuseppe Di Vittorio, himself a day labourer and the most influential syndicalist leader in the region, made a positive virtue of the absence of an elaborate theory, on the ground that no political movement should possess a doctrine beyond the comprehension of its members. The implications, he argued, would otherwise prove corrosive of internal democracy. The roots of anarcho-syndicalism in Apulia lay not in theory but in the conditions the labourers faced.

One important source of the appeal of syndicalism was that,

from the time of the crystallization of a coherent syndicalist current within the PSI between 1902 and 1904, the movement formed the left wing of the Italian labour movement. To be a syndicalist thereafter was to take a stand against the compromises with the established order made by the socialist leadership under Turati. To Apulian union activists the PSI had fundamentally betrayed the revolutionary cause and the rights of southerners. In their view, the party had become not a vehicle for fundamental change but a pressure group winning concessions on behalf of a nothern working-class elite. The concessions achieved by the PSI and the unions of the CGL did not extend to the South, where the toleration of strikes, the policy of high wages, the enactment of social-security provisions, and the achievement of universal suffrage did not apply. The Apulian left denied that the party had made any genuine attempt to deal with the "Southern Question". The northern socialist comrades, they claimed, had made their peace with the status quo. The PSI provided no analysis of the agrarian structures of the Mezzogiorno. The party sent no speakers, no organizers, and no money. The socialist press relegated information about the labour movement south of Rome to the back pages. The socialist deputies in parliament, far from supporting the Apulian strike movement enthusiastically, denied that the day labourers in the region constituted a "real" proletariat. They chastised the leagues for illegal methods, their "hotheadedness", and their "primitive impulsiveness".[20] Their recommendations were for greater patience and respect for the law.[21]

In the aftermath of the famous San Severo massacre in 1908, when troops opened fire on strikers, the socialist parliamentary group took an ambiguous position. They condemned the action of the state, but attributed much of the blame to the farm workers themselves. The deputies from the North called upon their comrades in Apulia to show "sentiments of moderation", to reject the tactic of repeated general strikes, and to rid themselves of "the impulsiveness that is harmful to all".[22] *Avanti!* loftily appealed against the "coarseness" (*rozzezza*) of the day labourers in the region.[23] Indeed, the paper argued that, in general, the "naive" recourse to the general strike attenuated, though it did not eliminate, the responsibility of troops who opened fire on strikers.[24]

In this climate, Apulian syndicalism was in part a protest against Turatian reformist politics – "monarchist reformism", in the words of the Apulian labour leadership.[25] Syndicalism, therefore, entailed a rejection of the bureaucratization and lack of internal democracy of the PSI and the national unions, of the parliamentarian path to socialism, and of the strategy of collaboration with Giovanni Giolitti, whom the Apulians called a "mafia boss" and the enemy of the South. According to the Bari-province union paper *La Conquista*, "The socialist deputies . . . are no different from any others. They too are bought and sold. And so Giolitti plays the tyrant, calm and undisturbed as always."[26]

The bitterness of feeling found expression in the resolution adopted by the Bitonto farm workers' league in 1907, which called for a total break with the existing PSI and the foundation of an alternative socialist party of the South. The reasons were clearly set forth in the text:

Here there is deep unrest, even indignation, directed against the leadership of the party because of the nonchalance with which it treats the vital interests of our region. As if insults were not enough, we now face the indifference of those whose sacred duty it is to promote the liberation of their comrades.[27]

Indeed, several attempts were made by the Apulian left during the first decade of the twentieth century to found such a southern socialist party. The effort failed, however, in the face of the insuperable problem that only in Apulia was there an organized mass peasant movement.[28] The only result of this initiative was the establishment in December 1910 of a "Federation of the proletarian organizations of the South", which lapsed into inactivity.[29]

Syndicalism, furthermore, fits the conditions of political life in the region. The precariousness of the structures of agriculture in

Apulia and the profitability constraints under which farmers operated precluded easy concessions and a successful politics of reformism. This factor, combined with the sheer misery and desperation of the mass of farm workers, radicalized the labour movement and confirmed the sway of revolutionary leaders within it.

The syndicalist reliance on unions instead of a party as the instruments for the emancipation of labour was also a response to the sociology of Apulian latifundism. Organization on an occupational rather than a geographical basis had much to recommend it in a socially homogeneous area where virtually all of the working class was engaged in a single activity and where there was almost no stratification within the ranks of the rural proletariat. For workers so deprived of resources, moreover, the lightning general strike at harvest time was the only weapon available to the farm workers capable of bringing sufficient pressure to bear upon the landlords. Direct action, in addition, was relatively easy to conduct in the teeming agro-cities where a single man with a trumpet sufficed to call the workers into the streets.

The local general strike was also well suited to the opponents the unions faced. The Apulian landlords, in contrast to their counterparts in the Po Valley or in Tuscany, lacked cohesion and organization. There was no equivalent of the provincial agrarian associations of Parma, Bologna, and Ferrara; of the Interprovincial Landowners' Federation, which linked employers throughout the Po Valley; or of the highly centralized and disciplined Tuscan Agrarian Association that emerged to confront the threat of mass unionization after the Great War. The leagues confronted isolated local employers who were especially vulnerable to union pressure because they lacked the support of an authoritative association.

The importance of this disorganization can be appreciated if one recalls the contrasting fate of syndicalist organization in the northern province of Parma. In Parma, the syndicalist stronghold in the northern countryside, the movement suffered a crushing defeat in 1908. A major factor in the defeat, a recent study has shown, was the fact that the landlords of the province, led by Lino Carrara, were powerfully organized and prepared for a prolonged state of siege. When the employers in the Po Valley confronted an all-out provincial general strike, they enjoyed the benefits of strike insurance to offset losses in production and of a collectively planned and coordinated resistance. They were therefore prepared to endure a labour stoppage lasting for months. In Apulia, by contrast, the landlords were vulnerable to the pressure of the strike at harvest time. As in the Po Valley, the early waves of agitation and unionization in the first decades of the twentieth century led to a series of attempts to found agrarian associations. Local employers' associations on the communal level were founded in the tense year of 1907 at a handful of major centres – Cerignola, Spinazzola, and Canosa. These were followed in 1913 and 1915 by similar associations at Corato and San Severo.[30] Not until the postwar years, however, were provincial associations established, and a regional federation, though widely discussed, never came into being.

To list the agrarian associations operating in the region is misleading in the implication that the organizations were effective. In fact, the provincial and communal employers' organizations in Apulia never gained the authority of their counterparts in northern and central Italy. They were associations that led a difficult and fitful life in the midst of the general apathy of the landlords. The organizations, once founded, were unable to impose discipline on their members; they were financially weak; and they often existed primarily on paper.

The most obvious influence which undermined the sporadic efforts at organization was the violent fluctuations typical of Mediterranean dry farming. Output in Apulia oscillated widely from year to year, and with these swings the bargaining power of the unions ebbed and flowed. It was all too easy, therefore, for landlords who saw the need for unity in 1906 and 1907, when the leagues gained victory after victory, then to relapse into a sense of apathy during the poor harvests between 1909 and 1912 when there was hardly a strike anywhere in the region and landlords seemed to have regained the upper hand.

A further reason for this striking and characteristic disorganization of the Apulian landed elite was absenteeism. Scattered throughout the Italian peninsula and abroad, ignorant of agriculture and of conditions in Apulia, the *latifondisti* were nearly impossible to organize. There was no regional capital where their interests converged, and where they met to form a network of contacts, clubs, and societies. No Apulian city performed the functions of Florence in Tuscany or Bologna in Emilia. Bari, the Apulian capital, was not the focal point of agrarian interests. On the contrary, the most common place of residence for the *latifondisti* was Naples, and there the Apulians were submerged in the great metropolis of the South as a whole. On the side of the *massari*, a corresponding factor which inhibited organization was the extreme brevity of leases. Settled on an estate for only three years, the capitalist farmer had little interest in long-term association.

A further source of disaggregation was the division between landlords and farmers, who were separated by a long history of bitter disputes over rent, the renewal of contracts, and the upkeep of the estates. Far from forming a united front with the proprietors in the face of the challenge of unionization, the *massari* quarrelled bitterly with them over the issue of which party should bear the financial burden imposed by the leagues. Land occupations by union members in particular drove a wedge between the two great sub-classes of the landed interest. The legal responsibility for the losses sustained and for the costs imposed by the workers was unclear, and each side was determined not to bear the expense. In several communes the *massari* went so far as to abandon the estates *en masse* during agitations, in effect boycotting landlords who refused to pay for work performed illegally by the leagues.

An additional divisive factor was the diversity of Apulian agriculture. Most obvious was the gulf separating the besieged *latifondisti* to the north and west of Bari and the undisturbed proprietors of the *marina*. Even in the areas of latifundism and syndicalist unrest, however, there were important divergences of interest. From the standpoint of the labourers, social conditions in Santeramo, Spinazzola, and Foggia, where only wheat was grown, were similar to those prevailing in the mixed-crop centres such as Cerignola, Andria, and Barletta. From the standpoint of the landowners, however, there were substantial differences. Wheat growers were more backward in their methods, more susceptible to violent and sudden fluctuations in output, more vulnerable to increases in the costs of labour, more dependent on tariff protection than the exporting wine producers. As a result, wheat farmers tended to be more intransigent.

A similar opposition set small landlords and great *latifondisti* at odds. Big landlords could afford to take the long view, to make concessions to the unions in the interest of social peace. Small and financially insecure farmers, with their entire economic and social future hanging on the outcome of the current agricultural season, had little margin for reformism. In an environment marked by the intransigence of the proprietors as a whole, it was the lesser farmers who nonetheless stood out as the diehard extremists, who destroyed the results achieved in painful negotiations by refusing to honour the agreements signed.

Finally, within even a single commune, and among landowners operating comparable crop systems of similar dimensions, factionalism all too frequently prevailed over harmony or a rational calculation of class interest. Election as deputy and control of town hall were coveted prizes that brought enormous financial rewards and powers of patronage, as well as prestige and influence. The contest for these spoils divided powerful families into feuding factions. At San Severo, for instance, the dominant Masselli family and the Fraccacreta clan were bitter rivals, as were the Jatta and Cotugno factions at Ruvo and the Pavoncelli and Larochefoucauld estates at Cerignola.

The results were favourable to the tactics of syndicalism. Lacking an organization and authoritative spokesmen, the Apulian landlords were ill prepared to resist the general strike. In the panic of an all-out confrontation when the profits for a whole year were at risk, the Apulian proprietors found themselves reduced to the stark alternatives of capitulation or physical force. Both reactions radicalized the labour movement further.

The experience of the Po Valley also had a direct ideological influence on the emergence of Apulian syndicalism. Despite its ultimate débâcle, the Parma field workers' strike of 1908, when the labourers stayed out from 1 May until the first week of July, served as a model of the kind of combative solidarity and organization that day labourers could achieve.[31] This example occurred just at the moment when the Apulian leagues were successfully establishing a mass political base. The syndicalist leader Alceste De Ambris, secretary of the Parma Chamber of Labour during the high point of its success in 1907 and 1908, toured Apulia to explain the lessons of the experience of the North.[32] In 1913 he was invited to preside over the third Apulian regional socialist congress when it met at Bari in December.[33] Interestingly, syndicalism established itself in Apulia just at the time when it was experiencing a major crisis and decline at the national level.

In explaining the strength of syndicalism in Apulia, one must also mention the influence of Cerignola. "Red Cerignola" was the Bologna of Apulia, the guiding centre and model that union activists throughout the region studied, visited, and imitated. It was the Cerignola league that was the most disciplined, had the largest membership, and achieved the most lasting and significant victories. Once established at Cerignola, therefore, under such charismatic leaders as Giuseppe Di Vittorio, syndicalism became a natural reference point for unions throughout Foggia and Bari provinces.[34] The close similarity of social and economic conditions for labourers throughout the zones dominated by latifundia further promoted a uniformity of political direction.

Nevertheless, although the leagues were predominantly syndicalist, they were not exclusively so. There were substantial areas of revolutionary socialist strength and a pocket of reformism. The revolutionary socialist stronghold was the agricultural centre of San Severo at the far north of the Tavoliere, together with the

11 Cerignola, *ca.* 1890: Grape crushing.

neighbouring communes of San Nicandro Garganico, San Marco in Lamis, and S. Giovanni Rotondo. The difference in political direction from the southern Tavoliere and from the farm workers' movement in Bari province was partly the result of the personal influence of the very able socialist leaders Domenico Fioritto and Leone Mucci. More important, however, was a difference in social structure. San Severo was dominated by latifundia, but, unlike the rest of the Tavoliere, it also possessed a substantial number of small peasant proprietors.

On the extreme northern end of the Foggia plateau, the establishment of vineyards in the 1870's and the 1880's had been accomplished on more favourable terms for the peasants. The improvement contracts provided for the *versurieri* to become the owners or leaseholders of the small plots of land they transformed. The result was a heterogeneous work force with substantial strata of peasants possessing or leasing land, as well as landless labourers.[35] For the local landlord A. Fraccacreta, San Severo – in marked contrast with Cerignola – presented a picture of "rural democracy" with a "healthy flowering of small [peasant] proprietors". By his calculation, 3,765 peasants in the commune owned 9,064 hectares of land in 1912.[36] The amounts owned were small, but the possession of even a tiny plot made a marked difference in social structure which transformed the task confronting labour organizers. At San Severo too many peasants had a direct interest in the harvest to make the general strike at harvest time a viable tactic, and too many cultivators fulfilled too many different agricultural roles to make syndicalist organization by occupational grouping a reasonable prospect.

Furthermore, the San Severo socialists set themselves the task of organizing the impoverished peasants of the nearby hills of the Gargano then in the final throes of expropriation as indebtedness, enclosure, taxation, and competition from the great estates forced them off the land and into the labour gangs of the plain. San Nicandro, S. Marco, and S. Giovanni were communes with large numbers of peasant cultivators, many of whom migrated at harvest time to work as day labourers on the nearby Tavoliere. Here revolutionary syndicalism and the leagues gave way to more traditional political initiatives. Geography replaced occupation as the basis of peasant resistance to the landlord. Issues such as housing, taxation, enclosure, health, and the reform of local government formed the core of socialist propaganda rather than the closed shop.[37] For the same reasons, the fragile union structures in Lecce province were socialist rather than syndicalist, despite the fact that they developed under the aegis of the syndicalist Bari Chamber of Labour.

The small reformist socialist current in Apulia was entirely *sui generis*, and was inseparable from its greatest leader, Gaetano Salvemini. His influence was strongest in the hinterland of Bari, and especially in the communes of Molfetta and Bitonto. This zone was unlike the areas where syndicalism and revolutionary socialism were based. It was not a zone of latifundism, but of dispersed landownership. Here there was also a sizeable number of artisans and industrial workers. In this context Salvemini built an electoral coalition – unique in Apulia – of radical professionals, republican artisans, reformist peasants, and socialist day labourers.

It should be stressed, however, that, despite political differences, the overriding feature of the labour movement in Apulia was its solidarity. There was a general awareness that the Apulian left was in an isolated and exposed position, that it could ill afford the luxury of factional struggles. Furthermore, as southerners, Apulian reformists, marxists, and syndicalists shared a common opposition to Turati's acceptance of the Giolittian political framework. The reformist Salvemini shared many of the political viewpoints of the revolutionaries. It was Salvemini who was the foremost spokesman for the Southern Question within the PSI, who labelled Giolitti's government "the ministry of the underworld". Salvemini was a critical, combative reformist.[38] The solidarity of the left in the region was symbolized by the activity of the syndicalist Di Vittorio, who campaigned on his bicycle for the election of Salvemini to parliament. Similarly, the socialists at San Severo were greatly influenced by the experience of the Cerignola organization. Luigi Allegato, leader of the San Severo farm workers' union, journeyed to Cerignola to study the organizational methods developed there. The differences were primarily a question of organizational structures rather than of objectives. In the heterogeneous society of the northern Tavoliere and the Gargano, revolutionaries turned to collectivism and the use of the powers of local government to achieve the socialization of the land rather than the general strike.

The great breakthrough for the labour movement occurred in the years 1906–8, when the workers' movement successfully established a stable organizational presence and a disciplined following. In nearly every centre of Bari and Foggia provinces a "peasant league" was founded, and linked to province-wide union federations, to a local chamber of labour, and to the chambers of labour in the two provincial capitals. By the second regional congress in 1908, 65,000 farm workers had been unionized – 39,000 in Bari province; 25,000 in Foggia; and just 1,200 in Lecce.[39] The leagues were forged in a wave of agricultural strikes that made Apulia the second leading region of agrarian union activity in Italy after Emilia. In 1906 there were 37 strikes involving 18,000 strikers; in 1907, 45 strikes and 109,000 strikers.[40] The socialist party, by contrast, remained primarily an electoral label with a frail organization and anaemic membership lists, as the figures in Table 8 reveal.[41] The party, furthermore, took no part in the organization of strikes and agitations.[42]

The progress of the unions should not be imagined as an unbroken run of successes. The difference between victory and defeat in any given year hung in the balance and was decided by such imponderables as the weather, the degree of state inter-

Table 8. *Number of socialist-party branches and members in Foggia, Bari, and Lecce provinces*

Province	Branches	Members
1906		
Foggia	7	178
Bari	14	220
Lecce	10	177
1907		
Foggia	10	185
Bari	22	421
Lecce	9	101

vention, and the resolve of the lo✴l employers. In the years between 1901 and the Great War, the years of advance by the movement were 1901–2, 1904, 1906–8, and 1913–15. In the intervals there were serious setbacks and failures, especially in the aftermath of 1908, when crop failure followed by a cholera epidemic and a major counter-offensive by employers led to severe reversals. For the years between 1901 and 1912, Angelo Fraccacreta produced the figures for strikes and strikers in Foggia province shown in Table 9.[43]

The strikes organized by the Apulian leagues were unrivalled for determination and reciprocal ferocity. The agitations rapidly acquired a characteristic pattern. Since disputes began with the onset of the peak periods in the agricultural year, just after long months of unemployment and hunger, the reserves of the men were nonexistent. To succeed, the labourers had to apply the maximum pressure as rapidly as possible. Furthermore, they had to deny the employers the possibility of importing "foreigners" to continue production. To overcome these difficulties in their bargaining position, the leagues resorted to the general strike.

Table 9. *Strikes and strikers in Foggia
province, 1901–11*

Year	Strikes	Strikers
1901	1	600
1902	7	1,780
1903	none	none
1904	3	8,000
1905	2	7,400
1906	6	4,000
1907	16	48,000
1908	16	20,000
1909	3	400
1910	none	none
1911	none	none

Pickets sealed off the commune with barricades, while teams of union men armed with their work tools patrolled the countryside to ensure that the *annaroli* adhered to the movement and to prevent the importation of blacklegs. The leagues also imposed closure on all commercial premises. At Minervino Murge in 1907, for instance, the press reported that the league "functions as a committee of public safety which decrees the closing of shops; orders bricklayers, tailors, and cobblers to suspend work; issues written permimssion for the operation of bakeries and the transportation of cadavers to the cemetery; and occasionally issues safe conduct passes".[44]

Such tactics were successful in these early years. From about 1906, wages began to improve as a direct result of union activity. The increases, moreover, were substantial. Assessing the situation at Spinazzola, for instance, the chairman of the farm workers' league, Raffaele Pastore, calculated that between 1901 and 1911 the monthly earnings of labourers at high season nearly doubled – from 31.7 lire to 60.5 lire.[45] A greater general well-being found expression also in an increased average annual per capita consumption of wheat, which rose to 156 kilos during the years 1908–12 – the highest levels since unification.[46]

The *massari* were caught off balance, unorganized and unprepared. If the workers chose their moment well, delay by just a few days could put an entire harvest in jeopardy. Mules, horses, and sheep were also at risk. The sealing off of the towns prevented the carters from supplying the estates with provisions and forced the *annaroli* to return to town, leaving their animals unattended. An additional important purpose of the blockade was to cut off the supply of water, which was brought to town in barrels by merchants. The aim was to use thirst to force the *massari* to yield. "Hunger", argued De Falco, "is the weapon of the bosses; thirst is the arm of the proletariat."[47]

Furthermore, every day that a strike involving thousands of hungry men and women continued, tensions mounted, violent incidents escalated, and there was the ever-present threat – planned by none but implicit in the situation – of a full-scale uprising. Indeed, the possibility was realized when landlords sought to import *marinesi* as blacklegs, or corporals attempted to force the picket lines. Then pitched battles and savage scenes were enacted. Such events occurred at Ruvo in 1907 and 1908, at Foggia in 1907, and at Cerignola in 1910 and 1914. Union members launched manhunts against "foreigners", attacking them with axes, knives, and clubs. In each instance several outsiders were killed, and scores were seriously injured.[48]

What were the demands of the strikers? The most important and frequent demands were:

(1) Union recognition.
(2) Wage increases, often of the order of 50–100 per cent. To prevent abuse, the unions also called for wages to be paid entirely in cash rather than in kind.
(3) Written rather than oral agreements. The establishment of formal contracts was a means to limit the arbitrary power of the overseers, and to abolish such practices as "free contracting" and the "deposit".
(4) A ban on the hiring of outsiders.
(5) The establishment of labour exchanges (*uffici di collocamento*) under the auspices of the leagues. The task of the exchange was to control and discipline the labour market. In each municipality the exchange would set up rosters of union members, who would be assigned in turn to the fields as employment became available. The *massari* would lose their right to pick and choose their men, and the piazzas would be circumvented entirely, putting an end to the regime of the corporals.

In addition to the five principal demands of the union agitation, the leagues pressed for a variety of specific reforms – accommodation for those who slept in the fields; transport; payment for time lost through travel or inclement weather; improvements in the quality of rations; regular rest periods during the work day; the observance of the first of May as a recognized holiday; the presence of a league representative on each estate to guarantee compliance with the agreed terms of contract; the confiscation of privately owned firearms; and the cultivation of broad beans in the winter to provide employment during the slack season.[49]

Simultaneously with the strike movement, the leagues sought to reverse the enclosure and usurpation of common land. They carried out a series of land invasions as union members occupied and cultivated the former commons and sheep highways. The immediate impetus behind the occupations was economic – the attempt to relieve unemployment – but the assault on the institution of private property itself was apparent when thousands of workers re-appropriated land they regarded as their own. These occupations had a grand ceremonial quality as columns of families marched to the fields in procession to the accompaniment of bands, floats, and red banners. In several places, producers' cooperatives were established to negotiate leases directly with the landlord, bypassing the *massaro* entirely as a "superfluous intermediary". The ultimate aim announced by the first regional congress of farm labourers at Foggia in 1902 was the "socialization of the land".[50]

It would be a mistake, however, to overestimate the importance of economic demands. Just as vital were the aspirations to moral reform and social equality. Alongside the contest with the *latifondisti*, the leagues conducted a programme of self-discipline and improvement. There were campaigns against alcoholism and delinquency. Members were urged not to carry knives, and any union member found guilty of crime or anti-social behaviour was subject to dismissal from the movement.[51] Literacy classes were held in the evening, and the union constitutions frequently contained clauses stating that attendance was compulsory. A number of leagues opened libraries. Vocational training in agricultural skills was an official demand of the movement. For children, after-school centres were set up with the aim of removing the young from the influence of the streets and of placing them in an environment where they would be supervised while they prepared their lessons or took part in games and exercises.[52] On Sundays there were regular open-air assemblies and speeches. These were festive occasions that lasted for most of a day. The speakers were met at the station or the city gates by a band and a mass procession. There was then a rally in the central piazza. This was a major event during which union orators harangued thousands of assembled workers on such themes as the nefarious power of the clergy, divorce, socialism and art, the rights of women, and the experience of union organizations in other communes.[53] To teach the lesson of class solidarity, the leagues concluded these meetings with collections in support of workers' resistance elsewhere in Italy. In Cerignola in 1914, for instance, there were collections among the farm labourers on behalf of the railroad workers and the marble quarriers of Carrara in Tuscany, which was a major anarchist stronghold.[54] The order of priorities was correctly appraised by the *Corriere delle Puglie*, which reported that the organizers of the unions "think of improving the moral and intellectual conditions of the workers today, and their economic conditions tomorrow".[55]

The Sunday rallies reveal that the leagues fulfilled many of the ceremonial functions traditionally performed by the Church. In the grim life of the field workers on the latifundia there was a clear need for occasional release. Throughout the Mezzogiorno saints' days and festivals had provided the few great occasions in the life of the peasantry. The pageantry of the feast of the patron saint of Cerignola, the Madonna della Ripalta, in April and September of every year, was typical of such events. In Cerignola on each occasion there were three days of festivities with pyrotechnic displays from midnight until dawn, horse races, bands, dancing, and the solemn progress of the float of the Madonna through the city to the accompaniment of a brass band while the entire populace lined the streets.[56] This feast performed a deeply felt social function that had little to do with religion. As Presutti discovered, the population responded above all to the spectacle, the folklore, and the opportunity to socialize. The festival of the patron saint was a pagan celebration of the beginning and the end of the agricultural cycle.

If such festivals provided public ritual, there were also rare private occasions when even the poorest labourers earned the recognition of their human dignity. The most important of these occasions was death. As the parliamentary investigation reported, the farm labourers at the turn of the century were unwilling to allow a relation to be hurried unceremoniously into a pauper's grave at public expense. Workers who were, in the main, irreligious, preferred to pay for the attendance of priests, who organized music and a funeral procession. Formal recognition was given to the human worth of the deceased.[57]

Both ceremonial functions – the collective and the individual – were assumed by the leagues, which successfully replaced the clergy in the observance of the important movements in the workers' lives. The choreography of the major occasions of the political movement is unintelligible unless one remembers the legacy of the past. The leagues built on tradition and local usage. The observance of May Day or a union rally under the auspices of the Foggia Chamber of Labour was a recognizable adaptation of traditional southern saints' days or carnival observance. The props were largely unchanged – processions, bands, pyrotechnics, dances and flowers. The workers wore their best clothes and sported red ribbons in their button holes. Politics was not a dour affair, but provided the occasion for a day of open-air festivities.[58]

The relationship between carnivals and saints' day festivals on the one hand and the ceremonial rituals of the leagues on the other hand was organic. The earliest spontaneous farm workers' demonstrations of protest against unemployment and hunger often took place on public festivals. Grand gatherings, when thousands of people assembled and exchanged experiences, were natural occasions for a widely shared anger to find expression. In the 1880's and 1890's saints' days were nervously watched by the police, who reported that angry men whispered in advance of their intention of voicing their feelings when the workers were gathered in the streets. Typical was the case of Molfetta during the economic crisis, when the *carabinieri* viewed the approach of Lent and the carnival season with mounting apprehension. As the commander of the military police wrote in 1889, "In Molfetta people are talking openly of a demonstration on the occasion of the carnival festivities. The motivation is the continuing shortage of work, and the demonstration in this town would not have a peaceful character."[59] Given this background, it was only natural that the organized labour movement should have borne at its maturity the festival birthmarks of its origins.

As well as continuing the religious tradition of collective observance, the leagues took over the personal services once rendered by the parish priest. The leagues undertook, for instance, the funeral observances at the death of any of their members. The entire membership *en masse* accompanied the body to the cemetery, carrying red flags and singing union songs. Indeed, with thousands of people taking part, the unions could provide a more impressive and memorable occasion than the Church. The leagues, moreover – and this was important – provided this ritual free, whereas the priests charged heavy and deeply resented fees. From the moment the leagues were founded, the parliamentary enquiry observed, the priests suddenly found themselves without custom – even when, in competition with the unions, they began to officiate at burials without charge.[60]

The unions also tried to challenge the outward signs of the workers' social inferiority. The first political intervention of Di Vittorio at Cerignola, for instance, did not concern economic questions. His idea was to introduce equality into the Sunday stroll, or *passeggiata*. To achieve this aim, the workers exchanged their traditional winter dress, the cape and beret, for the same uniform – the overcoat and hat – that the *signori* wore. To complete the gesture of defiance, they stuck copies of the socialist paper *Avanti!*, which few could read, in their pockets and refused to take off their newly purchased hats to the landlords as they passed in the street.[61] The vitality and strength of the movement can be understood only if one recalls that it included this fierce element of new-found pride and self-respect. The league at Terlizzi stated simply in its constitution, "We wish to be regarded as men, and to claim as our first demand the right to sit at the common table of society."[62]

The strictly syndicalist or union struggle, which stressed the direct confrontation between workers and employers, was part of a wider strategy. A constant danger facing the leagues was the possibility of the development of fissures within the agricultural working class. The risk was that of a conflict of interest between, on the one hand, a privileged and unionized category of men with jobs and, on the other hand, a fluctuating and more amorphous mass consisting of the unemployed, non-union workers, women, the elderly, and the disabled. The agro-towns, so central to the social structure of latifundism, presented problems as well as opportunities. The concentration of the population in large centres multiplied contacts, aided the circulation of ideas, facilitated the task of organization, and fostered a sense of community. Great labour markets, however, also accentuated the competition for jobs and supported the economic bargaining power of the employers.

The potential for political division in such a situation was revealed on those occasions as at Andria in 1908 when the piazzas became the scenes of violent clashes among workers. The men left behind by the recruiters attacked those who had just been hired, and sought to prevent their departure by force. Crowds of labourers condemned to idleness and hunger gathered to the chant of "All of us or no one!"[63]

It was important to union success, therefore, to establish a broad class solidarity that would unite union and non-union men, the waged and the unemployed, men and women. Syndicalism in the narrow sense, with its stress on the occupational grouping, had to be complemented with anarcho-communism, which stressed the geographical identity of the commune as a collective body cutting across the occupational divide. The strategy was to defend workers in their broad capacity as citizens as well as in their narrow roles as employees.

One way in which this objective could be achieved was to use the power of the unions to build a broad base of support by the adoption of objectives wider than the immediate interests of their members. The labour exchanges provide a good example. In addition to establishing a closed-union shop, the exchanges aimed at instituting a wider system of social welfare for the community. The exchanges required estate managers to provide jobs for men who were otherwise unemployable – the elderly and the disabled. At the same time the leagues agitated for the extension of compulsory insurance against industrial accidents to cover agricultural workers. Pensions, too, they argued, could be funded by the abolition of the standing army and the diversion of the funds saved to the provision of social welfare.[64] Solidarity rather than competition was the basis of the principle that employment should be offered in order of need. The sense of geographical community was further reinforced by the exclusion of "foreigners" from the local labour market, while the general strike united the community as a whole against landlords and farmers.

Another means of strengthening class unity was organizational. The leagues, by definition, were the instrument for the emancipation of those in work and enrolled in the organization. To ensure the representation of the entire working class, a second institution was established – the chamber of labour. Whereas the union was based on occupation, the chamber was organized geographically and included everyone within the commune among its potential members. This institution played a central role in the Apulian farm worker's movement. It was normal practice for major agitations to be led by the chamber of labour as well as the category union. It was the chamber as well that carried out electoral campaigns for the control of town hall by the left. The network of local chambers of labour coordinated the various communal agitations at the provincial level under the leadership of the Bari and Foggia Chambers of Labour. (The frail union structures in Lecce province were affiliated with the Bari Chamber of Labour). The corresponding provincial federations of the category unions led, by contrast, a tenuous existence.

Not only was collective solidarity reinforced through the chamber of labour, but also the movement was able better to make use of the skills of sympathetic members of the community who were not day labourers. Leagues were composed exclusively of farm workers. Membership of the chambers of labour, however, included artisans, building workers, peasants, teachers, lawyers, and non-unionized women, all of whom provided the movement with essential support. The chambers of labour assumed the legal defence and medical care of strikers; drafted labour contracts; assisted union representatives in negotiations; arranged speakers; collected statistical information; and drafted resolutions. In many respects the chambers took over the functions of aggregation and leadership that in other regions were performed by the socialist party.

Through the chambers the revolutionary movement took up the defence of consumers, women, and slum dwellers. Particularly popular among workers in the company towns was the network of consumers' cooperatives. The cooperatives controlled the cost of living; provided guarantees of quality and hygiene; and put an end to the sway of the moneylenders. Prices in the cooperatives remained constant from one harvest to the next. Pressure was also brought to bear on local government to enforce health regulations in the market place. In a society where a small fluctuation in the price of bread could spell widespread hunger and where the market was a constant danger to health, the defence of the consumer had a wide appeal. Many non-union workers joined the movement primarily to gain access to the cooperatives. The issue broadened the appeal of the movement beyond the natural union constituency of adult male farm workers to women in particular. In the established sexual division of labour in the region, women were most acutely subjected to the abuses of the vendors and usurers.

The appeal to women was not simply a tactic of convenience. Feminism was an integral part of the politics of anarcho-syndicalism. Hierarchy in any form was anathema to its libertarian ethos. A continuous effort was made to raise the consciousness of women's rights, to encourage women to take an active political role. In the rallies and open-air meetings that were a regular part of the politics of the left, issues such as divorce and the condition of women were often the chosen theme. One of the most effective speakers the movement possessed was the anarchist feminist Maria Rygier, whose oratory was so powerful that even landlords came out of curiosity to hear her. The issue of anti-clericalism as well had a special relevance to the subjection of Apulian women. The chambers also organized women's leagues.

Another campaign affected urban tenants. Housing was one of the greatest sources of human misery in Apulia. Appalling standards of sanitation, ventilation, and overcrowding were fatal to health, privacy, and family relations. The high level of rent weighed heavily on the family budget. The ownership of the workers' accommodation by employers also provided landlords with a powerful instrument of control, intimidation, and reprisal. The labourers' movement, therefore, organized tenants' resistance by means of rent strikes and tenants' cooperatives. The leagues sponsored the demand that every worker should own his own accommodation – a goal to be achieved through public-works contracts to be awarded to unions of building workers.[65]

Most ambitiously of all, the chambers challenged the power of the landlords in city hall. Electoral abstentionism was not a part of Apulian syndicalism. There was a deep distrust of parliamentary politics at the national level, but the capture of local power through the ballot was an important and accepted objective. The movement elaborated a large-scale programme of local-government reforms, including public works, abolition of the consumption levy, the municipalization of public services, abolition of the municipal police, the paving of streets, the building of schools, and the enforcement of public-health regulations. The strategy envisaged that control of local government would reinforce the power of the leagues and the labour exchanges. Through the control of the commune it would be easier to enforce the ban on outside labourers, for instance. Town hall would also assist the unions in their final objective of breaking up the latifundia. The tax powers of the commune would be used to expropriate the great landowners, while town hall would furnish credit and support for producers' cooperatives that would sweep the *massari* aside.

In the electoral battles the political appearance of the movement is misleading. Syndicalists stood under the socialist banner of the PSI at election time. Socialism, however, was only the name; syndicalism remained the substance. The socialist party, except on the northern Tavoliere, was little more than the name assumed by the chambers of labour on election day. Membership of the PSI was in the main an effort to reduce the isolation of the Apulian left. The chamber conducted the campaign and provided the mass of voters. The party branch normally had little independent existence and lapsed into inactivity between elections.

The first ephemeral electoral victory of the Apulian labour movement occurred at Gravina in 1902 when the socialist doctor Canio Musacchio became mayor.[66] This success, which was reversed in 1903 when the Liberals returned to power in the commune, was consolidated in 1911. Then the school teacher Giuseppe Musacchio, Canio's brother, was chosen as mayor and continued to hold the post without interruption until 1920. The example of Gravina was followed more widely in 1913–14, when several additional communes were captured by the left – Andria, Spinazzola, Cerignola.

The minutes of the town-council executive in Cerignola in the first year of socialist administration from the summer of 1914 convey an atmosphere very different from the old regime in 1912.[67] The precarious financial position that the new council inherited, with a slender tax base and a deficit of 27,892 lire, limited social experimentation. Under the leadership of the mayor, the lawyer Francesco Fiume, the *giunta* nevertheless took a series of immediate measures to confront the urgent needs of the residents of the "pigsty". The payments to sub-contractors for essential services, such as street sweeping, that were never performed were terminated. The town hired its own salaried personnel instead. Public scales were set up prominently in the market square, manned by the municipal guards. Now under the command of Antonio Misceo, the syndicalist councillor and secretary of the farm workers' league, the guards' task was to protect consumers from fraud. Teams of rural guards on bicycles were also formed to distribute quinine to workers in the fields. Doctor Casale at the

Russo Hospital was dismissed, and the vacancy was filled with a qualified doctor appointed through open competition and paid the normal physician's fees. In addition, the town opened a municipal clinic with four doctors in attendance. City hall also sought to combat child labour and illiteracy by funding grants to the children of labourers, so that their families could afford not to send them to work. A new and more accurate electoral list was commissioned. The council also purchased stores of wheat and grain as a means of undermining the black market and regulating the price of bread and flour. Finally, the administration adopted a new principle when it resolved, "It is the duty of the local authorities to intervene, even if only within the limits of what is possible, to alleviate the sufferings of the labouring population."[68]

7

WORK DISCIPLINE

Across the Tavoliere and in Bari province, employers responded with unbending opposition to the radicalization of the labourers and to their demands for change. One reason was psychological – the fear of so radical a reversal of deference. The social gulf between landlords and farm workers was so unbridgeable that it resembled the chasm of a caste or racial divide, and the proprietors were unwilling to tolerate any narrowing of the distance. A frequent problem in the path of union negotiations was the refusal of growers to sit down at the same table with the workers' representatives.

At San Severo in the dispute of 1907, deference was the prime consideration – to the great frustration of the deputy prefect, who feared that the uncompromising stubbornness of the landlords was likely to complicate his task of maintaining public order. The demand of the peasant league, the official complained to his superiors, "was just". The workers did not seek a wage increase. They asked only that wages be set in advance so that the labourers could count on an agreed sum instead of waiting for the farmers to determine on pay day what they could afford to give them. The great barrier to a settlement of the issue was that the employers – "little medieval lords" – refused to parley, on the grounds that "it was unacceptable that they should deal with the peasants as equals". The whole dispute, argued the deputy prefect, was "a simple question of mistakenly understood dignity".[1]

In a similar spirit the landlords at Lucera in 1902 rejected the union demand for a daily wage of 1.50 lire. The chief concern of

12 Cerignola, 1900: The Pavoncelli family palace, built in 1880.

the landlords was not economic. Indeed they announced publicly that such a wage was not excessive, and that they would be pre-pared to grant it to non-union workers. What they refused to con-template was the principle that a farm labourer should demand a voice in the determination of his own salary. Such self-assertiveness the employers regarded as "an infringement of their superiority" and "a new step in the local customs of our agriculture".[2]

Another important representative of lordly intransigence was the Larochefoucauld house at Cerignola. Giuseppe Pavoncelli had been a moderating influence in the city, urging modest conces-sions to de-fuse tensions and to avoid an all-out confrontation. The count's death in 1910, however, brought about the transfer of power in the commune, in the larger constituency, and in the Cerignola Agrarian Federation to the rival employers' faction dominated by the second great landowning family of the southern Tavoliere and the Pavoncellis' implacable enemies – the House of Larochefoucauld. Power passed from the family of the count to the family of the duke. Since the duke was resident in Paris, his power was exercised by his two plenipotentiaries in Italy – Georges Millet, his general administrator, and Eugene Maury, who succeeded Pavoncelli as deputy in the Chamber.

This palace revolution had a political as well as a personal significance. Millet and Maury were the hardest of employers, and the Larochefoucauld fields were feared by the working class. By Millet's own admission, the Larochefoucauld family was thought of locally as "the most retrograde enemies of the people", and was widely known as "the Bourbons".[3] Unlike the Pavoncellis, who attempted to introduce modern methods to increase yields, the Larochefoucauld estate was a model of backwardness that relied exclusively on a policy of low wages. Maury was also heavily involved in moneylending.[4]

Maury and Millet were the advocates of a direct and violent settling of accounts with the leagues, and they voiced their view publicly and unambiguously. Maury and his supporters, during the Frenchman's campaign for election to the Chamber, openly proclaimed the strategy he intended to pursue. They promised to starve the rabble into submission. "The rabble who oppose us", Maury said, "must either give way or disappear".[5] So vocal was Maury in his views that he radically influenced the political situation, earning the hatred of the workers against the foreigner who dominated the commune – their "boss from over the Alps".[6] He even lost the favour of the troops, who were torn between loyalty to order and sympathy for Italians oppressed by a foreigner. Maury's election in 1913 made no small contribution to the "municipal revolution" in Cerignola, which began with the stoning of the Larochefoucauld palace; continued with the great strike of December 1913 (the "Six Days of Cerignola");[7] and ended with the election of the socialist administration under Francesco Fiume in 1914.

Why were so many landlords, farmers, and administrators in Apulia so blindly uncompromising in the fashion of Millet and the proprietors of San Severo and Lucera? The parliamentary enquiry sought to explain such attitudes by noting that, "Accustomed to the long tradition of submission, the landlords are still not convinced that the peasants are men like them, and they fear a bloody rising of this dark and formless mass of proletarians with murder, havoc, and devastation."[8] In the same spirit the government commission on unemployment in Bari province remarked in 1920 that, "With rare exceptions, the mentality of the large landowners in the centres where agitations have been most serious is very backward. In their minds the idea of absolute property still holds sway, together with the notion that an employer's rule over the worker is not open to question. Only after violence and pressure do they adapt to new conditions."[9]

A more tangible factor was economic: Apulia had a backward and vulnerable system of agriculture, which, even behind the shelter of the great tariff of 1887, was able to survive in a world market only because of its ability to minimize costs, both of investment and of labour. As a leading representative of the Apulian landed interest, Domenico Andrea Spada the mayor of Ruvo explained, Apulian farmers could not afford to be trapped in a vice between uncertain harvests, which failed on average one year in four, and labour costs fixed at a high level. Table 10 showing wheat production in the communes of Altamura and Gravina in Bari province illustrates the wild fluctuations in output that made farming in the region such a risky undertaking.[10]

In Capitanata a comparison between the years 1909 and 1910 demonstrates the gamble involved. In 1909 the Tavoliere rivalled the most fertile areas in Europe with a harvest of 2,246,000 quintals of wheat. The yield per hectare was 16 quintals – well above the national average of 10.5, and approaching the Po Valley average of 17 quintals. In 1910, by contrast, production on the Tavoliere fell to 1,023,000 quintals – 7.3 quintals per hectare. Sharp variations in the annual rainfall were an important factor in these

Table 10. *Wheat production in Altamura*
and Gravina in Bari province

Year	Yield in quintals	
	Altamura	Gravina
1906	135,000	80,000
1907	79,000	70,000
1908	40,000	40,000
1909	94,000	160,000
1910	44,000	100,000
1911	figs. missing	220,000
1912	159,000	80,000
1913	65,000	70,000

violent oscillations. In the first thirty years of the twentieth century the annual rainfall at Foggia varied from 329.6 to 756.5
millimetres.[11]

Under such conditions, management considered wage rates set
in advance to be an intolerable burden. Constant themes of landlords' discussions were the impossibility of accepting the "regime
of labour contracts"[12] and the insistence on returning to what they
termed the "street price" for labour.[13] At stake were the essential
props of rent and profit. There were no margins for an easy
acceptance of unionization and high wages. The landlord from
Barletta, F. Casardi, wrote in alarm in 1911, "If the present
demands continue, our agriculture will go bankrupt. This is no
hyperbole."[14] The Apulian farmers' ignorance of sound agricultural
practice reinforced the determination to contain labour costs.
Employers maintained, furthermore, that politics turned the
labourers into poor workmen. The doctrine of class hatred, they
argued, led reapers and sowers to perform their tasks begrudgingly
or even to work badly intentionally as a kind of vendetta.[15]

The need for intransigence was underlined by an ecological

impasse. By the early twentieth century the progressive exhaustion of the soil had begun seriously to compromise productivity, which fell from an average of 14 hectolitres of wheat per hectare in 1870 to 12 in 1900 with no sign of a reversal of the trend.[16] The Pavoncelli family at Cerignola reported that it had become necessary to invest ever greater sums in chemical fertilizers – not to increase production but to maintain existing yields. Caught between increasing costs and rising wage bills, the Pavoncellis calculated in the new century that the estate risked losing money by planting wheat.

The financial basis of the bitter opposition of wheat growers to the principle of unionization is disclosed by the Pavoncelli estate records for 1903 – after the first rounds of labour victories in the commune. The family kept its accounts in the old Neapolitan units of measure, reckoning output in *tomoli* per *versura*. The *tomolo* was equal to 45 litres and the *versura* to 1.25 hectares. Expressed in these terms, the annual cost in lire for cultivating a *versura* of wheat was as follows:

ploughing	9.80 lire
sowing	3.50
animals	52.00
clod breaking	5.00
sowing machine	5.00
seed (5 *tomoli* at 11 lire per *tomolo*)	55.00
harrowing	0.50
weeding	12.79
harvesting (13 days at 2.75 lire per day)	33.75
cartage	2.00
killing locusts	2.25
threshing (36 *tomolo* at 0.85 lire per *tomolo*)	30.00
salary of fixed personnel	10.00
killing mice	4.00
excise	0.50

fallow	21.65
rent of fallow	20.00
cattle tax	0.80
fertilizer	41.65
depreciation of machines	3.00
depreciation of animals	5.00
repair of buildings and fences	3.00
fire insurance	4.00
interest	6.00
rent	60.00

Total expenses – 388.75 lire

Since the average yield per *versura* was 36 *tomoli* of wheat at 10 lira a *tomolo*, plus straw valued at 15 lire, the gross income per *versura* was 375 lire. The estate, therefore, sustained a loss of 13.75 lire per *versura*.[17]

It is worthy of note that, among the many costs of production, labour was by far the largest single factor, reaching a total of 135.24 lire per *versura*. Labour thus accounted for nearly half of the total cost of cultivation, far exceeding such other major items as rent, fertilizers, animals, and seed. A clear priority for management was to contain the pay of the workers. In a speech delivered in the aftermath of the massacre at Candela in 1902, Giuseppe Pavoncelli dispassionately explained the reasons for such tragic conflicts. It was a case of the clash of irreconcilable interests:

> The year was one of the worst of the decade: no crop was a success, whether of wheat or of fruit. It was an ill-advised moment to attempt to strike. The one side was pushed on by necessity to satisfy its needs. The other side was driven by the demands of self-preservation and so necessarily became miserly.[18]

A succession of natural disasters further hardened the landlords' resolve. Phylloxera, which first reached Apulia in 1889, devastated the vineyards of the region progressively, reducing them from 250,000 hectares in 1900 to 15,000 in 1920. The new American vines planted to replace the destroyed vineyards required up to seven years before becoming productive. Facing major losses and the expense of rebuilding the wine industry, employers were little inclined to generosity. More immediately, the calamitous drought of 1908, the worst in living memory, fortified their determination. The mayor of Ruvo, for instance, noted that the drought "has produced incalculable damage . . . totally destroying some crops and decimating others". The wheat harvest for the commune was 10,000 quintals, a quarter of the norm. Similar catastrophes occurred throughout the region. Bari province produced 50 per cent of the average wheat crop and Foggia province 40 per cent. Among the major centres, the extreme case was Spinazzola, where wheat production fell between 1907 and 1908 from 250,000 quintals to 8,000. In the aftermath of such a year, farmers urged new efforts of wage constraint.[19]

From the Pavoncelli estate accounts it is possible to explain some of the nuances of the reaction of different sectors of the landed elite to the workers' advance. A great landlord like Giuseppe Pavoncelli did not lose money in 1903. His estate was an enormously sophisticated and diversified operation in which wheat cultivation was only one activity. The Pavoncelli latifundium was a rustic equivalent of a monopoly-holding company in industry that minimized risks through a complex system of horizontal and vertical integration. In terms of this metaphor, the wheat-growing subsidiary was beginning to operate at a loss, but the parent company was still earning substantial profits. The latifundium as a whole was not solely dependent on wheat farming.[20]

Although the family owned land in more than one province in the South and maintained its principal family palace in Naples rather than in Apulia, its most extensive holdings were on the southern Tavoliere in the great centre of Cerignola and in the surrounding satellite communes of Stornara, Stornarella, and Ortanova. Here in southern Capitanata the Pavoncellis owned 7,335 hectares of land. Of this property, 3,450 hectares were devoted to cereals, 1,465 to vineyards, 1,850 to pasture, and 570 to olive and almond trees.

The possibility of offsetting the losses of wheat in a bad year or a period of labour unrest was a source of solidity for the enterprise as a whole. In 1903, when wheat cultivation yielded net losses, the vineyards made a profit of 37.15 lire per *versura* – enough in itself to write off the shortfall in wheat. In addition, Giuseppe Pavoncelli and his sons were major sheep farmers with 3,227 head, and this activity was almost wholly insulated from increases in the cost of labour. Shepherds were few in number, and they were fixed, non-union personnel. Indeed, while vineyards could not be easily expanded to meet short-term price fluctuations in the labour market, the trade-off of wheat and pasture was a permanent and easy option.

The security afforded by a variety of agricultural ventures was supplemented by a range of different contractual agreements designed to spread the burden of risk. In a good year the owner who leased his property at a fixed sum failed to profit from good fortune. On the other hand, in a year of crop failure he enjoyed a secure rent while his tenant absorbed the loss. The Pavoncellis hedged their bets by operating both systems at once. Of the land devoted to wheat, 2,203 hectares were let to *massari* on a three-year contract; the remaining 1,247 hectares were run directly by the count through salaried managers. The vineyards and pasture followed the same principle of divided risk.

Finally, the Pavoncellis extended their assets beyond agriculture. In addition to growing crops, the family possessed immense wine cellars and olive presses for the processing of their own wine and olive oil for export. They also owned urban property that they let to their labourers. Lastly, approximately a quarter of their total assets of 16,000,000 lire were invested in other sectors of the economy – moneylending and a large portfolio of industrial shares.

The political and economic implications of the Pavoncelli records are significant for the conflict between property and labour. Major *latifondisti* involved in a mixed production of wheat, grapes, and sheep found their level of profit undermined by the wage victories of the leagues, but until the completion of the phylloxera devastation during the Great War they retained margins of net profit. Partly for this reason, within the landed elite the great landlords and wine growers during the Giolittian period enjoyed a reputation for relative moderation. Giuseppe Pavoncelli, the former radical candidate, for instance, took the lead in urging farmers to listen to union grievances and to make limited concessions. Under his presidency, the Cerignola Agrarian Federation in 1907 set up a joint arbitration, grievance, and bargaining committee with representatives of the local farm workers' leagues. Pavoncelli opposed higher wages, but he was prepared to contemplate improved rations and accommodation, better educational provision, and a moderate increase in the area of land planted with wheat.[21]

For smaller landlords, for *massari*, and for men who operated a single crop wheat economy, the calculations involved were different. Their profits depended overall on the ability to keep labour costs low. Already in 1903, a "normal" agricultural year before the great wave of union agitations of 1906–8, profits for wheat farmers were in jeopardy. It is no accident that wheat growers and small landlords were more staunchly intransigent than Pavoncelli. In the later Giolittian period, moreover, conditions hardened. In 1909 the phylloxera lice, having begun their progress north from the Salento Peninsula, arrived at the Ofanto River. From this time, therefore, there were few margins for reformism even among the most sheltered sectors of the landed class. Grape growers rallied to the unyielding stance of their colleagues in wheat. 1909 witnessed the launching of an employers' counter-offensive against the leagues. Profitability was at stake.

The particular circumstances of their tenure inclined the *massari* further towards harshness in matters of labour relations. The proprietor's ambition was to maximize and regularize his rent. Accordingly, it was the task of his administrators to select as tenants those farmers who could be relied upon to squeeze the last *soldo* from the land. A reputation for firmness could establish a *massaro*'s reputation with the landlords of the zone, ensuring him first choice of the most desirable estates when his lease expired. A demonstration of weakness, on the other hand, could ruin a career.[22]

The apocalyptic character of labour agitations directly reflected the magnitude of the stakes involved in a strike. In contrast with industry, a work stoppage at harvest time jeopardized the yield of an entire year. Furthermore, since Apulian latifundism was overwhelmingly dependent on a single crop, the consequences of delay in bringing in the wheat would be disastrous. In a region where sporadic abundant harvests were essential to balance recurrent crop failures, a labour conflict menacing the crop in a good year directly threatened the *massari* with financial ruin. The paramount importance of timing easily gave conflicts launched at strategic moments the significance of a final showdown.

What were the means adopted to counter the union peril? One important means of circumventing the workers' demands was to avoid the piazzas entirely. What was involved was a major change in entrepreneurial strategy as well as a new development in Apulian social history. The idea was to create a new class of peasant cultivators to replace the *giornatari*, now so dangerously afflicted with the syndicalist contagion. The method was to import the sharecropping system of *mezzadria*, which was widely regarded as the social foundation for the calm of the countryside in central Italy. Tuscany, the classic region of *mezzadria*, stood out for its social stability and the absence of rural subversion. In the Tuscan provinces there were no stable labour organizations in the countryside in the Giolittian period. It was this history of political calm that attracted the attention of Apulian landlords.[23]

Sharecropping, "that magnificent alliance of capital and labour",[24] would offer a solution to the social question, diverting peasants from the "utopian aspiration" of land reform. Croppers promoted from the ranks of the day labourers and settled on the land, or recruited directly from the provinces of central Italy, would form a privileged class of conservative individualists insulated from the collective sympathies of the agricultural proletariat. The landlord Francesco Casardi, one of the foremost representatives of the landed interest in Bari province, was the leading advocate of the sharecropping venture. He knew the social structure of central Italy well, having grown up in Florence and taken a degree in agronomy at Perugia.[25] His argument was: "The old conflict between masters and slaves will be replaced by harmony and peace." Profit sharing, partnership, and the end of day labour were the catch-phrases of the employers' offensive.[26]

In the decade after 1910, the experiment was taken up by landlords on a large scale. A government commission examining the causes of unemployment in Bari province after the Great War noted the magnitude of the transformation which took place in the years between 1911 and 1920. According to the findings of the commission, there was a population increase in the province during that decade. Nevertheless, the number of wage labourers declined in absolute terms from 150,000 to 95,000 as they were replaced by various categories of newly established peasants – sharecroppers and leaseholders. The census returns do not reveal a change of the same magnitude. The reason, one suspects, is that the new peasants were not pure sharecroppers or leaseholders who subsisted exclusively by cultivating the plots they leased. Rather, they were mixed figures who supplemented their income as day labourers by tilling a small area of their own.

It was unrealistic for Apulian landlords to expect to imitate the classical *mezzadria* system exactly as it was known in central Italy. There the croppers lived on the land and subsisted entirely by cultivating their family plots. To establish such autonomous peasant farms, however, was an impossibility in the system of single crop agriculture that prevailed in the zones of Apulian latifundism. Furthermore, the capital outlay which would have been demanded of the owners was prodigious. Peasant houses, extensive irrigation, boundaries, and roads would all have been required. What was introduced, therefore, was a bastard *mezzadria* of a kind common in other areas of the South. "The contracts", said De Falco, "are the rottenest one could imagine".[27] The Apulian croppers were not independent farmers. They cultivated small plots to which they commuted from the towns and for which they paid what was, in effect, a rent in kind. Sharecropping formed a part rather than the whole of their labouring activity.

In the process of introducing new labour contracts, however, the landlords did succeed in creating a new element of complexity and division within the working class. The contractual terms of the new sharecropping system were onerous, but in the harsh conditions of the Apulian countryside the newly promoted croppers saw themselves as an elite with at least steady employment and a measure of security. They were estranged from the leagues, whose aim was to dispossess and to re-proletarianize them. From the outset, therefore, the croppers and leaseholders were a force of conservatism. The leagues responded by renaming themselves "anti-sharecropping unions", and proclaimed their intention of resisting the spread of *mezzadria*.[28]

If sharecropping was one weapon in the campaign to contain the union threat, there were other means as well.[29] One device was to boycott local workers by hiring non-union migrants from the *marina* or Basilicata. Simultaneously employers systematically reduced the number of operations performed in the agricultural cycle – a practice they openly referred to as a "lock-out". As Casardi explained, "This consists of suspending work for as many weeks as are necessary to teach the workers wisdom . . . In the present circumstances it is not a question of humanity but of profit."[31] Applying the method with exemplary rigour, the landlords at Corato in 1908 suspended all farming operations for five months. The Bari province union paper commented, "Only those who know the conditions in which our peasants live can appreciate the ferocity of such a reprisal. What it means is five months of hunger, indebtedness and humiliation!"[32]

Partial lockouts were adopted more widely. One was the extension of pasture at the expense of wheat so that sheep replaced men in the fields.[33] Another was the increasing reliance on the so-called "raw fallow" without a covering fodder crop requiring labour.[34] In many places employers insisted that all negotiations over wages, hours, and conditions be conducted in the winter, when the bargaining power of the labourers was weakest.[35] One of the most important techniques attempted on a large scale was the introduction of machines, especially harvesters and threshers. By the eve of the Great War, the San Severo landlord Angelo Fraccacreta boasted that Capitanata possessed as many agricultural machines as any province in Italy.[36] Here mechanization was entirely distinct from the rationalization of production. The most modern harvesters were deployed on estates that used neither fertilizers nor irrigation and where the soil was dangerously eroded.

Additional forms of wage control were the increase of urban rents; the lengthening of the work day; and the large-scale employment of women. Women were seldom unionized, and they earned less than a lire a day at a time when the going wage for men was 2½ lire. Frequently the women could also be allotted half rations. Such differences, the *massari* argued, were only natural because for women "bringing in the harvest is only a pastime – a *divertimento*".[37] Employers also resorted to direct methods. When the workers at Cerignola downed their tools in 1906 and in 1907 to enforce the eight-hour day, the *curatoli* forced them to continue until sunset at gunpoint.[38] Most simply of all, the agreements signed with the leagues were not observed. As the prefect of Foggia noted, "No pact between farmers and labourers is to be relied upon. The experience of over a decade demonstrates that all contracts are frustrated as soon as the high season approaches."[39] At the same time union activists were blacklisted and evicted from their homes.

As part of the farmers' offensive, a new and harsher regime of discipline and surveillance came into being in the fields. Surviving workers from Minervino Murge and Cerignola have recalled a new atmosphere in which it was no longer permissible for workers to gather in groups during breaks, when they might talk politics or plot agitation. A worker who was caught with a watch was dismissed on the spot as an agitator bent on reforming the work day.[40]

At Gravina, the first commune to be controlled by the left, the landlords systematically obstructed the new administration. The opposition boycotted meetings of the town council, refused to comply with its decisions, and began a tax strike. The intention was to reduce the socialist experiment to chaos in the hope of forcing the mayor to resign or of inducing the prefect to dissolve the offending town council. The Liberal deputy Caso, fearful for his seat if the subversive pestilence spread, orchestrated the campaign to discredit the majority led by Canio Musacchio.[41]

A macabre struggle even developed over the dead. Since funeral services were an occasion for the mobilization of union support, the local authorities, in the name of public order, sometimes commanded a rapid public interment. With the cemetery occupied by troops, the officials transported the body of a dead league member to the grave and hurried it into the ground before the union could stage a subversive demonstration. An example was furnished by Bitonto in 1907. There the union organizer Domenico Rossiello was ambushed and murdered in mysterious circumstances. The league intended to take charge of the funeral in order to use it as a demonstration of public outrage. The mayor forestalled the event by laying Rossiello to rest in a pauper's grave accompanied not by red banners but by the *carabinieri*.[42]

Finally, there was corruption. Where union organizers were open to temptation, farmers simply bought them out. Such apostasy could be arranged by the offer of a steady job on the yearly staff of a *masseria* or a sinecure at town hall, where a domesticated activist could live in comfort at public expense.[43]

All of these measures encountered violent opposition. Cattle were poisoned and stolen on a massive scale. There were waves of incendiarism and machine breaking. General strikes were called against the employment of outsiders, women, and sharecroppers. Carters were assaulted, the shelters of croppers were burned down, and the homes of non-union men were attacked. Landlords became the targets of angry crowds, as Spada learned to his cost when his carriage appeared unwisely during a strike. In 1907 at Ruvo the press reported the "delirium of civil war".[44]

To succeed, managerial strategy required force. Violence became a regular feature of social control. This violence took a number of forms. One was the use of the repressive instruments of the state. Night-time searches of militants' homes were a harassment and a warning. A simple punishment was for the police to confiscate the work tools of labourers whom they regarded as trouble makers. More persistent and defiant activists could be arrested, beaten, and charged with fictitious crimes. Such was the fate of the Andria union leaders, including the secretary of the farm workers' league, Giulio Corsi. Fourteen league officials in the city were indicted for homicide.[45]

Even if the charges in such cases were eventually dropped or dismissed in court, the effect of a lengthy spell in prison awaiting trial and the costs of legal defence could be ruinous for a defendant and his family. The wave of emigrants from Apulia included a small but steady trickle of political exiles attempting to escape police intimidation. An example was the secretary of the farm workers' union at Barletta, Antonio Napoletano, who left for America in 1907. He was reported to have been "the victim of continuous persecution by Giolitti's police, the local bourgeoisie, and the clergy".[46] Victimization was a form of political prophylaxis.

When prevention failed and organized resistance occurred, the police regularly deployed columns of mounted troops and *carabinieri* with fixed bayonets to charge pickets, dismantle barricades, and enforce the "right to work". When occupiers seized common land or uncultivated pasture, the cavalry cleared the fields. From the outset, the state broke strikes with notable ferocity. Agricultural disputes were all too frequently the prelude to a local reign of terror. At Candela in September 1902, for instance, eight workers were killed and twenty wounded when the *carabinieri* opened fire on unarmed pickets during a strike. Centanni, the officer in command, was decorated for bravery and promoted, while the Chamber of Deputies voted a motion of praise for the troops.[47] At Conversano in 1908 the troops hacked their way through pickets with sabres and fixed bayonets in what journalists who witnessed the scene described as an "orgy of brutality". Similar events occurred with regularity, and were followed by mass arrests, beatings, and the military occupation of whole towns. On these occasions the troops were often plied liberally with alcohol before being sent into the piazzas in order to fortify their resolve.[48] The authorities then closed their eyes as employers selected organizers for punishment.

A well-documented illustration of the massive collusion between property owners and the state was the general strike at Cerignola in 1904.[49] The agitation began at the onset of the high season in the agricultural cycle. On Sunday 15 May the league presented a series of demands for increased wages and reduced hours. The landlords refused to consider the union proposals. The mayor of Cerignola, Francesco Vasciaveo, informed the league representatives that it was impossible to convene a meeting of the local landlords to discuss the issue.

This announcement was the signal for the start of the strike, which began at 8.00 p.m. on Sunday. During the night union pickets blocked the exits from Cerignola and sealed off the town. The escalation of the dispute began promptly at 4.50 a.m. on Monday when carters approaching the Melfi Gate were turned away by a crowd of union men. The police were called upon to enforce the right to work, and a detachment of policemen, reinforced by a handful of soldiers and municipal guards, arrived under the command of Captain Stanziano and Lieutenant Rusconi. The crowd, now several hundred strong, greeted the police with shouts, jeers, and a barrage of stones. Stanziano was hit in the head and knocked unconscious. Rusconi panicked and gave the order to fire. The local paper, *Il Pugliese*, reported the event:

The fatal moment defied description. There was a continuous firing of rifles that spread shock and terror. There was a general flight amidst shouts and wails. The confusion could not be imagined, and here and there the dead and the wounded lay on the ground where they fell.[50]

As the news of the tragedy spread, people poured into the streets by the thousands, calling for revenge, screaming oaths, and shouting "Down with city hall!" As the crowd grew in size it gained confidence and converged on town hall. To placate the populace, the judges opened the jails and released the prisoners. The result was only to inflame the situation still more. Growing larger by the minute, the throng pressed tighter and tighter around the building, which it first besieged and then attempted to storm, overwhelming the *carabinieri* on guard. The mounted troops on duty were then ordered to charge. They broke up the demonstration at the gallop, dealing out blows to left and right with their swords. During the evening and the night reinforcements arrived, and Cerignola was transformed into an armed camp. A curfew was declared and the cavalry took control of the streets.

On Tuesday the strike continued. The market stalls were deserted, the shops were closed, and the water merchants failed to appear. At the city gates the balance of power swung back and forth. Barricades went up repeatedly, only to be torn down by troops who charged with fixed bayonets. Soldiers were stoned and at least one labourer was impaled.

The tide turned definitively on Wednesday 18 May, when special military trains arrived at the station. By late morning Cerignola was occupied by 2,000 soldiers, 300 *carabinieri*, and 68 officers, under the command of police commissioner Zaiotti, who declared himself "prepared to use whatever means are necessary to restore order and calm". Thus protected by the military occupation of the commune, the landlords finally met to consider the situation. Among the 100 proprietors and *massari* who assembled in the town hall, there were three points of view. The landlord F. Cirillo alone proposed a compromise settlement, and was shouted down. Vasciaveo, the mayor, suggested instead that a joint negotiating committee of union leaders and landlords be elected to study the views of both sides in an atmosphere of greater calm. He too was greeted by angry shouts of protest and jeers. The position of the overwhelming majority was stated by R. Palieri, one of the three great landowners of Cerignola, and by the *massaro* Pugliese. Palieri remarked, "It is enough to see the peasants on feast days to realize that they live in luxury. Those who demand an increase are the poor workmen. The diligent hands are happy with the pay due to them, and consider it sufficient."[51] Pugliese added, "It is out of the question to consider the economic condition of the workers because the whole issue depends on the demand for labour, and this is always satisfactory."[52]

On Monday 23 May the issue was put to the vote. The intransigent view triumphed by 101 to 4, with one abstention. Thus the landlords imposed their will by military force.

The use of military repression against the Apulian union movement was a consistent policy under Giovanni Giolitti, who dominated Italian politics between 1900 and the Great War. Giolitti is best known for his attempt to broaden the social bases of the Liberal regime by a wide spectrum of reforms. He attempted to de-fuse the problem of public order and subversion at the national level by domesticating the socialist party under the reformist leadership of F. Turati. Under Giolitti's initiative, the PSI and the unions were legalized; the state adopted a policy of non-intervention in industrial disputes; the suffrage was extended to include the literate working class; state support was provided to increase employment in both town and countryside; and the government pressed employers to pursue a policy of wage concessions. The economic boom of the period provided the margins necessary to finance Giolitti's ventures.

The difficulty with the liberalization programme was that it applied exclusively to the North of Italy. The PSI and the CGL, which entered into a political partnership with Giolitti, were almost exclusively northern in their membership. What took place, therefore, was the creation of a privileged labour elite. The cost of the benefits newly extended to northern workers and peasants was borne by the largely unorganized and unrepresented peasants of the rest of the peninsula.

In economic terms, public as well as private investment took place almost entirely either in the industrial triangle bounded by Milan, Genoa and Turin, or in the land reclamation projects of the Po Valley. Despite the evident need of the South for investment, government fiscal policy drained the region of capital for the

13 Cerignola, 1900: Underground grain silos in the Piano S. Rocco in the city. This square was also the scene of the massacre of 1904.

benefit of wealthier northern provinces. In Nitti's famous phrase, the taxation of the Liberal state was "regionally progressive in reverse". Capitanata, for instance, paid more than twice as much in taxes to the state as it received in government expenditure. In the fiscal year 1902–3 the province was assessed for 14,000,000 lire, principally through the land tax. In return it received only 6,500,000 lire in total public spending. Such treatment contrasted sharply with the province of Milan, one of the most prosperous in the country. In the same financial year Milan enjoyed a net excess of state expenditure (180,000,000 lire) over taxation (140,000,000 lire). The Apulian provinces directly subsidized northern economic development. The benefits of employment, union representation, and high wages did not extend to the whole of Italy.

Politically, the extension of the suffrage in 1911 enlarged the electorate far more in the North than in the South. Under the terms of the reform, all adult male literates over twenty-one years of age gained the vote. Illiterates could vote only at the age of thirty or upon completion of military service. The literacy requirement together with a low life expectancy and a high rate of rejection by the army effectively disenfranchised the majority of the southern population. Similarly, the legalization of the political and trade-union movements of the left applied only to the North. In the South the state continued to crush agitations and strikes with vigour.

The calculations involved were clear. Liberalization and repression were indissolubly linked as the northern and southern facets of the Giolittian political system. In Gramsci's analysis of *giolittismo*,

> The South was reduced to a semi-colonial status as a captive market and a source of savings and taxes. It was disciplined with two series of measures. The first was merciless police repression directed against every mass movement and involving the periodic slaughter of peasants . . . The other measures were personal favours to the class of "intellectuals" in straw hats, and took the form of jobs in the state bureaucracy, of permission to plunder local government . . . In this way the social stratum that could have organized the endemic discontent of the Mezzogiorno became instead an instrument of northern policy, a private accessory to the police.[53]

The reforms granted to the northern workers served to consolidate the moderate leadership within the PSI and to reduce the risk of a revolutionary confrontation. The opposition was tamed by being absorbed into the parliamentary system. The political cost for Giolitti was the possible loss of his majority hold upon the deputies elected in the North. He protected himself against this risk, however, by ensuring himself of an overall majority in the Chamber through the near unanimity of the deputies elected in the southern half of the peninsula. Liberalization in the North was balanced by authoritarian control of the political process in the Mezzogiorno. The South was the home of the deputies known as the *ascari*, after the native mercenary troops employed by the

Italian colonial army in Libya. These deputies, assured of the favouritism of the state, could be depended upon to vote in disciplined fashion for the government. In Salvemini's expression, Giolitti sold the prefect and bought the deputy.[54] Of all the regions in the South, Apulia bore most fully the weight of Giolitti's northern strategy. The reason was that in Apulia alone in this period was there a powerful challenge to the established Liberal hegemony. The overall calculations on which the Giolittian system rested explain the repressive collusion of the state authorities in Apulia with the landlords. Giolitti tolerated the "moral nihilism" of local government in Apulia. Rome allowed complete autonomy to the municipal administrations controlled by its supporters.

A number of specific features of the Apulian left guaranteed the unbending opposition of Rome. The leagues were unacceptable because they were, first of all, not reformist but revolutionary. Their syndicalist orientation made them further vulnerable. As radical critics of the reformist practice of the PSI and the CGL, the leagues could not count on the enthusiastic support of the socialist movement. This isolation in national politics made them an easy target. The tactic of the general strike, finally, ensured a direct confrontation with the forces of order. The blockading of entire towns and the infringement of the "right to work" were deliberate violations of the law and a challenge to authority.

The immediate interests of police officials in the region added to the rigour of repression. Apulia was the dumping ground and place of punishment for officials who had fallen into disfavour. The morale of the authorities in the three provinces was therefore low, and they resented risking their lives in violent affrays for little reward. The personal files of the members of the security forces in Bari province throughout the Giolittian period are an endless and revealing catalogue of discontents.[55] Police officers complained bitterly to their superiors about their postings in the region, citing the climate, the risk of infection, the high cost of accommodation, the lack of medical facilities, and the absence of schools for their children. They were well aware, furthermore, that assignment to such turbulent centres as Andria, Spinazzola, or Minervino Murge confronted them with tasks that were nearly impossible to accomplish. Even experienced and competent police commissioners, the deputy prefect of Barletta warned, soon found themselves in difficulty and invariably compromised their prospects for promotion – with disastrous effect on the enthusiasm and commitment of their successors.[56] For good reason the chief of police at Bari commented that he found the discipline of his officers and men "very deficient".[57]

The public prosecutor at Lucera confirmed that the conditions of service in Apulia seriously undermined the efficiency of the police. The force faced a severe crisis of recruitment. Applicants were poorly qualified, and enrolment was so low that in 1903 only 341 men (Pubblica Sicurezza and *carabinieri* combined) policed the whole of Foggia province. Furthermore, after a single tour of duty in the region most policemen abandoned the service in search of alternative employment. As a result, the security forces were demoralized, undermanned, and inexperienced. Overwork, the stress of duty in the midst of the hostility of the population, and sheer incompetence were all factors contributing to the penchant for opening fire.[58]

In a similar spirit, police officers thought only of obtaining a transfer to a more favourable post. A revealing example is the sheer glee of Benedetto Amari, the deputy prefect of Barletta, at the news of his transfer from the region in 1910. He wrote to a friend, "I've finally done it! . . . And now you'll see that my complete moral repair will begin! For certain!"[59] For men with such ideas, the deputy was a crucial figure. The deputy had access to the ministries in Rome. He could secure a new assignment and re-establish a career that had led only to San Severo or Barletta. It was only prudent, then, to secure the favour of the landlords and notables.

State officials, finally, shared with landlords a settler's view of the "native question". For prefects, police commissioners, and captains in the *carabinieri*, all of whom normally came from distant provinces and were new to the region, the farm workers were a race apart – lower down the evolutionary scale and in need of a firm, civilizing hand. Terzi, the deputy prefect of Barletta, for instance, openly expressed his opinion of the people he administered. The population of Apulia, he wrote in 1914, "is almost totally composed of impulsive peasants who have not yet evolved". It was only natural that he feared disorder and called for more troops and equipment.[60]

On their side, landowners were not slow to seek the goodwill of state officials. Police commissioners and *carabiniere* officers were entertained at the palaces of the *signori*. They rode the landlords' horses and joined in local hunts. The world of the proprietors was a world they knew and understood. In this manner a web of contacts and mutual interests was established between local state authorities and men of property. The violent hostility of the leagues towards the police completed the process. Law and order, all observers agreed, were enforced in Apulia with a systematic and violent bias in favour of the landlords.

The parliamentary enquiry, while predictably excusing Rome of direct collusion, noted the extraordinary conduct of the police in Apulia. In what was ostensibly a modern Liberal state, Presutti wrote,

In the early years of agitations, when orders from Rome called for a policy of liberty, still in places exactly the opposite occurred. Police officers, tied to the landlord by bonds of both friendship and kinship, very often contrary to central government instructions, carried out their intention of crushing the workers' movement.[61]

Only with regard to the innocence of the central government is this statement less than candid.

Perhaps the most blatant manifestation of the illiberalism of the southern face of Giolitti's Janus-headed political system was the electoral process. In Apulia Giolitti's faithful *ascari* and their clients on the local councils within their constituencies were rewarded with full licence to secure re-election by any means necessary. Every refinement of corruption, fraud, and violence was permitted, and never more so than when the opposition included syndicalists and revolutionary socialists. A representative comment was that of the prefect on the victory in the mayoralty contest of 1913 at Foggia by the incumbent Valentini over the socialist candidate Castellino. Valentini, reported the official, "openly and unhesitatingly employed every legal and illegal means".[62]

The variety of methods employed demonstrated considerable ingenuity.[63] A first device widely adopted was the manipulation of electoral registers. The municipal authorities were responsible by law for the drawing up of lists of eligible voters, the issuing of certificates which entitled them to gain access to the polls on election day, and the counting of ballots. It was an easy matter for the party in power to falsify the lists of voters, excluding opponents from the registers and denying them the necessary certificates. Alternatively, there was the system known as "the ladle". This consisted of increasing the number of sympathetic electors by "ladling" additional votes into the ballot boxes. Supporters of the dominant faction were allowed to vote more than once. Emigrants abroad and even the dead dutifully cast their votes. As a last resort, the count could be rigged since no representatives of the opposition were appointed as scrutineers.

A variety of ruses also kept opponents away from the polls. The voting day, chosen by the town council, could be set to coincide with high points in the crop cycle so that large numbers of farm workers were away in the fields. Hostile electors were frequently corrupted. A popular method was to give them lira notes divided in half, one portion of each note given as a deposit, the other retained until a successful outcome had been announced. So widespread was the buying of votes that a man eligible to vote was said always to have financial resources, and was regarded almost as a man of property. Alternatively, a voter could be granted exemption from military service for himself and his sons. Such bribery was commonly supplemented with intimidation. Work gangs were told prior to voting day that they need not bother to apply for work after election day if the opposition won. Many labourers were threatened with eviction from their homes.

Violence was also employed to make campaigning impossible for the opposition. In Apulia squadrism was not an invention of the fascists. The word *squadriglia* was already part of everyday language in pre-war usage. Gangs of men were recruited by the authorities to secure the desired outcome. These men were the notorious Apulian *mazzieri,* known after the *mazza* or club that was the tool of their trade. At Terlizzi the going wage was 2 lire a day during the campaign, plus 50 lire as a bonus when the happy result was known. With such incentives, the *mazzieri* instituted local reigns of terror. Electoral meetings of the opposition were broken up by men wielding clubs, throwing stones, and firing shots. Enemy candidates and their supporters were ambushed and beaten, and their homes were stormed in the night. The opposition press disappeared from circulation.[64]

Where necessary, the *mazzieri* were supported by official collusion. The members of the municipal guard joined them in sorties, and assisted them in selecting targets. The regular police and *carabinieri*, widely described in the prefects' files as "partisan", pretended not to see. On some memorable occasions, when a powerful deputy found his position in jeopardy, the authorities took a more active role. At Gioia del Colle in 1909 Salvemini was unceremoniously forbidden to enter the commune by police commissioner Prina, the strike-breaker *par excellence*. Gioia, Prina informed the socialist leader, belonged to the Honourable De Bellis, and the police were at his service.[65]

Nicola De Bellis, the "king, the tsar, the god of Gioia", had established an infallible combination of corruption and intimidation to secure his election as the most notorious of Giolitti's parliamentary mercenaries.[66] This deputy, who had nothing to say on larger public issues in the Chamber, was beyond challenge in his constituency. He established his satrapy in the 1890's with the creation of the De Bellis Bank. The bank lent endless sums to worthy electors from the local petty bourgeoisie – artisans, townhall clerks, retailers. The bank soon declared bankruptcy, but not before the deputy's faithful clientele had been able to purchase land with their irregular money. Thus initially wooed and thereafter favoured with employment, contracts, and assistance, these men knew how to vote on polling day.

Intimidation completed the process. Election day at Gioia del Colle passed in unnatural silence and order. The peace was guaranteed by the police and gangs of armed men hired by De Bellis and led by the criminal Rocco d'Aprile. Grouped into the so-called "Workers' Club", D'Aprile's *mazzieri* were recruited from the underworld of professional crime. In exchange for their services they were pardoned, granted impunity, and put on the municipal payroll. On election day they enforced a curfew. Residents of the city were not allowed out of their homes unless they were electors known to favour the good cause. Anyone else was set upon and beaten senseless. At least one rival candidate was assassinated. It was small wonder, Salvemini reported, that the commune of Gioia voted *unanimously* for De Bellis in 1908![67]

At San Severo, the fief of the major landlord Antonio Masselli, the reform party known as "the Reds" – a coalition of republicans and radicals with the support of the leagues – mounted a serious challenge in 1908. The socialist paper *Avanti!* described the "massacre of San Severo", which occurred when the opposition attempted a mass rally:

> The *carabinieri* were deployed in a long line. In a single movement they all raised their sabres in the air. For a moment they stood still, and then they advanced on the crowd.
>
> What happened next was indescribable. The swordsmen competed with each other to see who could strike the most blows, indiscriminately, to backs, legs, and heads.
>
> Some members of the crowd fell; others tripped in their flight and fell as well. Over these poor unarmed people stretched on the ground the *carabinieri* bent double in their frenzy to strike better with their unsheathed weapons.

If on occasion the Ministry of the Interior nonetheless proved over-delicate, farmers could turn to the less efficient but wholly reliable municipal and rural police, who were hired, paid, and commanded by local notables. The guards were legendary for their harsh conduct. It was common practice for the guards to operate "protection" rackets, and to arrest on fabricated charges anyone who refused to pay.[68] At Andria, in the words of the deputy prefect, they were composed of "individuals whose past renders them unworthy to wear a uniform". The fact that, to enlist in the local force, the applicant had to demonstrate literacy, to deposit 100 lire as security, and to maintain his own horse effectively insulated the municipal police from subversive influence.[69] A surviving record of the social background of the 197 men of the Cerignola municipal guard in 1829 gives further confirmation of the middle- and lower-middle-class composition of the force. There was not a single peasant, farm worker or manual labourer of any sort among them. The Cerignola guards were grocers, notaries, carpenters, pharmacists, and landlords.[70] These men were further alienated from the labouring population by the system of rewards for service. As an incentive to diligence, the guards were given a percentage of all fines that they collected and a bonus for each arrest. The effect was to encourage abuse.[71]

The commissioner sent by the prefect of Foggia in 1907 to examine the state of local government at San Giovanni Rotondo gave particular attention to the municipal police. "This force", he explained, "performs no useful service. It is made up of undisciplined and easily corruptible elements, and commands no respect in the town . . . If the guards occasionally do their duty, it is always at the expense of poor peasants who have refused to tolerate their irregular demands for gifts and money."[72] In some communes, furthermore, the local guards were reinforced by private security guards hired by the local agrarian association. Their functions were to defend property and to break strikes.

Apart from the municipal and security guards, there were irregular and illegal instruments of rural terror. Especially ominous were the night riders organized in monarchist societies financed by estate managers, such as the "Work and Freedom Club" of Ruvo,[73] the "Victor Emmanuel Club" of Foggia,[74] the "Labour and Justice Club" of Andria,[75] and the "Work and Progress Club" of Canosa.[76] These societies recruited among the employees of town hall, the fixed hands of the estates, the newly promoted sharecroppers, and the unemployed. Their purposes were to carry out punitive expeditions against the activists of the leagues, to "make" elections, and to break up rallies and strikes.

In this fashion, Apulia, in the view of some labour leaders, bore comparison with Alessandro Manzoni's famous novel of oppression in seventeenth-century Lombardy, *I promessi sposi* (The Betrothed). For them the prototype of the Apulian *latifondista* was the warlord villain Don Rodrigo, who surrounded himself with a swarm of hired toughs prepared to undertake any violent mission at the peasants' expense. Like Don Rodrigo, the Apulian landlords retained the services of their *mazzieri*. According to the Foggia trade unions,

Our Don Rodrigos and their thugs are more horrible and more menacing than those described by Manzoni . . .
There are shadowy organizations directed by powerful men that consistently terrorize people and attack their belongings, that condemn people to punishment by fire, by the knife, and by death.[77]

In a similar but less literary vein, the proprietors were described as "jackals".[78]

Giuseppe De Falco described the work of the Ruvo "Work and Freedom Club" during the general strike of September 1907. The club members – 200 *annaroli* from the estate of the deputy Antonio Jatta – fought pitched battles with the strikers with the full support of the police. Ruvo, wrote the syndicalist leader of the labourers of Bari province, "assumed the aspect of a state of siege. Soldiers and policemen conducted a hunt for strikers while the thugs of Jatta's club roamed freely through the city attacking workers and opening fire on them."[79] While Jatta's men – "heroes with the knife"[80] – chastised militants, the Ruvo employers agreed to offer the wage and hours concessions demanded by the unions to any labourers willing to join the club.

Nor were individual hit men unknown. The assassination of Silvestro Fiore, the leader of the farm workers' union at Foggia, was a notable example. Fiore, himself a day labourer, had long been a torment to the employers of the province. One of the earliest and most active union organizers, he founded the league at Foggia in 1901, and led it into the first general strike in the region in the summer. He then took the chief role in calling the first regional farm workers' congress, and played an important part in union administration thereafter. In 1911 he was murdered by the anarchist Antonio Caretta, who revealed at his trial that he had been hired by local landlords to eliminate Fiore.[81]

On occasion the landlords took matters directly into their own hands. The Canosa farmer Francesco Massa, accompanied by his three sons and a handful of croppers armed with hunting rifles and shotguns, forced picket lines in 1907 by opening fire on the strikers,[82] as did Domenico Andrea Spada at Ruvo.[83] In Lucera the owner Michele Schiavone attempted to assassinate the local union secretary with his rifle in 1908.[84] The most famous occasion, however, was the massacre at Gioia de Colle in 1920, when fifty mounted landlords ambushed a hundred unarmed labourers on pay day. The *signori* opened fire on the men and hunted them down as they fled across the fields, killing ten and wounding thirty.[85]

Between 1900 and 1915, the threatened bases of the landlords' power were propped up by violence. Labour relations were unstable and easily degenerated into rebellion and waves of mutual reprisals. The leagues succeeded in leading a series of victorious mass agitations, particularly in the years between 1901 and 1908. As tensions accumulated, however, the landlords remained able to dominate politics and the labour market because the state reinforced the self-help of the employers.

From 1909 until 1911 the balance of power tilted in the landlords' favour. In these years, taking advantage of bad harvests and mass unemployment, the employers mounted a major counteroffensive in which many of the gains earlier registered by the leagues were reversed. The rise of Millet and Maury to power at Cerignola was part of a broad swing to the right. The pact signed between the Cerignola Agrarian Federation and the labourers' union in 1909 revealed the extent to which the workers' bargaining power had been eroded. Wages, it was agreed, would no longer be fixed in advance. Both pay scales and hours would be governed instead by "the old local customs". The worker, furthermore, committed himself to a more intensive work rhythm, which he agreed would be "conscientious, exact, and productive". In that dark year of 1909 even the First of May passed unobserved in Cerignola for the first time in a decade.

The electoral reform of 1911 opened new possibilities of popular mobilization, while better harvests strengthened the unions' bargaining power. A new wave of strikes began in 1912. In 1913 the left took control of municipal government in a handful of union strongholds. A precarious balance had been reached in which the landlords continued to control most of the region, but the syndicalists and revolutionary socialists seized local power in Gravina, Spinazzola, Andria, and Cerignola. The outgoing Liberal mayor of Cerignola described in great distress the local transformation he witnessed:

> Numerous offences and crimes go unpunished because the mob is more powerful than the police and has become absolute master of the city. We are now on the verge of a civil war that the extremist parties proclaim in their meetings. Every word is an insult, when it is not an out-and-out crime. They have reached the point of declaring that the blood about to flow in the streets of Cerignola will give the signal for the general Italian revolution![86]

In alarm at this municipal revolution, the Duke of Larochefoucauld sold off a large portion of his holdings. He was in haste to realize their value before the deluge.[87] For him, as for many other *latifondisti*, Giolitti had betrayed them at last by giving votes to the *cafoneria* – the peasant scum.[88] As the labourers used the new right to vote to extend their control to local government in other communes, the panic demonstrated by the French duke took hold of many other proprietors.

A new phase in the struggle was introduced by the Great War, which provided the farm hands with a new sense of injustice and a new self-confidence that raised the workers' movement into a single disciplined attempt to overthrow the social order throughout the region. In the aftermath of the international conflict, the long-awaited civil war came into being.

8

••

THE GREAT WAR

Nationally, the Great War marked a turning point in the politics of the countryside. The Italian army consisted overwhelmingly of peasant soldiers – especially the men in the line. The war, that is, placed a disproportionate share of sacrifice on the very sectors of the population least enthusiastic about participation.

It was the peasants above all who swelled the lists of the dead and the maimed. It was they who experienced the worst conditions of any soldiers on the Western Front. Under the command of General Luigi Cadorna, an autocratic martinet, the Italian troops were hurled in waves against the entrenched machine-gun positions of the Austrians. Of all the soldiers in Western Europe, they were the most inadequately clothed, fed and equipped, and they endured the longest tours of duty in the line.[1]

Alone among European armies, the Italian High Command made no attempt to provide recreational facilities or to provide the troops with a sense of mission. Between intervention in May 1915 and the autumn of 1917 there was no military newspaper and no effort to explain the reasons for the conflict in order to reinforce discipline with patriotic zeal. For the Italian Command, intoxicated with the military dogma of the offensive, and committed to an aristocratic view of war as a test of valour, the infantryman was an infinitely expendable commodity.

The Italian peasants in uniform were driven into battle by a mixture of alcohol – the soldiers' "petrol" – and terror. When morale failed, the officers turned to disciplinary measures that culminated in the stationing of detachments of military-police

14 The Tavoliere, 1900: A team of labourers at rest during the work of
gleaning after the harvest.

units armed with machine guns behind the lines, in the summary
justice of the regime of special tribunals, and finally in the practice
of the *decimazione*, by which every tenth man in a unit that dis-
obeyed orders was executed by firing squad on the spot.

It was in these conditions that the Italian army experienced the
nightmare of the Isonzo front, where, after three-quarters of a
million casualties and two winters of frost-bite, lice, and disease,
the line separating the enemy forces remained utterly static. During
this period the front moved no more than twenty kilometres at
any point along a line stretching four hundred miles. Even the
names of the battles were unchanged as no fewer than twelve
battles of the Isonzo were fought.

In the countryside that the Apulian farm workers had left
behind, hardships increased and social inequalities widened. The
signori prospered while shortages accumulated, and wages and
family allowances – already low at 0.65 lire a day as the basic pay
of the private soldier in 1915, plus 0.30 lire for a dependent wife

and 0.15 lire for each child – were not kept in pace with a rampant wartime inflation. The *massari*, by contrast, grew wealthy. Under the emergency measures adopted by the government to maintain agricultural yields, farmers enjoyed exemption from service. They then made their fortunes from the freezing of rent contracts while prices soared, and from handsome bonuses paid by the state to provide incentives for the planting of wheat. Frequently the *massari* pocketed the bonus without cultivating at all, preferring the low-cost alternative of expanding pasture. Never before had the reality of class inequality been so strikingly evident.

The war also deepened the chasm that separated consumers from farmers and retailers. In a time of requisitioning and rationing, there was a constant temptation to hoard grain and speculate on the black market which the authorities could do little to control. So widespread was such conduct that some town councils reported that their chief preoccupations during the conflict were to guarantee supplies, to contain prices within the official limits, and to prevent famine. Summing up the activity of the town council at Gravina during the war, Giuseppe Musacchio, the mayor, described a situation of bitter tension. Despite legal price ceilings, the cost of necessities in the shops increased daily and almost without restraint. Suppliers withheld goods to create panic among the population. When the town council reacted by banning the export of foodstuffs from the township and by opening municipally run stores, the retailers retaliated by closing their shops and by selling only produce of the worst quality. By 1917 the labourers at Gravina had lost their patience and Musacchio feared disorder and riot.[2]

Inevitably in such circumstances, hardship deepened still further through the ending of all the prewar attempts at municipal reform. The wave of hope that had crossed the region when the first socialist councils had been elected was followed from 1915 by years of disillusionment. Gravina, the first commune to elect a socialist administration, is an important example. In 1914 the executive of the town council had promised an ambitious programme of social reforms – tax reform, full employment through public works, sanitation, primary education for all, and strict codes of practice for housing and hygiene in the market place.³ By 1916, however, the council formally abandoned any further attempt to improve conditions in the city. The choice, the acting mayor Domenico Derobertis publicly proclaimed, was between reform and war. Under war conditions, the council, starved of funds and personnel, opted to defer all discussion of social amelioration.⁴ In practice, standards of housing, sanitation, education, and welfare all deteriorated through neglect.

Not surprisingly, all observers were united in viewing the war years as a time of political radicalization of the peasant soldiers. Some leaders of the postwar revolutionary movement stressed the influence of the years on the Isonzo front. Antonio Gramsci, for example, wrote that

A habit of social discipline was born: the peasants conceived of the State in its complex enormity and measureless power. Bonds of solidarity were created that otherwise only tens and dozens of years of historical struggle could have created. In four years in the mud and slaughter of the trenches a spiritual world was formed . . .⁵

Giuseppe Di Vittorio, by contrast, stressed the influence of the spectacle of widening social inequality behind the lines. The postwar revolutionary fervour, he argued, was founded upon the sense of rage and injustice that farm workers felt at the contrast between their hardship and mourning on the one hand and the comfort and safety of their profiteering employers on the other. In the Cerignola syndicalist's words,

The gentlemen *massari*, instead of spending in productive work the sums advanced by the State, put the money in their pockets. They did not carry out the cultivations for which the subsidies were intended.
The result was an enormous loss for the peasants whose jobs disappeared. It was also a considerable loss for the wheat production of the country. In such circumstances, illegal working . . . became an act of justice that prevented fraud at the expense of the State and the general economy.⁶

Similarly, the union paper *Puglia Rossa* asked, "Do you really think that . . . the people of Spinazzola have forgotten the corruption of the gentlemen shirkers who stayed at home while the people – against their will – found themselves in the trenches?"[7] Furthermore, contemporaries noted, the war completed the transformation of the role of women, who entered the labour market *en masse*. "With the war", observed one journalist in reference to Apulia, "feminism triumphed".[8]

The loyalty of the peasants in uniform cracked under the strain in 1917, when the army was routed at the front. There were mutinies, mass desertions, and a wave of officers shot from the rear. Behind the lines a series of spontaneous local rebellions across the peninsula culminated in the barricades of Turin in August. The military command at Bari reported that there were

criminal bands of deserters who roam the countryside and the woods spreading panic and turning against the police the weapons that they refused to take up in defence of their country.

The danger is serious and immediate, and it revives the unhappy memory of brigandage.[9]

Nowhere were the results more deeply felt and enduring than in Apulia. As a wholly agricultural region, it bore to the full the impact of the holocaust. According to the prefect, Bari province had the highest proportion of front-line troops in Italy.[10] Although the South suffered the highest levels of war casualties, it received the lowest amount of the vast sums spent by the state to finance the war effort.[11] Here was a military manifestation of the Southern Question in Italy history. Apulia, however, stood out from the rest of the South because, unlike other regions, it also had a strong and well-organized revolutionary movement to provide direction to popular discontent.

The organizations of the left in the region had long condemned militarism and called for the abolition of the standing army. In 1915, going far beyond the official PSI position on the war of "Neither support nor sabotage!", the Apulian league leaders unambiguously condemned Italian intervention. The decision to enter the war inspired all the less enthusiasm among farm workers because it was taken by one of their own employers – Antonio

Salandra, the authoritarian landlord and deputy from Lucera.
Everywhere in Foggia and Bari provinces anti-militarist posters
went up. The socialist-controlled communes organized mass
peace demonstrations and flew the flag at half-mast. The socialist
councillors further voted resolutions condemning Italian participation in the war,[12] and honouring Jean Jaurès as the "apostle
of peace". *Il Randello*, the union paper of Foggia, explained simply,
"The enemy is not abroad but here."[13]

In the event, the regime survived the crisis of 1917–18. It did
so, however, at the price of mortgaging the future. A massive
effort was begun at the front to persuade peasant soldiers that they
had a reason to return to the line, that victory in the war would be
followed by an era of social reform. A new instrument of
encouragement – the Propaganda Service – was set up within the
army to preach the message of land reform. The Leninist slogan of
"Land to the peasants!" was taken up not by the left but by junior
officers organizing rallies to improve morale.

Being national, however, the Propaganda Service was generic
in its blandishments. The specific consequences of victory for the
Apulian provinces were explained behind the lines, where a
massive effort was made to preach the heady gospel that victory
would be equivalent to revolution. In the great panic of 1917–18,
the army command at Bari called upon the "honest citizens" of
the region to undertake a major propaganda campaign, "forget-
ting nothing, omitting no one, and – above all – not neglecting the
lowest social classes". The message of patriotism and encouragement, the military authorities stressed, had to reach the countryside and the urban slum.[14] After such solicitation, the economic
organizations representing the Apulian landed classes – agrarian
associations and chambers of commerce – launched a series of
weekly Sunday conferences throughout 1918 to which the representatives of the farm workers were invited. These meetings
were then supplemented with speaking tours in the rural centres
and by a press campaign.

The constant theme of these occasions was that a new order was
dawning in Apulia. Major *latifondisti* such as Spada, whom we have

already encountered rifle in hand, and Casardi, the leading proponent of wage resistance and the lockout, now attempted patiently to explain to union activists the particulars of a grandiose vision. In this effort they were joined by such important notables as the deputy from Minervino Murge, Raffaele Cotugno; Antonio Di Tullio, the president of the Bari Chamber of Commerce; Domenico Zaccagnino, the deputy from San Nicandro Garganico; the "tsar of Gioia del Colle", De Bellis; and Sabino Fiorese, the president of the Industrialists' Association of Bari. The daily paper *Corriere delle Puglie* officially endorsed the venture and gave it the maximum publicity.

Under the rubric of "Land to the peasants!" a series of specific commitments were made, including the following:

- the completion of the great Apulian aqueduct first planned in 1896
- the break-up of the latifundia and the redistribution of the land
- the provision of credit to the new peasant cultivators
- the return of common land to public ownership
- the institution of a confiscatory inheritance tax
- the lowering of tariffs in the interest of consumers
- social-security provisions for farm workers
- the reform of labour contracts, including the gradual transformation of day labourers into leaseholders
- the compulsory cultivation of unplanted land
- large-scale public-works projects to provide full employment and to intensify production by land drainage and reclamation
- the supply of water to every household
- credit to permit every veteran to purchase his own house.

Domenico Spada, the paymaster of the "Work and Freedom Club" and mayor of Ruvo, announced, "We are at a turning point in the history of our region." The way forward was a combination of "distributive justive" and a "programme of democracy and social reform".[15] The "glorious veterans", recalled Di Vittorio, were promised "land, happiness, and every possible gift of God".[16]

Responding to these pledges with premature optimism, the socialist deputy from Andria, Nicola Barbato, announced in 1919,

The Italian bourgeoisie . . . has finally understood that the time has come for great social change. Through the press and through constitutional channels they have let it be known that they are prepared to concede what the working classes have requested. We take note of these statements and wait calmly for the commitments to be made good.[17]

As peace returned, the will to political change was further stimulated by the spectacle of revolution in Germany and Austria-Hungary.

9

••

THE CLOSED SHOP

It is in the light of such promises made to the troops that one can best understand the outburst of agrarian unrest after the armistice. Veterans from the Bari, Lecce, and Murge brigades encountered a reality vastly different from that pictured in the Sunday lectures of 1917 and 1918. With the passing of the emergency, the reforming zeal of the landed classes dissolved. Demobilization for the returning soldiers began with a visit to the moneylender. The veterans' separation pay was handed over to purchase tools and civilian clothes. Instead of land reform and full employment, they found convicts and Austrian prisoners of war being used in place of local workers to till the fields.[1]

Economic crisis dramatically polarized Apulian rural society and brought social tensions to the point of open civil war. 1919 and 1920 were years of unprecedented hardship for agriculture in the region. In part the crisis resulted from the general national problem of conversion to peacetime production. Agriculture was the stepchild of the war effort, when resources were systematically diverted from the countryside to industry. The war years, therefore, greatly accentuated the structural weaknesses of an already precarious regional economy. Productivity was compromised for an extended period.

The most obvious factor in this process was the sudden acute shortage of manpower. The absence of hands, however, ended in 1918; other influences were longer lasting. An important circumstance was the lack of important capital goods. Machinery, replacement parts, and chemical fertilizers were nearly unobtain-

15 The Tavoliere, 1900: Gathering in the wheat after the harvest.

able, with the result that farm equipment was not renewed and the erosion of the soil accelerated. These problems were then exacerbated by the requisitioning of work animals. Investment capital, in any case, was in short supply and was further curtailed by a rampant rate of inflation in which agricultural prices lagged far behind the general price level. Grain requisitioning and the freezing of rent contracts further undermined the prospects of the agricultural sector.

The general agricultural crisis was made more dramatic in Apulia by two specific regional calamities. The first was the completion of the phylloxera devastation. Beginning with the first infestations in the Salento peninsula at the turn of the century, the vine lice had spread irresistibly northward, accomplishing their work of destruction in geometric progression. The war years marked the furious culmination of the process. By 1919 the wine industry of the region had been virtually annihilated and reconstruction began almost from zero. Even the reconstitution of the vineyards was seriously affected by the social crisis: landlords deferred investment programmes until greater security of property had been established.

The second regional calamity was drought. The crop failure of 1920 was even worse than in 1908. In 1920 the ground was so hard and dry that in many areas it was impossible to plough, and planting was simply never begun.[2] Where cultivation was undertaken, the yield was so deficient that the police found themselves confronted with a new crime – arson carried out by the farmers themselves. With harvests so meagre that there was no hope of meeting more than a fraction of the costs of production, *massari* resorted on a large scale to the expedient of setting the crops ablaze in the fields in order to claim compensation fraudulently from their insurance policies.[3]

In such circumstances, the clash of interest between capital and labour in the countryside could not have been sharper. Employers faced massive losses and sought to cut costs; the labourers experienced unemployment on a scale without rival in Italy. In 1920 Apulia led the regional unemployment table with nearly 20 per cent of the work force wholly out of work while most of the remaining labourers worked a three-day week even during the high season. In Bari province, the 200,000 day labourers present in 1920 lost a total of 13,000,000 work days, or 65 days per man in comparison with an average year. The loss of work was not, however, evenly distributed, but was concentrated in the great centres. Andria alone had 5,560 adult male *giornatari* unemployed throughout the year.[4]

So great a collapse of the labour market was primarily the result of the general crisis of agriculture in the region. Other factors, however, accentuated the problem. One was the closing of emigration routes, both seasonal and transoceanic, so that the safety valve which had eased the pressure of rural overpopulation ceased to function. In the general crisis, moreover, a growing proportion of the population sought employment in the piazzas. Peasant proprietors, leaseholders, and sharecroppers were unable to achieve a subsistence yield in the drought. They therefore joined the casual hands in the labour market, as did artisans and shopkeepers who were unable to sell their wares because the purchasing power of their customers had vanished. Managerial strategy compounded the problem as many *masserie* were left uncultivated, as pasture was extended in place of wheat, and as women were hired instead of men.

The implications for earning power were dire. On average in 1920 farm labourers in Apulia lost between a third and a half of their normal yearly pay. The average labourer earned 1,600 lire for the year, when 3,000 were required for subsistence. To prevent mass starvation and to preserve public order, the government intervened, decreeing price controls, grain requisitioning, and rationing. To assist recovery, moreover, the state named certain goods, such as petrol, restricted items for sale to producers but not for private consumption. Such measures mitigated the crisis and saved lives.

On the other hand, state policy, as applied to Apulia, was anomalous in conception and inadequate in practice. A national ration of 350 grams of flour per person per day was decreed, and then lowered progressively to 250 and then to 200 grams. The problem, as the Apulian deputies explained in parliament, was that such rations, sufficient to meet the urgent requirements of regions of Italy where wheat-based products were only one item in the diet, were wholly inappropriate in Apulia, where bread was the only foodstuff regularly eaten by the rural population.[5]

Thus deficient in conception, the government programme depended in practice on enforcement by local government. Except for the few communes controlled by the PSI, the effect was that landlords and farmers were asked to regulate themselves. The results were scandalous. The requisitioning of grain at official prices was a task to which local authorities never fully applied themselves. Massive quantities of wheat were directed into flourishing and profitable black-market outlets. Consequently, the distribution of supplies was highly irregular, and in some places there were intervals of several weeks between deliveries. In these intervals black-market prices reached astronomical levels. Interminable queues became universal while hoarders and speculators prospered.

According to the authorities, however, the cause of popular outrage was not the amount and irregularity of rations but the conditions under which they were delivered. There were, in the words of the Andria Chamber of Labour, "infinite tricks and abuses". Frequently the flour was augmented with additives, and was damp and mouldy. At Canosa, Ceglie, and Cassano only supporters of the local party in office could expect supplies. The women of Altamura were given ration coupons only in exchange for sexual favours with members of the municipal guard. There were even scenes of public humiliation when women queued for flour in the piazzas only to be called in turn by the guards, who lifted their skirts and called out, "Come along, little sheep, and be milked." In some places there were no registry files on which to base the issue of coupons and where the illiteracy rate was such that the residents were unable to comprehend the system. Inevitably, social inequalities became more pronounced than ever. While workers went hungry and did without light and heat, notables were able mysteriously to purchase pastries and even illegal petrol for their automobiles. In these various ways, hardship was brutalized and embittered. "Our population", Gaetano Salvemini declared in parliament, "no longer has any faith in the honesty of local government, which has been dishonoured and discredited, and is now dead in the minds of the people".[6]

Terminal "municipalitis" destroyed government efforts at public works as well as rationing. During 1919 and 1920 the state allocated substantial sums of money to relieve unemployment by creating jobs. The funding of public works through the intermediary of municipal government, however, negated the purpose of the programme. The government commission on unemployment in Bari province explained that the state had no means of establishing an effective system of public works because it had no control over the system of subcontracting. Funds budgeted disappeared without trace or were spent "in accord with the criterion of political opportunism".[7] Unemployment, the commission stressed, was not the sole cause of the crisis. The emergency laid bare the chronic weakness of the articulation of the state in the region, together with the long-term defects of latifundism. The response of the labourers took the form of one of the most powerful agrarian revolts in Italian history. In the prewar era the landlords had managed to contain the force of popular unrest. During the "Red Years" 1919–21[8] they lost control of events. The countryside of Bari and Foggia provinces, together with restricted areas of Lecce province, was engulfed in an insurrectionary upsurge. For the first time the movement extended to the *marina*, where several zones played a notable part in the ferment.

Nardò, the major farm labourers' centre in the Salento, was the scene of one of the most determined uprisings of the period. The calling of a general strike by the farm workers' league in protest at unemployment and hunger in April 1920 provided the occasion for a local attempt to seize power. Acting in accord with a plan prepared well in advance by the union organizers Carlo Mauro and Fedele Liguori, the crowd on 9 April took control of the commune. The workers stormed the police barracks and disarmed the troops. Teams of workers then dynamited the bridge and road approaching the town; cut telephone and telegraph lines; set up carefully constructed barricades sealing all entrances; and raised the red flag over town hall. The rebels also seized the houses of the landlords, whom they arrested and paraded through the central piazza to be exposed to public ridicule and humiliation.

For nearly three weeks the insurgents held the city and fought pitched battles with army units sent to restore order. Only on 29 April could the prefect report the capitulation of the revolutionaries when the levelling of the barricades by the artillery and the arrival of armoured vehicles made further resistance impossible.[9] The silence of Lecce province had been dramatically broken.

Elsewhere the inflamed atmosphere was carefully described and charted by the prefects and the police. The prefect of Foggia reported in 1919 that tensions were growing day by day. The

population was "fed up with the apathy and the corruption of the
local administrators" and listened with interest to subversive talk
of violence and soviets. The labourers were "unruly, insolent,
insubordinate, and careless in their work". The situation was one
of "general disquiet" and "real danger". The malcontents in
every town were "reinforced and urged on by the mass of
demobilized soldiers" and they found that the population was
"eagerly listening to their message".[10] In Bari province the police
noted that the farm workers expected to go into the streets to
launch what they thought would be a general national uprising.
Like his counterpart at Foggia, the Bari prefect faced what he described as a "grave and dangerous situation". "Everywhere there
is a great open or subterranean ferment."[11]

The tension quickly found expression in individual deeds of
violence. Farm buildings were vandalized and work animals
killed. Angry workers set fire to grain stores and buildings.
Labourers attacked landlords in the streets. Harvesters and threshing machines had to be guarded day and night.

More significant was the explosion of collective protest. This
movement assumed several facets. One form of rebellion, led
initially by returning war veterans, was the occupation of land.
Although land seizures had occurred sporadically in Giolittian
Apulia, the pattern and the scale of the occupations in 1919, 1920,
and 1921 far outstripped any prewar precedents. No longer was
the movement confined to common land. Workers now took
possession of unplanted land of all sorts – fallow, pasture,
enclosed commons, even entire estates that had been left
uncultivated during the time of troubles. The occupations began
fitfully in the spring and summer of 1919 in scattered communes,
starting at Andria in April. There was then a pause during the winter
off-season. In 1920 they swept every major centre affected by
unemployment throughout the region, and continued well into
1921.[12]

The course of the occupations varied from commune to commune. The movement was a series of spontaneous and uncoor-
dinated local initiatives. The purposes of the occupiers varied

accordingly. In some localities occupation had above all a demonstrative and symbolic value as a gesture of protest and warning. At San Marco in Lamis, for instance, the crowd marched into the fields in procession and then returned directly and peacefully to town.[13] In Spinazzola, however, the occupation developed instead as a defensive measure in response to a lock-out. The local farmers had abandoned the fields, removing their sheep and work animals to neighbouring Basilicata. The occupation was the workers' response.[14] In the commune of Foggia the movement was a reply to the entrepreneurial tactic of expanding sheep grazing at the expense of planting. 3,000 occupiers took over the newly established pastures, where they set fire to the fields to deprive the animals of fodder and block the employers' initiative. In the commune of San Nicandro the workers practised what a local landlord termed "collective brigandage". They invaded Lake Lesina and the land surrounding it. There they fished, cut wood, and hunted game. In the majority of cases, however, the occupation was primarily a means to combat the acute crisis of unemployment. The occupiers normally planted the uncultivated fields unasked and then demanded payment.

This practice of *lavori abusivi* or "illegal working" enraged proprietors. The compulsory employment of large numbers of unwanted hands had obvious implications for profit and for managerial prerogative. To accept the arbitrary work was to give tacit recognition to a right to work on the part of the labourers. The violation of private-property rights also presented a dangerous breach of principle, while the burning of fodder crops was a costly exercise.

In addition, farmers were repelled by the impulsive and improvised fashion in which the labourers carried out the operation. Hastily launched in response to an immediate crisis, the compulsory labour policy inevitably produced anomalies, abuses, and damage to property. On some estates the work carried out by the union men was unnecessary or even positively destructive. Often workers carried out tasks for which they lacked the requisite skills. Occasionally, guaranteed a wage by their organizations, labourers spent their time smoking and playing cards.[15]

"Illegal working" also had a disruptive effect on the landlords' attempt to introduce sharecropping at the expense of wage labour. If union men achieved guaranteed employment, then the enthusiasm of potential croppers to accept onerous terms in order to gain access to individual plots would diminish. Indeed, at Andria the proprietors complained that the land hunger of the share tenants had been seriously compromised and that men were beginning to refuse the offer of contracts.

The means adopted by the occupiers to secure payment for their work further inflamed tensions. Moved by a desperate need and convinced that they were laying claim to a right that had been promised, the labourers did not intend to be thwarted. Recalcitrant landlords who refused to pay had their lives and their property threatened. Frequently the invaders organized the harvest on their own, deducting what they deemed appropriate as payment in kind for services rendered. Such self-payment was practised at Andria, Barletta, and Minervino.[16]

A second facet of the postwar movement took place in the towns rather than in the fields, and began as spontaneously as the occupations. This was the bread riot. Rioting began in the summer of 1919 in protest against the rising price of bread, inadequate rations, and the abuses of hoarders, speculators, and contractors. The movement then gathered momentum as the economic crisis deepened in 1920. Angry demonstrations escalated into all-out confrontations, general strikes, and local insurrections. In many places the workers went into the streets in the belief that they were taking part in the beginning of a general national rising.[17] Workers stoned police stations, attacked employers, overturned market stalls, pillaged shops, and seized town halls. In Bari province alone in 1920 such events took place at Andria, Spinazzola, Bitonto, Molfetta, Bari, Minervino Murge, Canosa, Gioia del Colle, and Terlizzi. On these occasions there was bloodshed with multiple deaths and scores of injuries. The prefect of Bari observed, "It is useless to hope to persuade these people to accept further sacrifices. Living on practically nothing but bread, they are seeking not superfluous extras but bare necessities."[18] The crowds gave symbolic expression to their feelings by forcibly evicting local councillors from their offices and confiscating their keys. The village of S. Michele in the commune of Lecce witnessed the entire populace assemble to demand political independence as an autonomous republic.

The third aspect of the agitation was organized under conscious political direction. Throughout the years 1919–21 there was a vast wave of strikes. The strikes began in 1919 as the unions and chambers of labour struggled to re-establish their presence after the interlude of the war. The first strikes were local affairs which took up again the demands of the Giolittian period. In 1919 the leagues added a few new demands that were attempts to counter the employers' recent wage-control offensive. Thus the workers called for priority for men over women in the labour market and restrictions on the use of farm machinery. They sought an eight-hour day and a ban on overtime.[19]

By 1920 the movement had become far more menacing to property owners and managers. The principal new feature of the postwar conflict was organizational. In the atmosphere of expectation and crisis in which the farm workers lived, the leagues seemed to overwhelm everything in their path. Enrolment in leading centres was nearly total. At Cerignola, for instance, the league achieved a membership of 18,000 numbering virtually every adult day labourer in its ranks. The prefect reported of the city that, "The organization of the working class is perfect."[20] Similar statements could have been made of Andria, Spinazzola, and Minervino. In the zones of latifundism even communes with a less militant labour history, such as Altamura and Lucera, witnessed the emergence of the local league as the dominant political force in the commune.

Along with its new scope and compactness, the union movement achieved an unprecedented coordination. Before the war and for much of 1919, strikes had taken the form of local agitations. In 1920 and 1921, by contrast, the movement coalesced into a single regionally organized challenge to the power of property. The strikes of these years were great province-wide general strikes which aimed at the standardization of conditions throughout Apulia. In many places the strikers were armed with rifles and revolvers. At Terlizzi they threw hand-grenades at strikebreakers, disclosing a material contribution that the war experience made to labour militancy.[21]

The ambition of the strikers was to establish a single regional labour contract guaranteeing a uniform minimal hourly wage, regularized terms of employment, and 250 days of work a year. The means to implement the new right to work was to be an agricultural census carried out under the auspices of the provincial chambers of labour. The census would determine the number of employees that each *masseria* could employ and would form the basis for a roster of union men, who would be allocated to the farms in turn. The Apulian latifundia were to be organized into a single great closed shop. At the local level employers who refused to hire through the labour exchanges were assaulted in the streets and adamant agrarian federations were besieged.[22]

Employers reacted initially in confusion and panic. Their fear was palpable. Emergency meetings of the agrarian associations gave a measure of their mood. Domenico Spada sounded the alarm when he announced that "The tide is rising, and it threatens our homes, our lands, and our families."[23] At Spinazzola the landlords warned the government of the "lunacy of the masses",[24] while at San Giovanni Rotondo they reported that "total anarchy" prevailed.[25] The clearest manifestation of their concern, however, was the widespread flight of *massari* from the land. Corato illustrated the phenomenon. There the *massari* of the commune assembled in June 1919 to announce a common decision "to invest no more capital in an industry that is ungrateful and exposed to so many dangers".[26] In Putignano fifty-five estates representing a third of the area of the commune were abandoned. Such actions were repeated throughout the region. The inevitable effect was to increase the general tension.[27]

During the early spring of 1920 the success of the unions was presaged by a series of local capitulations by the employers in particular communes. At Andria, for example, the farmers agreed to hire only through the hiring hall of the chamber of labour. They also gave an undertaking to employ one labourer for every ten hectares if the estate was operated directly by the proprietor, or one for every twenty-five hectares if the *masseria* was managed by a leaseholder.[28] In March the Altamura farmers signed an accord in which they agreed to the eight-hour day; time-and-a-third for overtime; payment for time lost commuting or through stoppages due to inclement weather; and priority in hiring for local male workers.[29] In Bari province Minervino, Gioia, and Putignano soon followed suit.[30]

The great victories of the leagues were achieved in May 1920 at Foggia and November 1920 at Bari. The respective provincial employers' federations signed province-wide pacts with representatives of the farm workers' leagues. Practical difficulties such as the continuing weakness of the leagues in the *marina* and the contrast between the relative uniformity of conditions in Capitanata and the enormous diversity of Bari had postponed a single regional contract. In other respects, however, the employers had completely capitulated. The closed provincial shop was recognized.

The Bari province agreement[31] announced a minimum hourly wage for adult men of 1.20 lire and a maximum wage which was not to exceed the minimum by more than 50 per cent. The right to work was established, and the employers agreed to cooperate with the leagues in carrying out surveys of all agricultural land and all farm labourers with the objective of practising the minimum work year of 250 days. The survey was to be completed by the end of December. At the same time a united provincial hiring hall was created to coordinate and direct the communal labour exchanges. Employers agreed to hire labour exclusively under its auspices. The commitment was to achieve "a rational allocation of agricultural manpower". Finally, all individual disputes were referred to a provincial arbitration committee.

Within the framework of the provincial pact, local employers and leagues were expected to reach communal agreements with respect to hours and conditions for particular tasks in the crop cycle. The leeway for individual farmers to manage their work force was to disappear. Commenting on the agreement, the union paper *Puglia Rossa* explained that,

> Leaving aside the issue of wages, the value of the victory consists chiefly in the abolition of medieval practices. The concordat clearly establishes that the landlord is no longer free to hire and fire as he pleases. Employment must be agreed with the Chamber of Labour, which will have a representative on every farm.

In Foggia province a similar accord was signed.[32] The chief difference was that it was a much longer and more detailed document than the Bari contract. In the great uniformity of the more northern province the leagues had decided to avoid the duality of general provincial guidelines and detailed local provisions. The Foggia pact set out at length the conditions of service for all operations in agriculture. From the farm workers' perspective, a new era was dawning. Raffaele Pastore, leader of the Foggia league, announced that "The farmers must get it into their heads that the time of individual bargaining is past."[33]

Just as they were negotiating such terms of surrender to the unions in the labour market, the Apulian landlords experienced electoral defeat. In 1919 a new electoral law came into effect. It swept aside the literacy requirement that had disenfranchised the mass of Apulian citizens and established instead unrestricted male suffrage and proportional representation. This reform, coinciding with the political mobilization of the postwar years, permitted a major breakthrough. The national elections of 1919 indicated the new strength of the left. At a time when not a single socialist deputy was returned in Sicily, Basilicata, Calabria or Sardinia, Apulia elected six socialists among its twenty-eight representatives. Electoral figures in the major union centres in Bari province reveal the strength of the leagues (see Table 11).

More important, however, were the local-government elections held in October and November 1920. In the autumn of 1920 the leagues effected a municipal revolution. In the Giolittian era the PSI had won only a handful of strongholds. Now the move-

Table 11. *Electoral figures in major union centres in Bari province*

Commune	Votes, 1919					
	ANC	PSI	Opp.	PPI	Usc.	Lib.–Dem.
Andria	258	4,860	1,072	824	44	1,312
Barletta	1,193	2,402	1,005	857	12	386
Minervino	147	1,972	89	30	12	691
Spinazzola	266	1,390	152	116	6	1,310

ment gained control of local government throughout a vast "red belt" in the wheat-growing zones of Foggia and Bari provinces. In Bari province the PSI emerged victorious in the communes of Acquaviva, Alberobello, Andria, Barletta, Canosa, Conversano, Minervino, Noci, Santeramo, and Spinazzola. The party claimed in addition that only electoral fraud had deprived it of the majority at Ruvo, Gioia del Colle, Putigno, and Terlizzi, where union members were prevented from voting. The landlords' bases of political and economic power were crumbling.

An important illustration of the reaction of employers to the experience of socialist local government is provided by San Severo. There, within months of the autumn election, the defeated Liberals and the agrarian association drafted a formal list of their grievances against government by the "abhorrent Leninist minority".[34] The complaints concerned, first of all, symbols of the passing of the old order and the erosion of established authority. The employers of the northern Tavoliere thus objected to the recognition extended by the commune to the Soviet Union, to the sacking of the former employees of town hall, to the refusal of the socialist administration to build new barracks for the *carabinieri*, and to the fact that the new councillors were atheists. They denounced the new political direction given to education in the local schools. More significantly, they condemned the reform of local taxation, the municipalization of public services, the imposition of fines, and the sanction given by town hall to union land occupations. Most of all, however, farmers feared the increase in bargaining power that control of town hall could provide the leagues in the labour market. In the words of the letter drafted by the outgoing "democrats", "In the name of the Chamber of Labour, almost the entire local work force was monopolized by force, with the support and encouragement of the local government."[35]

The honest citizens of San Severo therefore appealed to the state to come to their assistance. Otherwise, they threatened, they "would be compelled to oppose force to force and bullying to bullying, repeating what like-thinking men have done in Bologna, Florence, Modena and other cities of Italy".[36] The intention to resort to squadrism could not have been more explicit.

At the same time the position of the landlords was challenged in so comprehensive and systematic a fashion that they came to feel they were no longer able to rely upon the state to protect their interests. The views of Apulian property owners on the correct response to the postwar agitations were unequivocal. The prefect of Bari, Camillo De Fabritiis, reported in July 1920:

> The landlords – and here they make no mystery of their views – believe that the only way to put an end to the invasions is violence, whether public or private.
>
> Most commonly they deplore the fact that a certain number of extremists has not been eliminated in every centre; that there have been no mass arrests; that our rifles have not been fired. This is their mentality. And naturally they oppose attempts at moderation and conciliation.[37]

The Cerignola Agrarian Federation was explicit in its requirements. In a resolution sent to the Ministry of the Interior, the federation called for infantry troops, cavalry, armoured vehicles, and tanks. The purpose was "to reduce the turbulent elements to impotence".[38]

Until the postwar period, the police and *carabinieri* had been regularly deployed to defend the "right to work". In the face of the massive and regionally organized challenge of the postwar years, the state adopted instead a new policy of non-intervention. On the grounds that an attempt at police repression would prove counter-productive, would in fact touch off the general rising that it was hoped to avoid, the prefects stood aside. Particularly troubling was the short supply of mounted troops.[39] Thus the prefect at Bari informed Rome that, "My hands are tied." Similarly, his colleague Ferrara at Foggia announced, "With the limited forces at my disposal, it is utterly impossible to prevent and to repress. Energetic action is impossible because the means are unequal to the task. . . It is impossible", lamented Ferrara, "for me to act."[40]

Far from repressing the leagues, the prefects of Bari and Foggia used every means available to urge the agrarian associations to negotiate with the strikers and to make concessions in the interest of public order. De Fabritiis openly called for "a breath of democracy in keeping with modern times".[41] As he described his policy, the prefect of Bari explained,

> Vigorous action was out of the question because of the lack of means to deal with the situation and because of the origins and cause of the phenomenon. Therefore I took care to lead the action of the masses away from possible disorders, directing them into legal paths, promoting agreements, setting up arbitration boards to settle conflicts . . .[42]

Where possible, he continued, "I tried . . . to facilitate the concession by the owners of land to the peasants."[43]

The government in Rome actively encouraged such a policy of conciliation. Fearful of the threat to public order posed by the first wave of land occupations in mid-1919, the state issued the famous Visocchi Decree of September 1919. The decree allowed prefects at their discretion provisionally to legalize the occupations that had already taken place and to assign land to the peasants for a period of four years, provided that the land affected was uncultivated and that the occupiers were war veterans.[44] The aim of the decree was to ease tensions by a timely if guarded concession. In practice the measure was seldom applied in Apulia. The impression made on landlords, however, was one of weakness and betrayal. The view that the state was no longer prepared to defend property soon received apparent further corroboration when the government folded its hands during the occupation of the factories in September 1920.[45]

This "absenteeism" of the state provoked the fury of the landlords and the *massari*. Already in mid-1920 the farmers of Bari province warned the prefect that, unless he acted vigorously to defend the rights of property, they would be forced to a "desperate reaction, which will have the most serious consequences". The Agrarian Association of Andria protested angrily, "The state authorities have turned their offices into bolshevik chambers of labour, supinely obeying any directives given to them by the turbulent elements. They have taken no measures to check and repress the greed of the masses."[46] The association demanded the dismissal of the officials responsible for law enforcement.

It was only in the face of a crisis of this magnitude in which they were deserted by the state that the landlords succeeded in overcoming their internal divisions and factional quarrels sufficiently to launch an organizational offensive to re-establish their control. A provincial agrarian federation was founded at Bari in 1919, and counterparts were set up in Foggia in 1920 and, at greater leisure, in Lecce in 1921. Under their auspices the fascist campaign of terror began in 1921. As the prefect of Foggia commented in January 1921, "All the farmers [have] joined together in an association in order to fight violence with violence."[47] The commercialization of the latifundia, war, and economic crisis had thoroughly eroded the traditional power bases of the *latifondisti*. The *ad hoc* and sporadic violence of prewar labour discipline gave way to a systematic military assault to destroy the workers' movement.

10

FASCISM

Fascist violence in 1921 and 1922 marked the final resolution of the confrontation between farmers and labourers on the Apulian latifundia. Between the first farm workers' strikes in 1901 and the dramatic successes of the leagues in the "Red Years" after the Great War, employers had progressively lost the ability to control the two great resources of Apulian society – the land and the flow of patronage from Rome. 1920 marked the culmination of this process for three reasons. First, the labour contracts of that year and the institution of the closed shop implied a revolution in labour relations and heralded the end of the established practices of farming. Second, the election of socialist local governments and of socialist deputies to parliament threatened to cut off the flow of favours, contracts and exemptions at their source – to be replaced by a confiscatory surtax on land. Finally, the state, which had underpinned an unstable social order by its willingness to intervene militarily on the landlords' behalf, adopted a new policy of neutrality in the contest. For landlords to resign themselves to the changes brought about in 1920 was tantamount to accepting the end of the old order. Instead they discovered a new means to restore their position. The only region in the South to have produced an organized revolutionary challenge to the established social order, Apulia also became the only area of the Mezzogiorno to experience the squadrist counter-offensive.

Initially proprietors responded by relying on the established local vigilante gangs of *mazzieri*. As the league challenge gathered momentum while the state refused to intervene, the existing self-

175

16 Cerignola, 1900: Wells for the supply of water for the city. In the foreground are water merchants, a municipal guard, and health inspectors.

defence mechanisms of the great estates proved inadequate to the task. A better organized and more powerful instrument was required. The solution was fascism, whose purpose, more ambitious than that of the monarchist clubs, was to destroy subversion at its source. Whereas earlier forms of repression in Apulia had aimed to combat particular strikes and agitations, fascism set itself the task of purging the countryside once and for all of the institutions, the symbols, and the leaders of the workers' movement.

The inspiration for the new course that Apulian farmers soon adopted came from the North. *Latifondisti* in Bari and Foggia provinces discovered Mussolini's movement only after it had already demonstrated its usefulness to landowners in the distant Po Valley. The first para-military assaults by armed gangs of black shirts on the strongholds of agrarian socialism at Bologna and Ferrara in November and December of 1920 provided new hope, a model to emulate, and offers of material assistance in the violent redemption of the South.

The emergence of fascism as an effective political force in Apulia, therefore, occurred later than in any other region of Italy where it established solid bases. In the North and Centre of Italy, the fascist offensive against rural socialism began in the winter of 1920–1, reached a paroxysm of ferocity in the spring, and triumphed before the end of the summer. In Apulia, by contrast, fascism began hesitatingly in a handful of communes, and then progressed haltingly out from them in concentric circles. Not before the winter of 1921–2 did the balance tip clearly in favour of the reactionary reconquest, and the last stronghold of the left in the region – the city of Bari – fell only in the summer of 1922.

That fascism in the Apulian countryside was the instrument of the *latifondisti* to destroy the challenge of the farm workers' leagues is beyond dispute. Streams of reports from the state authorities throughout the region leave no room for doubt. Wherever a fascist branch sprang up in the interior of the three provinces, the initiative came from local landowners and employers. As the movement developed thereafter, proprietors gave it their full and unconditional support. In centre after centre those responsible for public order reached identical conclusions. The *fascio* and the political organizations representing the landed interest merged to form a single organization; landlords massively financed the new movement; and leading men of property personally directed the black shirts in their work.

The rise of fascism in the major agricultural centre of Andria was representative. Instructed to investigate the origins of the movement in the commune for the benefit of the Ministry of the Interior, Police Inspector General D'Orazi reached the following conclusions in his account of July 1922:

For some time in Andria farmers and large landlords, together with the part of the population that follows in their wake, felt unable any longer to tolerate the presence of socialist administrators in the commune. They accused the socialists of abuses, blackmail, and favouritism.

Their discontent grew daily until a series of incidents . . . convinced the landlords to adopt new methods of resistance.

For this purpose in April a branch of the fascist party was founded at Andria, and forty young men enrolled.[1]

Thereafter, according to the prefect of the province, the Andria fascists were fully supported by the landlords and their clients. The increase in the membership of the movement was "largely determined by the massive financial assistance that is repeatedly supplied by the landowners. The proprietors have merged with the fascists, and the local nobility takes part in their activities."[2] "I confirm", the prefect added, "the attitude of total commitment of the agrarians to the fascists and the substantial subsidies they provide them."[3]

The first to act were employers in three of the centres where the revolutionary challenge was strongest – Cerignola, Minervino Murge, and Spinazzola. In these three communes fascist branches were organized in the last days of 1920 and the early weeks of 1921. At Cerignola, which gave rise to the earliest and most powerful fascist organization in the region, the initiative came from the young farmer Giuseppe Caradonna.[4] Caradonna, who became in rapid succession secretary of the Cerignola party branch, president of the Foggia provincial fascist federation, and fascist deputy to parliament, was the key figure in the development of the movement throughout the region. A man who was the victim of land occupations and strikes, and who had seen his own grain stores and wine cellars destroyed by fire in union reprisals for his intransigence, Caradonna had abundant personal reasons to welcome the violent initiative of his colleagues in Emilia. As an officer who had served in the trenches during the war, Caradonna also hated the unions for their defeatism and lack of patriotism.

Since Caradonna had ample experience in the use of weapons and the command of men and possessed invaluable contacts through his positions as a member of the executive of the Cerignola Agrarian Federation and as president of the Cerignola

Veterans' Association, he was ideally placed to preside over the new venture. Behind him stood the farmers of the chief union stronghold in the region. In 1921 Caradonna offered them the means to restore their control, and they seized the chance. The sphere of influence of the "Duce of Cerignola", however, was primarily Foggia province, at least during the early months of the counter-offensive. Caradonna's counterparts in Bari province were Mario Limongelli at Minervino Murge and Salvatore Addis at Spinazzola.

In Minervino, reported the police, "Fascism is Limongellism".[5] The dominant figure in the landlords' politics in the commune and a relative of the prefect at Lecce, Limongelli had enormous resources to bring to the movement. He played a key role as the founding father of the Minervino *fascio* and then as president of the Bari-province fascist federation. Having broken the hold of the left at Minervino, he organized the fascist assault throughout southern Apulia.

If as landlord and squadrist Limongelli was the counterpart of Caradonna in Bari province, the third great figure in Apulian fascism was of very different social origins. Salvatore Addis, the hero of the reaction in Spinazzola, had no history of direct involvement in the contest for power on the latifundia. He was a soldier of fortune, a fascist *condottiere*. Addis was a Sardinian captain in the *arditi*, the shock troops of the Italian army. After demobilization and a spell of unemployment at Genoa, he discovered a new career by selling his military experience and his ideas of rescuing the beleaguered landlords of Spinazzola by an organized campaign of force. By the end of 1921, this "captain on forty lire a day", had set up a highly efficient para-military organization. He had also been elected to the executive of the Agrarian Association of Bari province.[6]

If, under the guidance of these three men, fascism first took root in the region in early 1921 as an imitation of squadrist success in the North, the movement in Apulia had its own distinctive pattern of development. In the North of Italy, fascism was a form of reactionary populism. It destroyed the socialist and union challenge of the day labourers not simply by sheer physical force. In addition, fascism in the Po Valley recruited a mass popular following. It exploited the social heterogeneity of the northern countryside in order to build support for a reactionary crusade. The fascist organizers appealed against the day labourers on the modern capitalist estates to those relatively privileged strata of intermediate peasants with a stable position in the social order and a stake in the harvest – sharecroppers, leaseholders, small peasant proprietors. In this way the fascists in the Po Valley succeeded in splitting the ranks of the rural work force, in spreading doubt and dissension, and in constructing broadly based union and party organizations. Conventional political organization supplemented the physical intimidation of the "punitive expeditions".[7]

In Apulia, however, the marked social homogeneity of the zones of latifundism precluded a similar development. The lines of class division in the countryside were too clearly drawn between the narrow elite of great estate owners at one pole and the mass of casual day labourers at the other. In between there were no substantial numbers of traditional peasants whose ambiguous relationship with the unions could be developed into a system of class alliances in defence of property. Fascism in the heel of the Italian peninsula, therefore, was not a populist movement with an aroused plebeian following. Apulian fascism was exclusively the political instrument of the landed elite. There was no possibility of making the defence of latifundism a popular cause. There was no way to bridge what the prefect of Bari termed the "implacable hatred between the farm workers and the landowners, who are the supporters of the *fasci*".

It was symptomatic of the nature of Apulian fascism that it failed to adopt the demagogic slogans employed by the reaction elsewhere. In the North the *fasci* promised land reform, and took up the popular rallying cries of "Land to the peasant!" and "To every peasant the entire fruit of his sacred labour!" In Apulia, significantly, the fascists openly defended latifundism and proclaimed the very different slogan of "The land to the farmer!"[8]

Also indicative of the inability of the *fasci* in the region to generate broad support was the lack of attention given to the development of lateral organizations flanking the party. In the North and Centre, for instance, a union movement played an important role in the fascist offensive. The fascist unions, which followed in the wake of the squads, were partly mere instruments of repression and regimentation. In addition, however, they served the function of reassuring farm workers and peasants that the emerging new order had something to offer them. The unions outside of Apulia arranged employment for their members; made conciliatory promises of land and "rural democracy"; and affected an attitude of independence from the employers.

In Bari, Foggia and Lecce provinces, by contrast, little attempt was made to appease the farm labourers or to spread soothing blandishments in their midst. Thus in 1923 the prefect of Bari observed that in the province under his responsibility the fascist unions were "almost zero". They were, he held, ineffective and badly led. They repelled the masses and created an atmosphere of distrust inimical to popular enthusiasm for fascism.[9]

The very narrowness of the appeal of fascism in the region is one key to its slow and painful development. Apulian fascism lagged a full year behind the triumph of the counter-revolution elsewhere in Italy. Even in the centres where fascism was strongest, the local branch invariably consisted of fewer than a hundred members who lived surrounded by the hatred of the local populace. At Andria, for instance, even on the eve of the March on Rome, the *fascio* was composed of a few dozen "exalted youths" who feared for their lives when they walked the streets of the town and slept for protection on the premises of the party headquarters. The director general of public security at the Ministry of the Interior described the situation of fascism in the commune in the following terms in the summer of 1922:

The fascist party in Andria is composed of a handful of young men (roughly thirty) belonging to various social classes.

The socialist movement, instead, as is known, numbers in its ranks almost the whole of the immense mass of peasants and labourers.[10]

The fascists in Apulia, regarding the population of farm workers as irreducible enemies, never made a concerted effort to gain a broad popular following. The movement in the region developed no theory, no political platform, and no agrarian programme. There was virtually no effort to construct a fascist trade-union organization. The summation of the daily *Corriere delle Puglie* on the first year of fascist activity in Capitanata is apt. "They do nothing", the paper commented, "to win over the masses . . . Neither the organization of the landlords nor that of the fascists has been able to change the spiritual condition of the political climate there."[11] It was highly revealing that Caradonna's solution to the social question, as he explained it to the regional congress of farmers in 1921, was to demand a military dictatorship.

The very lack of popularity of fascism in Apulia is a major factor in explaining its overwhelming reliance on violence. An emphasis on sheer terror reflected the inability to rely on conventional political appeal and moral suasion. In Apulia, fascism was squadrism and nothing else. With good reason the historian of the postwar years in the region, Simona Colarizi, concludes that the fascists in the three provinces possessed no positive vision and enacted only one policy – resistance to agrarian socialism. As Police Inspector General Secchi reported of the establishment of fascist domination at Minervino under Limongelli's leadership, "Their supremacy is not due just to smiles and persuasion. It is the result of action that relies on material force."[12]

Those who applied this force were a small and disparate social grouping. Throughout the civil war landlords and farmers provided the organizational backbone of the movement. They summoned, financed and directed the squads. They furnished horses, rifles and motor cars. They supplied the names of targets and smoothed the relations between the fascists and the state authorities. Seldom, however, did they personally accompany the squads on their expeditions. Apulian fascism recruited its squads from more humble sources.

First of all, the movement made use of the skills of men who had experience in the use of force and could be relied upon for their hatred of socialism. The underworld of the agricultural centres was accordingly one of the most important recruiting grounds. All contemporary observers of the unfolding civil war in the Apulian countryside underlined the fascist reliance on the "lower depths" of the world of crime. Police reports on the appeal of fascism are filled with references to "the worst elements", "hired thugs", "ex-convicts", "individuals notorious for their violence", the *bassi fondi*, and "paid criminals".[13] In the words of the socialist mayor of Corato on the eve of his defenestration, "There has been a continuous effort to stir up the lowest depths of local thuggery."[14] Even the fascists themselves noted the heavy dependence of the movement on the murky underworld of the *malavita*. In the autumn of 1921 the secretary of the Bari *fascio*, Francesco Fato, informed the Milan leadership of the fascist party that the branch in the Apulian capital was "made up of criminal elements of every type and gradation".[15]

Whole squads were formed of professional criminals hired to travel from commune to commune spreading fear and carrying out political vendettas. At Barletta, one of the earliest and most important *fasci* in the region, the "action squads" were formed under the direction of the convicted killer and racketeer Gaetano Altomare and two of his underworld associates – Filomeno Corvasce, known as "the Mummy", and Giovanni D'Ascanio. This trio set up a special team of professional hit men for hire by landlords throughout Bari province.[16]

For such men fascism offered the chance of being put on the payroll of the landlords' associations, of gaining access to a ready supply of weapons, and of covering a career of crime by joining a movement that would secure them immunity from arrest and prosecution. City gangs originally formed for "protection" and extortion gained respectability and powerful protection by joining the *fasci*. Furthermore, since the funding for the movement was secret and unaccountable, there was every opportunity of diverting political contributions into private use. Indeed, money regularly vanished from the tills of the movement. The entire executive of the Bari *fascio* in 1921, an internal investigation revealed, lived off funds stolen from the branch.[17]

In addition to the underworld, the veterans' associations provided fascism with a steady supply of men prepared to take arms in the name of reaction. Particularly in Foggia province, where Caradonna himself was the leader of the ex-combatants' organization (ANC), the local branches of the ANC and of the fascist movement were interchangeable. Often they operated from the same premises, had the same leaders, and formed joint-action squads.[18]

With regard to the politics of veterans, however, it is important to make two distinctions. The first concerns military rank. Ordinary demobilized soldiers were peasants and day labourers with subversive sympathies antithetical to fascism. The squads recruited not among the rank and file of the returning veterans but among the elite of the young officers. Particularly inclined to pro-fascist sentiments were the junior officers – demobilized lieutenants and captains like Caradonna, Addis, and the "boss of San Nicandro", Giuseppe Tozzi. These men were likely to be property owners and to have a violent hatred of socialism both for reasons of class interest and for a sense of outraged patriotism.

In Capitanata, therefore, where the ANC was the organization of the officers, the veterans' organization and fascism formed a seamless web. In Bari province, however, the picture was more complicated. South of the Ofanto River the ex-combatants' association was split along lines of rank and political sympathy. Frequently, as at Andria, the ANC was divided into two warring factions – a "Proletarian League" of the rank and file affiliated with the Bari Chamber of Labour and the official veterans' branch, which openly supported property, fatherland, and fascism.

Criminals and veterans, then, provided the movement with the use of their special skills and experience. A further and overlapping source of recruitment was the network of *mazzieri*, the vigilantes already organized in local monarchist clubs during the Giolittian years before the war. These men had a long history of violent service in the defence of property, and it was only natural for them to merge with the fascist squads. The way in which this could occur is well illustrated by the *fascio* at San Nicandro. There the nerve centre of fascist operations was the monarchist club "Umberto I", founded as a self-defence association by the local landowners. The premises of the club housed at once the San Nicandro Agrarian Association, the local branch of the ANC, and the *fascio*. Here was the meeting ground for the "professional heroes" of the reaction. [19]

If young men who made a profession of violence were the backbone of Apulian fascism, the movement also attracted support from other sources. One was the narrow clientele following of the proprietors both on the estates and in the towns. On the estates, the fascists won a following among the supervisory personnel of the *masserie*. Fixed personnel, guards, and overseers had a favoured position to defend against the levelling pretensions of the unions. They had steady work, independence, and a plot of land to protect. Having a vested interest in the harvest, they also bitterly resented the general strikes imposed by the leagues. Many had been involved in armed clashes with the union "red guards" during the agitations of the Giolittian era or of the "Red Years" following the war. Some had been the victims of union reprisals, and were anxious to settle accounts. All feared that the new regime of producers' cooperatives and the closed shop would sweep them aside. Safely in the good graces of the employers, they rallied to fascism in order to defend latifundism and social hierarchy.

In town as well as on the estates there was a small minority of privileged social groups, many of whose members were prepared to support fascism. The advent of socialist local administration jeopardized the livelihood of followers of the traditional parties of order. Town councillors, clerks, teachers, and municipal guards all risked being sacked. Excise men, builders and contractors feared the loss of contracts. Shopkeepers and vendors faced the threat of losing their licences, the enforcement of regulations protecting consumers, and the competition of the cooperative movement. Lawyers, doctors, and pharmacists foresaw the ruin of their most important clients and the enactment of a new and onerous progressive taxation. The friendly intercession of the mayor in obtaining employment for their sons or exemption from military service could no longer be taken for granted. For those of the middle classes who also leased a farm or who had purchased a market garden by taking advantage of the favourable terms available to land speculators in a time of crop failure and social unrest, social revolution signified confiscation and financial ruin. For all of them fascism promised to defend a way of life, to restore the *belle époque* with its privileges, its entertainments, and its sinecures. For their sons, fascism was an investment to guarantee their future prospects. Throughout Apulia, therefore, the active squadrists included large numbers of students at both the secondary and university levels. Given the sociology of education in the region, these young fascists were clearly the sons of notables and the members of their clienteles.

Representing such a narrow constellation of social interests and failing to appeal to the mass of the population of farm labourers, the fascists applied force massively and systematically. The primary objective of Apulian squadrism was to disrupt the organization of the farm workers' unions. Large-scale military raids provided an impressive first step. Using the early strongholds of Cerignola, Minervino and Spinazzola as their bases, large gangs of well-armed men commanded by military veterans and reinforced by squadrists from the North and Centre, converged by train and lorry on the great league strongholds in the region. Arriving without warning at their destinations in the small hours of the night, the fascists acted rapidly to spread fear and destruction. The premises of the leagues, the chambers of labour, socialist-controlled town halls, and labour exchanges were raided, ransacked and set ablaze with petrol bombs. The supplies of cooperative stores were devastated. Printing facilities, work rosters, membership lists and files were confiscated. The houses of left-wing town councillors and union activists were stormed, and the occupants beaten and sometimes shot. Having demolished the focal points of subversive activity and delivered the unequivocal message that to join the organizations of the left was to risk one's life, the black shirts vanished again into the night, unknown and therefore unassailable.

The Andria *fascio* began its reconquest of the commune in mid-1922 with such a visitation. In the early morning of 4 July some 600 fascists from outside the commune arrived to reinforce the handful of hopelessly outnumbered local supporters. For the occasion several of the most experienced veterans of the civil war in other centres and other regions arrived in Andria – Achille Starace, the deputy secretary of the fascist movement at the national level and the hero of the fascist offensive in the North; Dino Perrone Compagni, the infamous "Grand Duke" of fascism in Tuscany, now charged with the organization of squadrism in Apulia;[20] and the ubiquitous Giuseppe Caradonna. Under their command, the fascists rampaged through the town, devastating buildings sheltering subversives, burning the chamber of labour to the ground, and taking over city hall, where the red banner was replaced by the Italian flag.[21]

The disorientating effect upon the labourers of such occurrences as the "events of Andria" was reinforced by constant harassment and terror in an effort to make the internal life of the leagues impossible and to block the channels of communication between the union leaders and their following. The Sunday rallies, funeral processions, May Day festivities, strikes and demonstrations that had played so important a part in the rise of the left were broken up wherever they occurred. Gangs of outsiders brandishing rifles and revolvers suddenly appeared and opened fire on the crowd. At the same time the *fasci* acted as recruitment agencies for black-legs who broke strikes under armed escort.

Fascism also made life impossible for the leaders and known activists of the left. The aim was to decapitate the leagues by driving their known organizers into exile. Union leaders were attacked in the streets, their homes were raided, and their families were threatened. Labourers who had played a major role in the strikes of the "Red Years" now feared the journey to work through the open countryside. Landlords set up mounted squads of black shirts to patrol the fields and punish men with a reputation for causing trouble. Militants who persisted in their cause were physically eliminated. The most famous case was the assassination of the socialist deputy Giuseppe Di Vagno as he delivered a speech in the village of Mola di Bari in September 1921. His murder was carried out by a team of professional killers employed by the landlords of Gioia del Colle.[22]

Under such intense pressure there was a flood of political refugees from the rural centres seeking refuge in the regional capital at Bari. As usual, the first town to experience such a development was Cerignola. There by the summer of 1921 the mayor Adolfo Salminci, the socialist town councillors, the members of the executive of the labourers' league, and the deputy Di Vittorio had all resigned their posts and fled for their lives. With good reason the deputy Arturo Vella, who had himself been the victim of a fascist beating the month before, complained to the Ministry of the Interior in May 1921 of the "hellish situation" in the Apulian provinces and of the "unheard of violence against the working class". "Life", he wrote, "is impossible for men of the socialist party."[23]

With regard to local government, violence was supplemented with other forms of pressure intended to destabilize the socialist administrations. The objective was to reduce the affairs of the newly elected authorities to chaos. For this purpose the fascists organized a boycott. Employees with a knowledge of administration resigned *en masse*. All decisions of the town council were declared inoperative, and meetings were disrupted. Tax resistance began as men of property refused to pay the new levies and surtaxes announced by the communes. The idea was to create such confusion in the conduct of local affairs and such a breakdown in law and order that the prefect would have a pretext to intervene, dissolving the socialist town councils and placing the conduct of local government securely in the hands of temporary commissioners chosen from the ranks of the parties of order. One by one in the course of 1922, therefore, the local officials elected in the heady days of 1920 were replaced by notables appointed from above. The effects on the rank and file of the leagues of such a systematic campaign of terror were profound. As the chambers of labour and union offices went up in flames, as socialist mayors and league officials resigned and fled, as activists were beaten senseless, and as the established lines of communication were broken, fear and confusion took hold. By the end of 1921 at Cerignola, the first centre in Apulia to experience the full weight of squadrist intimidation, the prefect reported a deep sense of bewilderment among the workers. They had not changed their political views. Fascism had made no converts. Deprived of their known organizers and spokesmen, however, they felt impotent and abandoned, and lapsed into a sullen despair. The same, argued Inspector General Secchi, was true in every commune he visited in these years. The farm workers were overwhelmed by "bloody events", "systematic terror", and "fear". They were never persuaded. Concluding his gloomy survey of the political situation in the region, Secchi ventured a prediction: "Fascism deceives itself with the belief that it can build on a foundation of violence and intimidation. Unknowingly it is preparing a sad future for itself because to sow the wind is to reap the whirlwind."[24]

Landlords seized the opportunity to destroy the contractual revolution of 1920 and 1921. In the wake of the squadrist offensive, employers throughout the region denounced the provincial pacts so recently signed. The closed shop was systematically dismantled. Entrusting labour relations and negotiations to the fascists, the estate managers insisted on a return to local agreements, which invariably sanctioned a repudiation of all of the union gains of the preceding decades. Where the new contracts were written, as at Stornarella in Foggia province, it is possible to chart the course of the contractual counter-revolution. At Stornarella, union recognition was revoked and employers insisted on the return to freedom of hiring with no commitment to give preference to local workers. All wages agreed in advance were reduced by 18 per cent with regard to the pay scales established in

1920. More sinister, however, was the provision that wage rates for the most important and costly tasks such as reaping and threshing were not to be determined in advance, but were to be settled on the basis of the former practice of "free contracting". In a similar spirit, hours were to be regulated by "local custom".[25]

In the case of Stornarella, therefore, there was clearly a reversion to the bargaining relations prevalent before the strikes of 1901. The workers of Stornarella were fortunate, however, in having a written document. Frequently the new agreements were oral, as they had been in the nineteenth century, with dire results on the labourers' conditions of living. At times even the fascists rebuked the employers for their evangelical parsimony. Luigi Granata, the secretary of the Andria *fascio*, complained that the worst enemies of fascism were the landlords. In their zeal, he wrote in the summer of 1922, "They prevent the flowering of our organizations and undermine the *fascio* by their determination to reduce the workers to slavery."[26]

Not surprisingly, when so much was at stake and when the reaction was so uncompromising, the fascist reconquest met a fierce but poorly organized resistance. In this respect again Apulia stood apart from the Italian norm. In the fascist strongholds in the Po Valley, the structures of agrarian socialism collapsed with astonishing rapidity in the first wave of squadrism. As the communist paper of Turin, *Ordine Nuovo*, commented,

> The fascist experiment was first tried in the city considered the red stronghold of Italy, Bologna, and the proletariat there knew no way to resist except in a weak and half-hearted manner. There was an occasional scuffle, the odd fight waged by a small group, and nothing more. Bologna, like the other centres of Emilia, did not lend itself to the effort.[27]

In the Po Valley a bureaucratic and reformist trade-union leadership had not prepared its membership either morally or materially for a trial of physical force. A major reason for the débâcle of 1921, *Ordine Nuovo* stressed, was the distance that had developed between the unions and their supporters. The unions of

Emilia had become centralized, undemocratic hierarchies standing above the masses like a new state power, levying taxes,
sanctioning non-compliance by the uncommitted, and administer-
ing fines. The union officials had so wrested the initiative from
their following that the task of reversing the process for the purpose of resisting the fascist offensive proved impossible. The
Turin paper explained,

> Organization was heavily centralized in the persons or the very small
> circle of the leaders. To bring chaos into the unions it was enough to
> strike down a few individuals. Worse still, this provoked no serious re-
> sponse from the masses . . . The reason was that the organization, in its
> recent colossal bureaucratic growth, became nothing more than an
> enormous central administration which had lost all contact with the
> masses, who no longer considered it the arm and standard of their
> faith.[28]

Furthermore, accustomed to the legality of the Giolittian era,
the northern labour movement was psychologically unprepared to
defend itself by force. Far from advocating resistance to fascism,
the northern socialist party and union organizers preached non-
violence and disarmament. Their followers, stunned by the
ferocity of squadrism and demoralized by the advice of their
leaders to turn the other cheek, were unable to improvise effective self-defence. The result was to facilitate fascist success.

In Apulia instead, the advance of Caradonna's troops was contested at every step. As Arturo Vella, the deputy from Bari, commented in bitter criticism of his northern comrades, "While
everywhere else people marked time in debate and argument,
here in Apulia we acted with lightning speed and with a unanimity
without equal."[29] The response of the farm workers in Apulia to
the early squadrist assaults fully supports Vella's statement. In
February 1921 the labourers staged a three-day general strike
throughout the region in protest against fascist intimidation. The
movement was on a scale unique in the peninsula. In the zones of
latifundism throughout the region production, trade, and public
services of every kind were halted. League members at the same

time attempted on their own initiative to settle scores with the *fascisti*. In their fury bands of union men roamed the region in search of vengeance. In the countryside they burned estate buildings to the ground, fought pitched battles with *annaroli* who sought to defend the property or continue work, and attacked any landlords or farmers who stood in their path. The strikes spontaneously developed into a manhunt for employers suspected of responsibility for the squads. The press reported that the days of the Great War were being relived. Several employers were lynched, and many were savagely beaten. When, as frequently occurred, the crowds were unable to find the men they sought, they took reprisals as best they could. They slashed vines, poisoned the drinking water of farm animals, slit the throats of sheep, and pillaged estate buildings.[30]

The events of February 1921 were the most dramatic example of anti-fascist resistance on such a scale. Throughout 1921, however, and with dwindling vigour down to the end of the summer of 1922, opposition to squadrism persisted at the local level. The most notable instance of such local resistance took place in the regional capital in August 1922, when large-scale popular resistance to fascism had virtually ceased elsewhere in the peninsula. In the working-class quarter of Old Bari, long a centre of subversive sympathies and the refuge of union militants from the whole of the region, a carefully organized Labour Alliance, grouping the remnants of the Apulian labour movement of all political persuasions under the leadership of Giuseppe Di Vittorio, prepared a desperate last stand. During the summer firearms were purchased and distributed to the workers, materials for the construction of barricades were assembled, and women were encouraged to arm their homes with rocks and burning oil. On 1 August the plans went into effect as the city rose in open rebellion against the fascist advance. Order was finally restored only on 4 August after three days of fierce street battles against the army and the fascists acting together. This rising, the police commented, revealed "the deadly hatred of the population of Old Bari for the fascists".[31]

If the general strike of February 1921 and the Bari uprising of

August 1922 marked the beginning and the end of armed resistance to fascism, the intervening eighteen months were filled with spontaneous local activity in the major agricultural centres. In all of the strongholds of the left the farm workers engaged in guerrilla warfare with the black shirts. As late as the spring of 1922 at Andria, for instance, the local fascist "boss", Luigi Terlizzi, and other members of the executive of the party branch were ambushed in the streets and thrashed nearly to death. Such assaults, the leaders of the Andria *fascio* lamented, had long been almost a daily occurrence in the commune. The branch itself bore the appearance of an armed camp in enemy territory, and its members never went abroad alone or unarmed.

Such was the reality throughout the Apulian interior. Nor did opposition confine itself to acts of vengeance against individual fascist leaders. There were also occasions when squadrists arriving on an expedition found that their visit had been anticipated and a furious reception prepared. Labourers armed with scythes and spades then overwhelmed the intruders by sheer force of numbers and hacked at them with their tools.

The difficulty for the labourers in this civil war was that the contest proved unequal and asymmetrical. A major new factor in the final confrontation of 1921–2 was the success of the landlords but not the workers in making an organizational leap forward. The left remained fundamentally local in orientation. The communally based leagues were the decisive units in the contest for power with only a loose coordinating superstructure of provincial chambers of labour and union federations. In the Giolittian era such an emphasis on the commune was no disadvantage since the employers were also organized only at the local level. Furthermore, the syndicalist organizational pattern with the commune as its focus had the positive advantages of making the movement highly responsive to local conditions and of preventing the development of a bureaucratic ossification which was anathema to the libertarian ethos.

A new danger in the postwar crisis, however, was that the landlords had effectively organized. In the peril of the postwar agitations, landlords and farmers for the first time overcame their internal divisions sufficiently to found provincial agrarian associations to coordinate their resistance to the advance of agrarian socialism. Taking this process a step further, the fascist movement introduced a fundamental innovation in Apulian politics. The *fasci* were the first political movement in the region to have a solid organizational presence at the regional and national levels.

Thanks to this organizational factor, the counter-revolution was able to bring powerful outside resources to bear on the power struggle in particular centres. At Andria, Barletta, and San Severo, therefore, the landlords and their allies in the commune were not dependent in the showdown with the leagues upon the meagre local recruitment of fascists. On the contrary, they could rely on the concentration of men and material from the whole of the region and even from other areas of Italy. While the leagues could expect no assistance from the national leadership of the socialist party, the fascist movement sent to Apulia whole squads from the North and experienced organizers.

On the terrain of open civil war, moreover, fascism possessed a number of advantages that the leagues could never match. Massively supplied with funds by the most powerful economic interests in Apulia, the *fasci* were well armed and amply provided with transport, with the result that they possessed the vital assets of surprise and superior firepower. Here the leagues could not hope to compete. Financial stringency was a perennial weakness of the unions, which were dependent on the contributions of destitute labourers. The very postwar economic crisis that helped to spark the revolutionary ferment of 1920 and 1921 stretched the resistance funds of the field hands to breaking point. As a result, although the syndicalist and revolutionary socialist leaders preached armed resistance to fascism, the resistance in practice was hastily improvised and hopelessly equipped. Heavily armed squadrists under military command faced crowds of labourers wielding their work tools or throwing rocks.

Furthermore, instead of receiving outside assistance, the Apulian labour movement found its violent opposition to fascism

condemned by an embarrassed socialist party. At the national level
the PSI was convinced that fascism was a mere mechanical reaction to the challenge of revolution and that it would therefore
recede as the wave of strikes and occupations passed. The party
therefore advocated a policy of non-resistance to fascism. The
pitched battles and general strikes of Apulia were highly
unwelcome. The party leadership denounced such activity as
dangerous and counter-productive, as more likely to prolong
squadrist violence than to defeat it. The newly founded communist party (PCI), for its part, was still too weak to provide practical aid in distant Apulia. In any event, the PCI, although
committed in principle to armed resistance to fascism, stood in
favour of an ideal resistance under party control. The desperate
scenes enacted by non-party labourers and syndicalists evoked
little enthusiasm. Palmiro Togliatti, the communist leader who
castigated the PSI for its passive resignation and who praised the
sporadic attempts at self-defence by his comrades in Tuscany and
Emilia, was silent about Apulia. In its conflict with fascism,
therefore, the labour movement in the region stood isolated
and alone.

Fascism also possessed the inestimable advantage of physical
invulnerability. The organizational centres of agrarian socialism –
the town hall, the chamber of labour and the union offices – were
highly visible, while the leaders of the movement were local and
well known. It was relatively easy for the fascists to disrupt and
demoralize the unions by destroying their premises and driving
their leaders into exile. The fascists, by contrast, were very difficult to find and strike. As a result, the reaction was able to attack
the nerve centres of the left while the unions in their resistance
had to content themselves with largely symbolic reprisals. The
workers could burn down estate buildings and poison sheep, but
the leaders of the movement remained beyond their reach. The
reaction, reinforced by economic crisis and large-scale unemployment, thus kept up a relentless pressure on the labourers.

The most important factor of all, however, in the victory of the
fasci and the re-imposition of the autocracy of latifundism was the

massive collusion of the state apparatus in the region. In the trial of strength of 1921 and 1922 the farm workers faced not one enemy but two – the agrarian counter-offensive and the power of the state. So important was the collaboration between fascism and state authorities, that, in discussing the violent end of the union movement at Cerignola, Di Vittorio commented, "We were defeated not by the fascists but by the *carabinieri*."[32]

Here it is important to make a distinction between Rome and the Apulian provinces. At the national level the governments headed by the prime ministers who presided over the crisis of the Liberal regime – Nitti, Giolitti, Bonomi, Facta – did not directly support the fascist movement in its rise to power. To have done so would have been deeply self-destructive because the *fasci* were a subversive challenge to their authority and to the rule of law. Accordingly, there was a constant stream of telegrams from the Ministry of the Interior to its subordinates in the provinces enjoining them to enforce the law and to arrest and prosecute fascists guilty of illegality. There is no evidence of direct sympathy between the governments of postwar Italy and Mussolini's movement.

On the other hand, in a time of revolutionary crisis, the Liberal political leadership was guilty of a preoccupation with the threat from the left and of a serious underestimation of the danger from the radical right. For the authorities in Rome, fascism was a useful if troublesome political force in the defence of the social order against bolshevism. The challenge was to "constitutionalize" Mussolini's movement, repressing its violent excesses and steering it into the path of legality. For this purpose Giolitti even included the fascists in 1921 in the notorious National Bloc, the electoral alliance of the parties of order against revolution. The result was to give Mussolini's movement a legitimacy and a respectability it could not have acquired otherwise.

At the same time, a weak and vacillating government failed to support subordinate officials who attempted to apply the full rigour of the law against the fascists. When powerful landowners protested at the action of prefects who arrested black shirts and when the squads threatened retaliation and disorder, Giolitti adopted the course of least resistance, removing the offending official and putting more pliant officers in his place. The most notorious case was the replacement of the prefect of Bologna, Cesare Mori, at the insistence of landlords and their allies.

In such circumstances, the message transmitted to officials in the provinces was highly ambiguous. On the one hand, telegrams and official instructions called for an impartial enforcement of the law. On the other hand, the government had clearly indicated to subordinates that the fascists were a respectable force that enjoyed favour in high places. To wink at their misdeeds was to risk little, while to repress them conscientiously was to risk a career.

In the Apulian provinces the lack of firm direction from Rome had the most fatal consequences. In the three provinces the force of the state had long been put at the disposal of the landed interest. In the process a network of bonds of interest and friendship had been established that made a benevolent attitude to fascism almost automatic and that could not be broken by the occasional cable from Rome. Indeed, it was hardly from Apulian officials, demoralized and undermanned in a hostile environment they regarded as a place of punishment, that the state could reasonably expect a vigorous attempt to apply the uncertain and shifting policy of Giolittian non-intervention.

For their part, the prefects and police were unanimous in their opposition to the unions. It was true that in 1919 and 1920 the three prefects in the region had adopted a policy of non-intervention in labour disputes. This policy, however, implied no change of sympathy and no weakening of their attachment to the parties of order. On the contrary, Limongelli, the prefect of Lecce and relative of the Minervino landlord, declared that he regarded agricultural strikes as a "crime against the national economy".[33] In line with this view, the Apulian prefects had prepared in 1920 a contingency plan to break the strikes of the leagues by calling in the army to harvest the grain.[34] If the plan was not applied, it was only because of tactical calculations: De Fabritiis at Bari, Regard in Foggia, and Limongelli at Lecce agreed that they lacked the manpower necessary for the performance of so delicate a task.

When in 1921 the landlords, against the advice of the authorities, who recommended concessions, launched their own attempt to destroy the labourers' movement once and for all, the police greeted the initiative with warm approval. According to De Fabritiis, fascism, "an awakening of the healthy elements of the nation, must be greeted with sympathy by everyone".[35] He singled out Salvatore Addis in particular for praise for his role in halting the "rising bolshevik tide" and for his "healthy propaganda based on truly patriotic feeling".[36] At the same time, Regard defined fascism in Capitanata as a "justified protest against continuous acts of revenge and arbitrary power". With such unambiguous expressions of opinion by their masters, the state authorities below the prefects at every level gave virtually unqualified support to Caradonna's illegal initiative.

On this point the files of the Ministry of the Interior are eloquent. During 1921 and 1922 a series of inspectors were sent from Rome to investigate the political situation in Apulia. With regard to the relationship between the state officials and fascism, the reports were unanimous. The recurring phrases used to describe the behaviour of the police are "partisan behaviour", "inertia", "unclear understanding of their responsibility", "deficiency", and "inaction".[37]

What these terms meant in practice is that the police and *carabinieri* systematically closed their eyes to fascist violence, allowing the squads to harass, to threaten, and even to kill with total impunity. Crimes committed in the service of reaction were rarely investigated, and no arrests were made. In a more positive role, the police regularly intimidated and disarmed members of the unions. Serving officers provided the fascists with arms and transport, and often accompanied them in their operations. Subversives were arrested and beaten in their cells. In some communes, such as Gioia del Colle, the local fascist branch was actually founded by police officers.[38]

When complaints were filed with the Ministry or when particular police excesses caused public scandal, superior officers and prefects defended their subordinates' conduct. Especially loyal in this respect was Regard, the prefect of Foggia. In defiance of all the evidence of illegal conduct by the men under his command, Regard regularly denied all accusations as "socialist bias". His men, he wrote to Rome, were beyond all praise.[39]

The role that such complicity could play in the rise of fascism emerges in reports on the state of public order in specific communes. In Cerignola the success of Caradonna's *fascio* was due in no small measure to the zeal of the chief of police in the commune, Commissioner De Martino.[40] De Martino was a personal friend both of Caradonna and of the notorious squad commander Salvatore Izzi. The three together plotted the reconquest of the "Bologna of Apulia", and met regularly to coordinate their plan. The troops under De Martino's control actively promoted the fascist cause, and provided the squads with material aid. The *carabinieri* stationed in the city took part in punitive missions. On several occasions De Martino's police surrounded and cordoned off the working-class neighbourhoods of the city at night. Then teams of squadrists carried out house-by-house searches for known militants and weapons.[41] Such militant pro-fascism was by no means confined to Cerignola. Equally extensive and well-documented collusion between the police and the *fasci* occurred at Spinazzola, Barletta, Canosa, and Minervino.

With such powerful assistance, the fascists proceeded step by step to dismantle the structures of Apulian subversion. Once again Cerignola provided the model. In Di Vittorio's words, Cerignola was "the centre from which fascism radiates throughout the region". By early 1922 the politics of the commune had been radically reversed. The union organizers had been driven into exile; the league offices and cooperatives had been destroyed; and the work force had been purged. The opposition press had disappeared from circulation, and the rallies and demonstrations of the leagues had been banned. The mayor and the town councillors elected by the leagues had resigned, and local government was in the hands of a commissioner acceptable to the employers. The recognition extended to the unions had been revoked and the contract of 1920 annulled. In place of the labour exchange under the auspices of the chamber of labour, the labour market was regulated by the new Union of Independent Workers – a classic company union operated by the fascists for the recruitment of deferential outsiders as blacklegs. Workers who refused to accept the return to free contracting, the twelve-hour work day, and the regime of the corporals were blacklisted. If they protested, they were threatened and visited by Caradonna's men or arrested by De Martino's police. The last desperate attempts to defend the gains achieved in two decades of union action were broken up and followed by terrifying reprisals. In February 1922 the attempt by determined militants to call a general strike inspired by the fierce resistance of the year before was a dismal failure. No one dared any longer to protest.

The silence which first fell on Cerignola was progressively extended to every agricultural centre in Apulia where a union movement had contested the power of the employers. By August 1922 the era of strikes, cooperatives, and socialist local government was over. Such was the nature of fascism.

Latifundism in Apulia had emerged as a form of commercial agricultural enterprise adapted to the particular conditions of the local environment. In a region of dry farming, easy communications, and high but erratic yields per acre, profits could be made extensively – as a return on money invested in bringing more land under cultivation rather than in intensifying the method of production. The possibility of profit, however, depended on a ready supply of cheap free labour. Labour in Apulia had been made free by the destruction of subsistence peasant agriculture throughout the South. Under the relentless pressure after unification from enclosure, the extinction of *usi civici*, regressive taxation, and a series of commercial and natural disasters from the tariff war with France to phylloxera, peasant producers were driven from the land on to the labour market. As peasant society was smashed, a steady flow of labour trickled down from the surrounding hills and from the coast on to the great plain of the Tavoliere and the

17 Ascoli Satriano, Foggia province, 1900: A flock of "Merinos" sheep at the *masseria* S. Carlo.

open fields of the north and west of Bari province. There labour was kept cheap by the "natural" defences of the latifundia – the irregular demand for labour, the competition for work generated by overpopulation, and the ability of the estates to expand or contract the area under cultivation by turning to sheep. These "natural" defences were supplemented by the autocracy of the employers in the interior of Apulia founded on their control of local government, their command of the repressive force of the state, and the possession of private instruments of intimidation. Violence and the repression of labour were inherent in latifundism.

In the early twentieth century the calculations of profitability were profoundly altered to the detriment of property owners. Yields were undermined by soil erosion and, above all, the supply and control of labour were threatened. Emigration and the organization of the work force radically transformed the balance of power in the labour market, overwhelmed the mechanisms of control built into the estates, and threatened the very survival of latifundism as a system of production. Fascism was the final defence of the great estates.

The emerging dictatorship in Apulia was not simply a response to the threat of revolution in the postwar crisis. Its roots lay in the whole evolution of labour relations in the agricultural centres between 1901 and 1922. Latifundia could not co-exist with a unionized work force, and the local instruments of force available to employers could no longer contain the threat of the emancipation of labour. What was novel about the movement launched by Caradonna was not its violence but its organization of repression on a systematic and regional basis. Fascism was a long-term settling of accounts between property and labour. It enabled employers to abolish union recognition and to restore the absolutism of management first challenged when the Cerignola farm hands struck in 1901. Fascism in Apulia was a repressive method to maintain the profits of a commercialized extensive agriculture. Mussolini's dictatorship gave the great estates a twenty-year lease of life. The collapse of the regime, a new wave of emigration to the cities, and a renewed contest for power in the labour market in the 1940's and the 1950's sounded the death knell of the great estates.

NOTES AND SOURCES

1 Wheat and sheep

1 Lecce province throughout the period considered in this work included the three present-day provinces of Lecce, Brindisi, and Taranto. The term was synonymous with the geographical designation Terra d'Otranto.

2 "Il congresso dei contadini", *La Conquista*, 19 April 1908.

3 An excellent study of Lecce province in the Giolittian period is Fabio Grassi, *Il Tramonto dell'età giolittiana nel Salento* (Bari, 1973). Chapter 3 is entitled "The Silence of the Peasants".

4 Angelo Fraccacreta, *Le forme del progresso economico in Capitanata* (Naples, 1912), p. 75.

5 The crop rotations in use in the commune of Foggia are discussed in Antonio Pompa, *Inchiesta sul latifondo: Agro di Foggia* (Foggia, 1932), p. 18.

6 An interesting account of agriculture in Bari province is Franco De Felice, *L'agricoltura in Terra di Bari* (Bari, 1971).

7 This discussion of the Tavoliere is based on the following works: Fraccacreta, *Le forme del progresso economico*; Carlo De Cesare, *Delle condizioni economiche e morali delle classi agricole nelle tre provincie di Puglia* (Naples, 1859); Michele Papa, *Valori e progressi economici della Capitanata, 1866–1936* (Foggia, 1936); Giovanni Praitano, *Il Tavoliere di Puglia* (Bari, 1908); and Vincenzo Ricchioni, *Lavoro agricolo e trasformazione fondiaria in Terra di Bari* (Bari, 1929).

8 "Nelle tre Puglie", *Corriere delle Puglie*, 18 May 1913.

9 "L'agricoltura nelle Puglie e i pugliesi", *La Conquista*, 23 July 1911.

10 Letter of Vito Orofino to Sig. Sindaco di Altamura, 9 June 1863, Archivio di Stato di Bari, Demani comunali ex feudali, b. 10, fasc.

119 (Operazioni demaniali del comune di Altamura eseguite dall'agente Vito Orofino dal maggio 1863 a maggio 1964).

11 The difficult climate is considered by Pompa, *Inchiesta sul latifondo*, pp. 7–9; and in "Alcuni cenni statistici sulla Capitanata", *Scienza e Diletto*, 11 February 1894.

12 On the geography of malaria, see "Il Tavoliere di Puglia", *Il Foglietto*, 31 October 1901.

13 A. Jatta, "La produzione del frumento nel barese", *Rassegna Pugliese*, II (1885), pp. 291–2.

14 On the movement of rent in Bari province, see Archivio di Stato di Bari, Agricoltura, Industria e Commercio, b. 17, fasc. 18 (Variazioni nel fitto dei terreni).

15 Emanuele Fizzarotti, "Il Banco di Napoli e le Puglie", *Corriere delle Puglie*, 2 August 1907. Cf. also Luca Gentile, "Agricoltura e contadini", *Corriere delle Puglie*, 31 August 1907. These observations require verification in the archives of the banks.

16 "Patrimonio della famiglia Pavoncelli al 31 dicembre del 1903", Archivio Privato Pavoncelli, fondo Gaetano Pavoncelli fu Giuseppe.

   At the time when I made use of the Pavoncelli archive at Cerignola in the summer of 1981, the documents had not been fully catalogued. The papers were grouped according to major series or *fondi*, but individual boxes of documents and single entries were not numbered.

17 "Notizie biografiche", Archivio Privato Pavoncelli, fondo Giuseppe Pavoncelli fu Federico: Atti amministrativi. A funeral oration by Pavoncelli's friend Raffaele De Cesare is also full of biographical information. Cf. "Discorso pronunziato a Cerignola", 11 June 1911, Archivio Privato Pavoncelli, fondo Giuseppe Pavoncelli fu Federico.

18 Letter of Giuseppe Pavoncelli to Antonio Salandra, 30 August 1881, Archivio Privato Pavoncelli, fondo Giuseppe Pavoncelli fu Federico.

19 The conditions of peasants in the South of Italy were the subject of a report by a parliamentary commission headed by Senator Faina, *Inchiesta parlamentare sulle condizioni dei contadini nelle provincie meridionali e nella Sicilia* (Rome, 1910). The volume on Apulia was drawn up by Errico Pressutti, and will henceforth be referred to in the notes as *Inchiesta*. The reference here is to p.19.

20 "Un progetto di contratto agrario", *L'Agricoltore Pugliese*, 15 September 1904, p.257.
21 On the role of the administrator, see Ricchioni, *Lavoro agricolo*, pp.119–20.
22 On the contracts prevailing in Apulia, cf. Vittorio Curato, "I patti colonici in Puglia", *Corriere delle Puglie*, 20 and 21 March 1904.
23 *Ibid.*
24 On the origins of the *massari*, see *Inchiesta*, pp.33–4.
25 Angelo Fraccacreta, *Le forme del progresso economico*, p.15.
26 The managerial methods widely in use in Apulia are discussed in "Concetto amministrativo dei grandi latifondi in Capitanata", *L'Agricoltore Pugliese*, 15 May 1904, pp.129–31; and A. Jatta, "La produzione del frumento nel barese", *Rassegna Pugliese*, II (1885), pp.323–5 and 355–7; and *Rassegna Pugliese*, III (1886), pp.67–71 and 83–5.

An excellent study of latifundism in the Crotonese zone of Calabria is Pino Arlacchi, *Mafia, Peasants and Great Estates: Society in Traditional Calabria* (Cambridge, 1983), chapter 3. The predatory practices of the Sicilian *gabelloti* – the counterparts of the Apulian *massari* – are described in the important article by Denis Mack Smith, "The Latifundia in Modern Sicilian History", *Proceedings of the British Academy*, LI (1965), pp.87–93.

27 "Le tre Puglie", *Il Foglietto*, 7 February 1901.
28 "Capitanata triste", *Scienza e Diletto*, 1 September 1895.
29 "La crisi a Troia", *Il Foglietto*, 19 October 1902.
30 "Un progetto di contratto agrario", *L'Agricoltore Pugliese*, 15 September 1904. Cf. also Sabino Fiorese, "Per la terra ai combattenti", *Corriere delle Puglie*, 28 February 1918.
31 Carlo De Cesare, *Delle condizioni economiche e morali*, p.81.

2 Day Labour

1 F. Casardi, "Acqua e pane", *L'Agricoltore Pugliese*, 31 January 1914, p.3.
2 Franco De Felice, *L'agricoltura in Terra di Bari*, p.52.
3 Ricchioni, *Lavoro agricolo*, p.114.
4 The system of corporals is discussed by Francesco Casardi, "Ripopoliamo le compagne!", *L'Agricoltura Pugliese*, 30 April 1914,

p.63. On the privileges of the *annaroli*, cf. also Ricchioni, *Lavoro agricolo*, p.121: and Raffaele Pastore, "Dopo dieci anni di lotte", *La Conquista*, 3 September 1911.

5 Francesco Casardi, "Ripopoliamo le campagne!" *L'Agricoltore Pugliese*, 30 April 1914, p.63.

6 Even in Sicily, the other great region of latifundism in the South, the work force consisted of impoverished peasant tenants rather than authentic proletarians. Cf. Mack Smith, *The Latifundia in Modern Sicilian History*.

7 The mayor of Altamura reported, for instance, that the farm workers in the commune "find work day by day with different landlords". Letter to the president of the Bari Chamber of Commerce, 30 July 1908, Archivio di Stato di Bari, Camera di Commercio, b.1. fasc. "Danni della siccità" (1908), n.2686.

8 Ministero di Agricoltura, Industria e Commercio; Direzione Generale della Statistica e del Lavoro, *Censimento della popolazione del Regno d'Italia al 10 giugno 1911*, vol. I (Rome, 1914), Table I.

9 De Cesare, *Delle condizioni economiche e morali*, pp.16–17.

10 "Relazione della commissione governativa per la disoccupazione in provincia di Bari", Archivio Centrale dello Stato, PS (1920), b. 77, fasc. "Bari: disoccupazione", p.52.

On the lack of skills of the day labourers, see also *Inchiesta*, pp.293–5. The inability to spin or weave is noted by Giulio Curato, *I contadini di Troja (Foggia) secondo l'inchiesta parlamentare* (Rome, 1916), p.12.

11 Giovanni Rinaldi and Paola Sobrero, eds., *La memoria che resta: vissuto quotidiano, mito e storia dei braccianti del basso Tavoliere* (Foggia, 1981), p.122.

12 *Inchiesta*, p.36.

13 For a description of the living conditions of the day labourers by the secretary of the Bari Chamber of Labour, see Giuseppe De Falco, "Il proletariato nel paese degli eccidi cronici", *La Conquista*, 3, 10 September and 1 October 1911.

A discussion of wages and conditions by the deputy and landlord A. Jatta is "Giornate e salarii nel barese", *L'Agricoltore Pugliese*, 15 August 1901, pp. 225–9.

14 *Inchiesta*, p.543.

15 *Ibid.*,p.296.

16 Report of Sottoprefetto di Sansevero to Prefetto di Foggia, 28

January 1876, Archivio di Stato di Foggia, Sottoprefettura di San Severo, fasc. 395, fascicolo 4–2/1876.

17 Report of Tenente Comandante del Circondario RR.CC. to Sottoprefetto di San Severo, 1 August 1879, Archivio di Stato di Foggia, Sottoprefettura di San Severo, fasc. 397, fascicolo 1879.

18 Fraccacreta, *Le forme del progresso economico*, p.87.

19 "Corriere foggiano", *Il Foglietto*, 13 May 1900.

20 *Inchiesta*, p.312.

21 Letter of Federazione Agraria di Cerignola to Sig. Sindaco di Cerignola, 7 June 1910, Archivio Comunale di Cerignola, Cat. 15 (Pubblica Sicurezza), cart. 345, fasc. 2 (Scioperi di contadini).

22 The "deposit" was an abuse specifically discussed by the Bari province union federation. Cf. "Congresso provinciale dei lavoratori della terra", *La Conquista*, 18 August 1907.

23 Ricchioni, *Lavoro agricolo*, p. 122. See also Jatta, "Giornate e salarii nel barese", p.226.

24 The course of the work day at Torremaggiore was described by the mayor of the commune. Cf. Sindaco di Torremaggiore, "Questionario per scioperi agricoli", 27 January 1908, Archivio di Stato di Foggia, Sottoprefettura di San Severo, fasc. 414, fascicolo 7–13(1908).

25 On the question of forced prayer, see the interview with Giuseppe Angione in Rinaldi and Sobrero, *La memoria che resta*, p.123, and the interview with Lucia Barbarossa, *ibid.*, p.125.

26 *Ibid.*, p.121.

27 *Ibid.*, p.186.

28 On the adulteration of bread and wine by the landlords at Candela, there is the direct testimony of F. Turati in a speech to the Chamber of Deputies on 31 March 1903. Cf. *Atti del parlamento italiano*, Camera dei Deputati, Legislatura XII, Discussioni, vol. VII, p.6933.

29 Jatta, "Giornate e salarii nel barese", p.228.

30 "Nelle tre Puglie", *Corriere delle Puglie*, 13 May 1903.

31 "Sulla breccia", *Il Randello*, 24 June 1906.

32 "Nelle tre Puglie", *Corriere delle Puglie*, 11 August 1911.

33 Report of Sindaco di Bari to Presidente della Camera di Commercio di Bari, "Prezzi medi mensili della vendita al minuto degli alimenti farinacei durante l'anno 1907", Archivio di Stato di Bari, Camera di Commercio, b.6.

34 Municipio di S. Paolo di Civitata, "Terza relazione agraria 1908", Archivio di Stato di Foggia, Sottoprefettura di San Severo, fascicolo 13, sottofasc. 2 (Relazioni agrarie, stati delle campagne, 1900–11).

35 Speech by F. Turati on 31 March 1903. *Atti del parlamento italiano*, Camera dei Deputati, Legislatura XII, Discussioni, vol. VII, p.6933.

36 Comune di Celenza Malfortore, "Relazione sullo stato delle campagne, 1904", Archivio di Stato di Foggia, Sottoprefettura di San Severo, fascicolo 13, sottofasc. 2 (Relazioni agrarie, stati delle campagne, 1900–16).

    The day labourer Domenico La Barbutta, who was born at Minervino Murge in 1900, vividly recalled his first days at work for 12 *soldi* (0.12 lire) in 1913. Interview at Minervino Murge on 20 September 1982.

37 Giuseppe De Falco, "Nella Puglia Nuova", *Avanti!*, 19 June 1908.

38 "Capitanata triste", *Scienza a Diletto*, 6 March 1898.

39 On the plight of elderly farm labourers, see *Inchiesta*, pp.314–35 and 539–40.

40 *Inchiesta*, pp.539–40.

41 On the functioning of the *opere pie* in Bari province, see Sabino Fiorese, *Le confraternite e la loro trasformazione civile* (Bari, 1884).

42 Report of Sottoprefetto di San Severo to Prefetto di Foggia, n.d., Archivio di Stato di Foggia, Sottoprefettura di San Severo, fasc. 394, fascicolo 1870.

43 This discussion of the Russo Hospital is based on "Tornata del 26 ottobre 1914", in Registro degli atti originali della Giunta Municipale dal 28 febbraio 1913 al 1915, Archivio Comunale di Cerignola.

44 For a description of the condition of the charities at Gravina, see the budget report for 1903 presented by mayor Canio Musacchio to the *giunta* on 8 December 1902 in Archivio Comunale di Gravina, "Convocazione e deliberazioni della Giunta", 1902, Cat. 1, cl. 7.

45 "Corriere di Cerignola", *Il Foglietto*, 8 April 1909.

46 Report of Delegato P.S. to Sottoprefetto di San Severo, 14 March 1905, Archivio di Stato di Foggia, Sottoprefettura di San Severo, fasc. 398, fascicolo 4-4 (1905), n.12.

47 Letter of Sindaco di Cerignola to Signor Presidente dell'Opera Orafonti, 19 February 1880, Archivio Comunale di Cerignola, Cat. 15 (Pubblica Sicurezza), cart. 344, fasc. 2 (Assistenza pubblica per i disoccupati).

48 On the causes of death, see below, pp.57–61.

3 Grapes

1 A discussion of these contracts is Giuseppe Tammeo, *I contratti agrari e la crisi pugliese* (Naples, 1890), part 3. For brief accounts of the transformation of the grape zone, see *Inchiesta*, pp. 106ff; and "Nuovi orizzonti della agricoltura pugliese", *Bollettino Agricolo*, 1 June 1911, pp.17–24.

The improvement contracts on the Pavoncelli estate are described in detail by Gaetano Pavoncelli, "Relazione sull'azienda", n.d., Archivio Privato Pavoncelli, fondo Giuseppe Pavoncelli fu Federico. The Pavoncelli example is particularly instructive because it was the Pavoncelli and Larochefoucauld estates that took the initiative in first establishing vineyards. Fraccacreta, *Le forme del progresso economico*, p.78 n. The account here closely follows the practices discussed by Gaetano Pavoncelli.

2 Pavoncelli, "Relazione sull'azienda", p.6.

3 Tammeo, *I contratti agrari*, part 3.

4 Pavoncelli, "Relazione sull'azienda".

5 *Inchiesta*, p.106.

6 Fraccacreta, *Le forme del progresso economico*, p.89.

4 The company town

1 "Da Cerignola", *Il Foglietto*, 19 October 1902.

2 *Inchiesta*, pp.498–9.

3 *Corriere delle Puglie*, 17 March 1904.

4 Curato, *I contadini di Troja*, p.12.

5 Casardi, "Ripopoliamo le campagne!", p.63.

6 *Inchiesta*, pp.498–9.

7 Ministero di Agricoltura, Industria e Commercio: Direzione Generale della Statistica, *Censimento della popolazione del Regno d'Italia al 10 febbraio 1901*, vol. II (Rome, 1902), Table XIV, pp.72ff.

8 "Rioni di Cerignola", *Scienza e Diletto*, 18 November 1894.

9 An article on the grottoes is "La vecchia Puglia e una vergogna che dura: le 'grotte' ", *Il Foglietto*, 11 February 1912.
10 "Da Sansevero", *Il Randello*, 19 August 1906. On urban rents see also F. Casardi, "Ripopoliamo le campagne!", p.63.
11 In his memoirs Luigi Allegato, secretary of the San Severo peasant league, has recorded his childhood experience of living in a room 25 metres square with another family of perfect strangers: *Socialismo e comunismo in Puglia: Ricordi di un militante (1904–1924)* (Rome, 1971), p.32.
12 "Rioni di Cerignola", *Scienza e Diletto*, 18 November 1894.
13 "Le case popolari", *Corriere delle Puglie*, 30 December 1902.
14 The text of the interview with Lucia Barbarossa is in Rinaldi and Sobrero, *La memoria che resta*, pp.125–7.
15 "Vita sanseverese", *Il Foglietto*, 25 January 1900.
16 Fraccacreta, *Le forme del progresso economico*, p.76.
17 "Il proletariato nel paese degli eccidi cronici", *La Conquista*, 3 September 1911.
18 Fraccacreta, *Le forme del progresso economico*, pp.36–7.
19 *Inchiesta*, p.541.
20 This observation was made of the theatre at Taranto. "Nelle tre Puglie", *Corriere delle Puglie*, 10 March 1903.

    On the lifestyle of the landlords, see also "Conflitti economici", *Il Foglietto*, 14 April 1907, and De Cesare, *Delle condizioni economiche e morali*, pp.78–9.
21 The opera programmes of these three cities in 1903 are reported in the column "Nelle tre Puglie", *Corriere delle Puglie* 14, 22, 26, 30 January 1903; 7, 16, 26 February 1903; and 30 March 1903. An angry protest against such luxury expenses is "La miseria a Corato", *La Ragione*, 19 May 1901.
22 "Corriere di Cerignola", *Il Foglietto*, 8 September, 1907.
23 "Patrimonio della famiglia Pavoncelli al 31 dicembre 1903", Archivio Privato Pavoncelli, fondo Gaetano Pavoncelli fu Giuseppe.
24 Text of speech by Giuseppe Pavoncelli, n.d., Archivio Privato Pavoncelli, fondo Giuseppe Pavoncelli fu Federico.
25 *Ibid.*
26 Istituto Centrale di Statistica del Regno d'Italia, *Il censimento generale della popolazione al 21 aprile 1936* (Rome, 1937), vol. IV, part 2, Table II.
27 Ministero di Agricoltura, Industria e Commercio: Direzione

Generale della Statistica e del Lavoro, *Censimento degli opifici e delle imprese industriali al 10 giugno 1911*, (Rome, 1914), vol. I, Table I.

28　Fraccacreta, *Le forme del progresso economico*, p.30.

29　For a description of the social composition of the non-agricultural population of the town of Troia, see "La crisi a Troia", *Il Foglietto*, 19 October 1902.

30　Report of 13 February 1908, Archivio Comunale di Gravina, Cat. 15, cl. 1 (Pubblica Sicurezza, 1901–24), fasc. "Legge sul riposo festivo" (1908)".

31　An investigation into the adulteration of food in the Cerignola market was carried out by M. Spezzati for the local paper *Scienza e Diletto*. For his conclusions, see "Adulterazioni e falsificazioni", *Scienza e Diletto*, 11 February and 4 March 1894. Other descriptions of the adulteration of bread and flour are "In Cerignola", *Il Pugliese*, 24 June 1900; and "Per la buona qualità dei viveri", *I. Randello*, 5 July 1908.

　　Laboratory reports on bread, flour, and pasta sold in the market at Gravina in 1905 are in Archivio Comunale di Gravina, Cat. 4, cl. 3, b. 51 (1905–16), fasc. "Vigilanza sanitaria sulle bevande e sugli alimenti, 1905".

32　Discussions of the lack of hygiene in city markets with regard to vegetables, meat, fish and water appear in the column "In Cerignola" in the paper *Il Pugliese* on the following dates: 24 June and 7 October 1900; 15 September 1901; 7 September 1902; and 2 August 1903. On the problem of lethal vegetables, cf. "Gli orti micidiali", *Corriere delle Puglie*, 20 September 1910.

33　Report of Sottoprefetto di San Severo to Prefetto di Foggia, 6 January 1890, Archivio di Stato di Foggia, Sottoprefettura di San Severo, fasc. 394, fascicolo 1890, n. 12 Gabinetto.

34　"Il Prefetto Bacco", *Il Foglietto*, 6 January 1904. An excellent discussion of the problems confronting local government in the region is Pietro Mossa, "L'amministrazione della provincia e dei comuni in Terra di Bari", *Rassegna Pugliese*, XVII (1900), pp.129–33 and 179–82. A brief mention of the quality of local government in the zones of latifundism in Sicily is Mack Smith, "The Latifundia in Modern Sicilian History", pp. 100–1.

35　The following account of the deliberations of the town council at Cerignola in 1912 is based on the minutes of the meetings of the executive (*giunta*), in "Amministrazione Comunale: Registro di deliberazioni originali, 1912–1913", Archivio Comunale di Cerignola.

36 "Estratto del bilancio preventivo pel 1888 del comune di Andria", Archivio di Stato di Bari, Agricoltura, Industria e Commercio, b. 75, fasc. "Dazio di consumo: statistica".

37 Pietro Mossa, "L'amministrazione della provincia e dei comuni in Terra di Bari", *Rassegna Pugliese*, XVII (1900), p.180.

38 A discussion of education at Cerignola while Remigo Palieri was mayor is "Da Cerignola", *Il Foglietto*, 30 November 1902.

39 Ministero di Agricoltura, Industria e Commercio: Direzione Generale della Statistica, *Movimento della popolazione secondo gli atti dello stato civile nell'anno 1903* (Rome, 1905), Prospectus XIII, p.xxii.

40 Ministero di Agricoltura, Industria e Commercio: Direzione Generale della Statistica de del Lavoro, *Censimento della popolazione del regno d'Italia al 10 giugno 1911* (Rome, 1914), vol. III, Table V.

41 See the series of articles "Il colera in Puglia", *Rivista Medica Pugliese*, V (1910), pp.305–7; 365–72; and 417–21.

42 "Il colera in Puglia", *Rivista Medica Pugliese*, V (1910), p.339.

43 "Da S. Marco in Lamis", *Il Foglietto*, 16 April 1903. There is now a plaque on the site of the old cemetery. The plaque bears an inscription explaining that the cemetery had to be destroyed because of its role in spreading pestilence.

44 Alfredo Violante, "Un pericolo: la tuberculosi", *Corriere delle Puglie*, 17 June 1920.

45 "Il colera in Puglia", *Rivista Medica Pugliese*, V (1910), p.307.

46 *Ibid.*, p.339.

47 Report of Sottoprefetto di San Severo to Prefetto di Foggia, 6 January 1890, Archivio di Stato di Foggia, Sottoprefettura di San Severo, fasc. 394, fascicolo 1890, n. 12 Gabinetto.

48 The official investigations into the finances of local government at Andria culminated in three reports: R. Commissario Carlo Calvi, "Relazione al consiglio comunale di Andria", 11 May 1902; Sottoprefetto Vincenzo Lugaresi, "Parole di commiato del R. Commissario straordinario al nuovo consiglio comunale di Andria", 25 June 1895; and Sottoprefetto Pietro Gardin, "Relazione del R. Commissario straordinario letta al ricostituito consiglio comunale di Andria", 10 September 1892. These reports are to be found in

Archivio di Stato di Bari, Gabinetto del Prefetto di Bari, cart. 68, fasc. "Amministrazione comunale: relazioni a stampa".

49 Report of Ispettore Generale Taddei to Sig. Prefetto di Bari, 20 February 1909, Archivio di Stato di Bari, Gabinetto del Prefetto di Bari, cart. 68, fasc. 6 (Altamura: amministrazione comunale, inchiesta).

50 Canio Musacchio, the socialist mayor of Gravina, described the *dazio consumo* as "hateful because of the police repression inevitable in its method of collection", and "harmful because it gives rise to tricks and swindles of every sort". "Tornata del 8 dicembre 1902", Archivio Comunale di Gravina, Deliberazioni della Giunta, 1902.

51 "Una sommossa popolare a Barletta", *Corriere delle Puglie*, 3 September 1910. For a similar report on the hostility to the medical authorities exhibited during the cholera epidemic by the inhabitants of the working-class quarters of Old Bari, see Letter of Commissario De Padova to Ispettore Generale Reggente la Questura di Bari, 3 October 1910, Archivio di Stato di Bari, Gabinetto del Prefetto, seconda serie, b. 291, fasc. 97 (Brogiotti Gaetano).

52 "Cronaca del capoluogo: vita impossibile", *Il Foglietto*, 7 February 1904.

53 "Da Troia", *Il Foglietto*, 9 October 1902.

54 Carlo Serpieri, "Le condizioni dei lavoratori della terra", *Corriere delle Puglie*, 5 July 1901.

55 Interview at Minervino Murge, 20 September 1982. What La Barbutta said was confirmed by twelve other day labourers from the town whom I interviewed on the same occasion. The majority of the men asked to remain anonymous, but six were prepared to have their testimony recorded. They were: Gennaro Balice (b. 1907), Giacomo Di Consolo (b. 1904), Nicola Piastro (b. 1909), Leandro Cossetta (b. 1908), Michelangelo Di Noia (b. 1904), and Agostino Ciantilli (b. 1924).

56 Text of a speech by Giuseppe Pavoncelli, n.d., Archivio Privato Pavoncelli, fondo Giuseppe Pavoncelli fu Federico.

57 The seasonal pattern of the major causes of death in 1909 is shown in Ministero di Agricoltura, Industria e Commercio; Direzione Generale di Statistica, *Statistica delle cause di morte nell'anno 1909* (Rome, 1911), Table II (Morti nel Regno in ciascun trimestre dell'anno 1909).

For 1907 the leading causes of death were considered in their incidence by age and sex. Cf. Ministero di Agricoltura, Industria e Commercio: Direzione Generale di Statistica, *Statistica delle cause di morte nell'anno 1907* (Rome, 1909), Prospetto N 11 (Morti nel Regno nell'anno 1907 classificati per età, sesso e cause di morte).

58 See, for example, the reports in the column "Nelle tre Puglie" in the *Corriere delle Puglie* for July 1905.

59 On trachoma in Apulia, see "La lotta contro il tracoma in Puglia", *Rivista Medica Pugliese*, V (1910), pp.440–3. The etiology of the disease is discussed briefly in Paul B. Beeson, Walsh McDermott, and James B. Wyngaarden, eds., *Cecil Textbook of Medicine* (London, 1979), pp. 332–5.

60 *Inchiesta*, p.539.

61 Antonio Pansini, "Infortuni nel lavoro dei contadini", *Rivista Medica Pugliese*, VI (1911), pp.7–8.

62 "I denutriti delle Puglie", *Il Foglietto*, 26 May 1904.

63 "La miseria igienica della Capitanata", *Il Foglietto*, 7 November 1912.

64 "Alcuni dati statistici in rapporto alle Puglie", *Rivista Media Pugliese*, II (1907), n. 21, p. 349. In the decade 1895–1905 Apulia led the list for the highest rate of death in 1895, 1898, 1899, 1901, and 1903.

65 Ministero di Agricoltura, Industria e Commercio: Direzione Generale della Statistica, *Statistica delle cause di morte nell'anno 1903* (Rome, 1906), Prospetto N 8, pp.xxvi–xxvii.

International comparisons for 1903 are to be found in Ministero di Agricoltura, Industria e Commercio, Direzione Generale della Statistica, *Statistica delle cause di morte nell'anno 1911* (Rome, 1913), p.lxxxv.

66 "Alcuni dati statistici in rapporto alle Puglie", *Rivista Medica Pugliese*, II (1907), n. 21, pp.342–9. The journal noted with regard to typhoid fever, "Apulia has the painful privilege of making the largest contribution to typhoid infection and to the resulting mortality."

67 Ministero di Agricoltura, Industria e Commercio: Direzione Generale della Statistica, *Statistica delle cause di morte nell'anno 1903* (Rome, 1906), Table V, p.68.

68 "La delinquenza in Italia", *Corriere delle Puglie*, 1 August 1902. On the pervasive presence of the criminal underworld in the

agricultural centres of the region, cf. "La malavita in Puglia", *La Ragione*, 1 May 1904.

69 "Il nuovo anno giudiziario", *Il Foglietto*, 13 January 1907.

70 "Il nuovo anno giuridico al Tribunale di Lucera", *Il Foglietto*, 14 January 1906.

71 An example was Federico Pavoncelli. Cf. "Corriere di Cerignola", *Il Foglietto*, 8 September 1907.

72 The best chronicle of crime is the column "Nelle tre Puglie", in the daily *Corriere delle Puglie*. The notices of such deeds are too numerous to list, but for example see 2, 16, 20 and 25 February 1907.

73 "Il proletariato nel paese degli eccidi cronici", *La Conquista*, 10 September 1911.

74 "Il nuovo anno giudiziario," *Il Foglietto*, 13 January 1907.

5 Seeds of rebellion

1 Sottoprefetto di San Severo, "Relazione agraria del primo quadrimestre 1908", Archivio di Stato di Foggia, Sottoprefettura di San Severo, fascicolo 13, sottofasc. 2 (Relazioni agrarie, stati delle campagne, 1900–16).

2 "L'emigrazione in Puglia", *Corriere delle Puglie*, 8 June 1913.

3 *Inchiesta*, pp.119–20.

4 Grassi, *Il Tramonto dell'età giolittiana*, p.89. Interesting general works on emigration are John W. Briggs, *An Italian Passage: Immigrants to Three American Cities, 1890–1930* (New Haven and London, 1978); and Michael Piore, *Birds of Passage: Migrant Labour and Industrial Societies* (Cambridge, 1974).

5 Istituto Nazionale di Economia Agraria, *Inchiesta sulla piccola proprietà coltivatrice formatasi nel dopoguerra* (Rome, 1935), vol. XI, Puglie, p.8. For emigration statistics, see Commissariato Generale dell'Emigrazione, *Annuario statistico della emigrazione italiana dal 1876 al 1925* (Rome, 1926).

6 Sabino Fiorese, "Salarii e emigrazione in Terra di Bari", *Corriere delle Puglie*, 27 May 1909.

7 "L'emigrazione in Puglia", *Corriere delle Puglie*, 8 June 1913. In 1902 steerage passage from Genoa or Naples to New York for a journey lasting 15½ days was 185 lire. R. Commissariato dell' Emigrazione, "Piroscafi che trasportano emigrati", 30 November 1902, Archivio

Comunale di Gravina, Cat. 3, cl. 3 e 5, b. 183, fasc. 1 (Istruzioni diverse, 1902).

8 Ministero di Agricoltura, Industria e Commercio, *Statistica della emigrazione italiana per l'estero negli anni 1904 e 1905* (Rome, 1906), Table IV.

9 Mario Altomare, "Molfetta nell'emigrazione all'estero", *Corriere delle Puglie*, 27 July 1913.

10 Jorge Balan, "Comments", *American Historical Review*, LXXXVIII, no. 2 (April 1983), p.333.

11 For the files of the emigrants from Gravina in 1904, see Archivio Comunale di Gravina, Cat. 13, cl. 2 ("Disciplina della emigrazione"), b. 181 (1903–15). Unfortunately, the records for most of the years in this period have not survived intact.

12 Herbert S. Klein, "The Integration of Italian Immigrants into the United States and Argentina: A Comparative Analysis", *American Historical Review*, LXXXVIII, no. 2 (April 1983), p. 325.

13 Sabino Fiorese, "Nuovi dissesti e maggiori depressioni", *Rassegna Pugliese*, XXIV (1908), pp.3–4.

14 *Ibid.*, pp.3–4.

15 *Ibid.*, pp.1–6.

16 Report of Prefetto di Foggia to Ministero dell'Interno, Direzione Generale della Pubblica Sicurezza, 2 May 1913, Archivio Centrale dello Stato, PS (1913), fascicolo 20, sottofasc. Bari, n. 792.

17 Camera di Commercio ed Arti della Provincia di Bari, *Inchiesta sulle condizioni di vita, sui salari e sull'emigrazione della Provincia di Bari nell'anno 1907* (Bari, 1907), p.56.

18 "Il proletariato nel paese degli eccidi cronici", *La Conquista*, 10 September 1911.

19 Letter of Prefetto di Bari to S.E. il Ministro di Agricoltura, Industria e Commercio, 5 October 1875, Archivio di Stato di Bari, Gabinetto del Prefetto, b. 8, fasc. 65 (Stato degli operai agricoli), n. 14623, allegato 20.

20 "Il movimento agrario", *Avanti!* 24 May 1908.

21 "Bari operaia", *La Conquista*, 9 June 1907.

22 Davide Lajolo, *Il volto umano di un rivoluzionario: la straordinaria avventura di Giuseppe Di Vittorio* (Florence, 1979).

23 Tenente Comandante il Circondario RR.CC., "Elenco degli appartenenti agl'internazionalisti", 2 May 1879, Archivio di Stato di Foggia, Sottoprefettura di San Severo, fasc. 395, fascicolo 1879, n.

66. Cf. also "Internazionalisti", Archivio di Stato di Foggia, Sotto-prefettura di San Severo, fasc. 396, fascicolo IV–2(1893).

24 Report of Tenente Comandante il Circondario to Sottoprefetto di San Severo, 11 April 1873, Archivio di Stato di Foggia, Sottoprefettura di San Severo, fasc. 395, fascicolo "Partiti politici dal 1867 al 1880", n. 1457.

25 The discussion here of the question of the *demani* owes much to the interesting work by Paolo Grossi, *An Alternative to Private Property: Collective Property in the Juridical Consciousness of the Nineteenth Century* (Chicago, 1981).

26 "I demani comunali", *La Ragione*, 15, 22, 29 March 1903.

27 The Sicilian equivalent to the *tratturi* – the sheepruns known as *truzzere* – are discussed by Mack Smith, "The Latifundia in Modern Sicilian History", pp.113–14.

28 Letter of Vito Orofino to Sig. Prefetto, 19 June 1863, Archivio di Stato di Bari, Demani comunali ex feudali, b. 10 fasc. 119 (Operazioni demaniali del comune di Altamura eseguite dall'agente Vito Orofino dal maggio 1863 a maggio 1864), n.3.

29 "I demani nel Mezzogiorno", *Corriere dell Puglie*, 4 February 1903

30 "Secondo congresso provinciale dei lavoratori della terra", *La Ragione*, 13 December 1903.

31 "La legge sui tratturi", *Il Foglietto*, 14 February 1909. A brief discussion of the problem of the *tratturi* is "Nelle tre Puglie", *Corriere delle Puglie*, 5 May 1914.

32 An official history of the issue of common land at San Nicandro is Comune di S. Nicandro Garganico, *Appello alla opinione pubblica*, 28 October 1920, in Archivio Centrale dello Stato, PS (1922), b. 67, fasc. Foggia ("Agitazione agraria").

33 For the electoral promises of Enrico Fraccacreta at San Severo, see "Relazione del Sindaco: Tornata del Consiglio Comunale di San Severo del 22 di settembre 1902", Archivio di Stato di Foggia, Sottoprefettura di San Severo, fasc. 454, fascicolo II–2(1902), n. 39343. On Cotugno's campaign at Ruvo di Puglia, cf. "Nelle tre Puglie", *Corriere delle Puglie*, 1 and 2 July 1907.

 The text of the radicals' electoral programme at Carpina is Unione Radicale Carpinese, "Discorso – Programma" (Lucera, 1910), in Biblioteca Lelio Basso, Archivio Domenico Fioritto.

34 Report of Sottoprefetto di San Severo to Prefetto di Foggia, 18

December 1912, Archivio di Stato di Foggia, Sottoprefettura di San Severo, fasc. 457, fascicolo II–3 (Amministrazioni: pratiche varie, 1904–6), n. 1952K.

35 Commissario Prefettizio, "Inchiesta sull'andamento dell'amministrazione comunale di S. Marco in Lamis", 18 September 1903, Archivio di Stato di Foggia, Sottoprefettura di San Severo, fasc. 464, fascicolo 4–4(1903).

36 Raffaele Mascolo, *La sinistra in Capitanata, 1866–1896* (Foggia, 1981).

37 Delegato P.S. to Sottoprefetto di San Severo, 14 March 1905, Archivio di Stato di Foggia, Sottoprefettura di San Severo, fasc. 398, fascicolo 4–4(1905).

38 Report of Sottoprefetto di San Severo to Prefetto di Foggia, 6 January 1886, Archivio di Stato di Foggia, Sottoprefettura di San Severo, fasc. 394, fascicolo 1886, n.3 Gab.

39 On Manfredi's conversion, see "Corriere cerignolese", *Il Foglietto*, 5 May 1904, and "I luttuosi fatti di Cerignola", *Il Foglietto*, 19 May 1904.

40 *Inchiesta*, pp.543–5.

41 "Da un colloquio con Gaetano Salvemini", *Il Foglietto*, 15 January 1911.

42 *Ibid.* On the decline of religious sentiment among the farm workers, see also "Le condizioni dei contadini pugliesi", *Il Foglietto*, 30 July 1911.

43 Report of Sottoprefetto di Barletta to Prefetto di Bari, July 1920, Archivio di Stato di Bari, Gabinetto del Prefetto di Bari, cart. 261, fasc. "Elezioni amministrative: circondario di Bari", n. 470.

44 Ministero di Agricoltura, Industria e Commercio: Direzione Generale della Statistica, *Censimento della popolazione del Regno d'Italia al 10 febbraio 1901* (Rome, 1902), Table IX ("Numero e popolazione delle diocesi. Numero delle parrocchie e loro classificazione secondo il numero degli abitanti presenti al 10 febbraio 1901").

45 "Da Troia", *Il Foglietto*, 9 October 1902.

46 "Corriere cerignolese", *Il Foglietto*, 17 March 1904.

47 "Il nuovo anno giuridico al tribunale di Lucera", *Il Foglietto*, 14 January 1906.

48 "Dai comuni della Capitanata", *Il Foglietto*, 6 October 1907.

49 "Il proletariato nel paese degli eccidi cronici", *La Conquista*, 3 September 1911.

50 *Ibid.*

51 "La disoccupazione dei contadini di Capitanata", *Il Foglietto*, 27 August 1908.

52 "La camorra bancaria", *Il Foglietto*, 19 May 1901.

53 "La grandiosa dimostrazione anticlericale di Cerignola", *Il Foglietto*, 27 February 1908.

54 "Corriere di Cerignola", *Il Foglietto*, 13 April 1913.

55 "Nelle tre Puglie", *Corriere delle Puglie*, 13 August 1901.

56 "Le votazioni del 7 marzo", *Il Foglietto*, 11 March 1909.

57 "La grandiosa dimostrazione anticlericale di Cerignola", and "La grandiosa manifestazione anticlericale di Cerignola", *Il Foglietto*, 27 February and 23 September 1909.

58 "Clericali e anticlericali a Cerignola", *Il Foglietto*, 24 March 1910.

59 For parallel observations on Andalusia, another region of latifundism and anarcho-syndicalism, see Temma Kaplan, *Anarchists of Andalusia, 1868–1903* (Princeton, 1977).

60 "Congresso provinciale dei lavoratori della terra", *La Conquista*, 18 August 1907.

In the same spirit Euclide Trematore, secretary of the Foggia Chamber of Labour, began his propaganda speeches by exposing the most recent "clerical scandals". "Nelle tre Puglie", *Corriere delle Puglie*, 6 August, 1907.

6 Revolutionary Syndicalism

1 Letter of Prefect of Bari to S.E. il Ministro di Agricoltura, Industria e Commercio, 5 October 1875, Archivio di Stato di Bari, Gabinetto del Prefetto, fasc. 65 (Stato degli operai agricoli), n. 14623, allegato 15.

2 *Ibid.*, allegato 69.

3 Report of Sottoprefetto di San Severo to Prefetto di Foggia, 28 January 1876, Archivio di Stato di Foggia, Sottoprefettura di San Severo, fasc. 395, fascicolo 4–2/1876.

4 Report of Tenente Comandante il Circondario di San Severo to Sottoprefetto del Circondario di San Severo, 4 July 1874, Archivio di Stato di Foggia, Sottoprefettura di San Severo, fasc. 394, fascicolo 1874, n. 4.

5 The view of employers in Basilicata towards Apulian workers is des-

cribed by the Telegram of Prefetto di Potenza to Ministero dell'Interno, Direzione Generale della Pubblica Sicurezza, 4 March 1920, Archivio Centrale dello Stato, PS (1920), b. 77, fasc. "Bari: agitazione agraria", n. 282.

6 Report of Sottoprefetto di San Severo to Prefetto di Foggia, 28 January 1876, Archivio di Stato di Foggia, Sottoprefettura di San Severo, fasc. 394, fascicolo 4–2/1876.

7 Letter of Prefetto di Foggia to Sottoprefetto di San Severo, 29 March 1879, Archivio di Stato di Foggia, Sottoprefettura di San Severo, fasc. 397, fascicolo 1879, n. 399–3–53.

8 For a report on the siege of the estate of the landlord Giuseppe Zaccagnino in the commune of San Nicandro Garganico, cf. "Nelle tre Puglie", *Corriere delle Puglie*, 5 January 1918.

9 *Inchiesta*, pp.541–2.

10 Letter of Sottoprefetto di Altamura to Prefetto di Bari, 9 February 1889, Archivio di Stato di Bari, Agricoltura, Industria e Commercio, b. 7, fasc. "Corato: ordine pubblico", sottofasc. "Circondario di Altamura: agitazione per la crisi", n. 14.

11 Report to Prefetto della Provincia, 10 March 1889, Archivio di Stato di Bari, Agricoltura, Industria e Commercio, b. 6, fasc. "Andria", n. 1536.

12 Report of Tte Colonello Caracciolo to Prefetto di Bari, 25 January 1889, Archivio di Stato di Bari, Agricoltura, Industria e Commercio, b. 6, fasc. 3 bis. (Corato: agitazione per la crisi), n. 506.

13 Municipio di Gravina di Puglia, "Verbale per voto al governo", 9 September 1888, Archivio di Stato di Bari, Agricoltura, Industria e Commercio, b. 6, fasc. 6.

14 "A proposito dell'abolizione del dazio sul grano", *Corriere delle Puglie*, 11 October 1913.

15 Report of Tte Colonello Caracciolo to Prefetto di Bari, 4 March 1889, Archivio di Stato di Bari, Agricoltura, Industria e Commercio, b. 6, fasc. "Andria", n. 1419.

16 "L'agitazione daziaria", *Corriere delle Puglie*, 3 January 1904.

17 The only general history of syndicalism in Italy is David D. Roberts, *The Syndicalist Tradition and Italian Fascism* (Manchester, 1979). This account, however, is marred by a one-sided preoccupation with syndicalist intellectuals. Roberts also seems unaware of the presence of syndicalism as a powerful force in Apulia.

A very interesting study of syndicalism among the peasants on the latifundia of Andalusia is Temma Kaplan, *Anarchists of Andalusia*

1868–1903 (Princeton, 1977). The conditions in Andalusia bore a remarkable similarity to those prevailing in Apulia, and the farm workers' movement which resulted had a similar political orientation. See also Gerald Brenan, *The Spanish Labyrinth* (Cambridge, 1980), chapters 6–8; E.J. Hobsbawm, *Primitive Rebels: Studies in Archaic Forms of Social Movements in the 19th and 20th Centuries* (Manchester, 1959); and Jerome R. Mintz, *The Anarchists of Casas Viejas* (Chicago, 1982).

18 Pistillo, *Giuseppe Di Vittorio*, p.90.
19 Allegato, *Socialismo e comunismo in Puglia*, p.41.
20 Cesare Aroldi, "Le agitazioni in Puglia", *Avanti!*, 28 September 1907.
21 Cesare Aroldi, "L'agitazione dei contadini in Puglia", *Il Foglietto*, 6 October 1907.
22 "Per gli eccidi di piazza del Gesù e di San Severo", *Avanti!*, 6 April 1908.
23 *Ibid.*
24 Francesco Ciccotti, "L'agitazione agraria nelle Puglie", *Avanti!*, 24 September 1907.
25 "Al bivio", *Il Randello*, 6 May 1903.
26 "Deputati di carriera", *La Conquista*, 24 June 1908.
27 "Per la propaganda nel Mezzogiorno", *La Conquista*, 19 January 1908.
28 For a report on the Second Southern Socialist Congress, see "Il secondo congresso socialista meridionale", *La Conquista*, 15 September 1907.
29 The founding of the federation is reported in "I lavoratori del mezzogiorno a congresso", *La Conquista*, 11 December 1910.
30 The founding of the various agrarian associations in Apulia is reported in the column "Nelle tre Puglie" of the Bari daily *Corriere delle Puglie*. Cf. 7 May, 20 May, and 13 October 1907; 15 November 1913; and 9 May and 17 September 1915.
31 For a discussion of the syndicalist strikes of 1907 and 1908 in Parma, see Thomas R. Sykes, "Revolutionary Syndicalism in the Italian Labor Movement: The Agrarian Strikes of 1907–1908 in the Province of Parma", *International Review of Social History*, XXI (1976), pp.186–211.
32 "Vittoriosa fine dello sciopero di Cerignola", *Il Foglietto*, 18 December 1913.
33 "Cronaca di Bari", *Corriere delle Puglie*, 14 December 1913.

34 Two biographies of Di Vittorio are Lajolo, *Il volto umano di un rivoluzionario*, and Michele Pistillo, *Giuseppe Di Vittorio, 1907–1924* (Rome, 1973). On the leading role of Cerignola, see Allegato, *Socialismo e comunismo in Puglia*, pp. 41, 53, 61.

35 For the conditions of the establishment of vineyards at San Severo, see the discussion by Fraccacreta, *Le forme del progresso economico*, pp. 82 ff.

36 Fraccacreta, *Le forme del progresso economico*, p.82.

37 For the text of the socialist programme at San Severo in 1906, see Comitato del Circolo Socialista e delle Leghe Operaie di San Severo, "Defendete i vostri diritti!", in Archivio di Stato di Foggia, Sottoprefettura di San Severo, fasc. 457, fascicolo II–3(1906).

38 On the affinity between Salvemini and the syndicalists, cf. Pistillo, *Giuseppe Di Vittorio*, p.45.

39 "80,000 vassalli a congresso", *Il Foglietto*, 4 November 1909.

40 "Scioperi e organizzazione", *Il Foglietto*, 4 November 1909.

41 Pistillo, *Giuseppe Di Vittorio*, p.24.

The Bari Liberal daily commented with special reference to San Severo but in terms that could be extended to all of Foggia province "The socialist party here is not strong in numbers with hardly fifty people enrolled. Its strength lies in the numbers of the leagues of peasants, grape pickers, and day labourers organized by the Chamber of Labour." "Nelle tre Puglie", *Corriere delle Puglie*, 27 May 1914.

42 G. De Falco, "L'on. Jatta si difende", *La Conquista*, 5 October 1907.

43 Fraccacreta, *Le forme del progresso economico*, pp.96–105.

44 "Nelle tre Puglie", *Corriere delle Puglie*, 11 September 1907.

45 Raffaele Pastore, "Dopo dieci anni di lotta", *La Conquista*, 3 September 1911.

46 "A proposito dell'abolizione del dazio sul grano", *Corriere delle Puglie*, 11 October 1913.

47 Giuseppe De Falco, "Il proletariato nel paese degli eccidi cronici", *La Conquista*, 1 October 1911.

48 For reports of battles between strikers and "foreign" workers, see "Nelle tre Puglie", *Corriere delle Puglie*, 18 May 1907 and 18 April 1914.

49 The demands of the league at Spinazzola in 1907, for instance, are reported in "Nelle tre Puglie", *Corriere delle Puglie*, 1 September

1907, and "Dalla Murgia al mare", *La Conquista*, 15 September 1907. For a list of the demands at Canosa in 1908, cf. "La triplice agitazione in Puglia", *Corriere delle Puglie*, 12 May 1908. The similar position of the league in Corato is considered in "Nelle tre Puglie", *Corriere delle Puglie*, 13 May 1907.
In August 1907 the Bari provincial union federation adopted a set of general demands for the whole province. Cf. "Congresso provinciale dei lavoratori della terra", *La Conquista*, 18 August 1907.

50 "Il congresso dei contadini", *Il Foglietto*, 6 April 1902.
51 "Statuto della lega di Carpino", n.d., article 8, Biblioteca Lelio Basso, Archivio Domenico Fioritto.
52 A discussion of the after-school activities of the labour movement at Cerignola is "Corriere di Cerignola", *Il Foglietto*, 13 April 1913.
53 The Ministry of the Interior followed these occasions with great interest. Reports on open-air rallies in various communes in 1911 in Bari province include: Telegram of Prefetto di Bari Gasperini to Ministero dell'Interno, 22 April 1911, n. 13249; Telegram of Gasperini to Ministero dell'Interno, 22 February 1911, n. 16887; Telegram to Ministero dell'Interno, 12 February 1911, n. 5590. All of these reports are to be found in Archivio Centrale dello Stato, PS (1911), b. 13, fasc. "Bari".
Corresponding reports for 1911 in Foggia province drawn up by the prefect Lualdi are to be found in Archivio Centrale dello Stato, PS (1911) b. 15, fasc. "Foggia".
54 Telegrams of the Prefetto di Foggia to Ministero dell'Interno, 6 April 1914, n. 460, and 14 June, n. 174, in Archivio Centrale dello Stato, PS (1914), b. 21, fasc. "Foggia", sottofasc. "Cerignola".
55 "Nelle tre Puglie", *Corriere delle Puglie*, 28 August 1901.
56 This account of the festival of the Madonna della Ripalta at Cerignola is based on personal experience of the feast in September 1982. The festival survives in a truncated form, and elderly inhabitants of the city explain how much grander the occasion was before the Second World War.
57 *Inchiesta*, p.543.
58 For descriptions of May Day at Foggia, see "Il primo maggio", *Il Randello*, 6 May 1906; and "Il primo maggio a Foggia", *Il Foglietto*, 4 May 1902.

59 Report of the Colonello Comandante la Divisione RR. CC., 2 March 1889, Archivio di Stato di Bari, Agricoltura, Industria e Commercio, b. 7, fasc. "Corato: ordine pubblico", sottofasc. "Agitazione in Molfetta", n.1356.
60 *Inchiesta*, p.543.
61 Lajolo, *Il volto umano di un rivoluzionario*, pp.11–12.
62 Quoted in *Inchiesta*, p.602.
63 "Nelle tre Puglie", *Corriere delle Puglie*, 11 May 1908.
64 "Il congresso dei contadini", *Il Foglietto*, 10 April 1902.
65 "Il congresso dei contadini", *Il Foglietto*, 10 April 1902.
66 "La vittoria socialista di Gravina", *La Conquista*, 23 July 1911.
67 The following account of the decisions of the town hall at Cerignola in the first year of socialist administration is based on "Registro degli atti originali della Giunta Municipale dal 28 febbraio 1913 al 1915", Archivio Comunale di Cerignola.
68 Adunanza del 22 settembre 1914, "Registro degli atti originali della Giunta Municipale dal 28 febbraio 1913 al 1915", Archivio Comunale di Cerignola.

7 Work discipline

1 Sottoprefetto di San Severo, "Rapporto relativo allo sciopero dei contadini di Sansevero", to Prefetto di Foggia, 20 June 1907, Archivio di Stato di Foggia, Sottoprefettura di San Severo, fasc. 398, fascicolo 1907, n. 505.
  The refusal of the landlords to sit at the same table with the farm workers is also recalled by the secretary of the San Severo peasants' union. Cf. Allegato, *Socialismo e comunismo in Puglia*, p.41.
2 "Il primo urto", *Il Foglietto*, 24 April 1902.
3 Letter of Georges Millet to Monsieur le Duc de Larochefoucauld, 30 June 1914, Archivio Privato Pavoncelli, Carteggio Larochefoucauld–Millet.
4 "Il viaggio e le conferenze dell'on. Luigi Luzzatti nelle Puglie", *La Ragione*, 28 April 1901.
5 "Lo sciopero generale a Cerignola", *Il Foglietto*, 14 December 1913.
6 "Corriere di Cerignola", *Il Foglietto*, 23 November 1913.
7 An account of the strike is "Lo sciopero generale a Cerignola", *Il Foglietto*, 14 December 1913. Cf. also "Vittoriosa fine dello sciopero di Cerignola", *Il Foglietto*, 18 December 1913.

8 *Inchiesta*, p.603. Cf. also *ibid.*, p.604.

9 "Relazione della commissione governativa per la disoccupazione in provincia di Bari", Archivio Centrale dello Stato, PS (1920), b. 77, fasc. "Bari: disoccupazione", pp.6–7.

10 Annual production figures for wheat production in various communes in Bari province were prepared for the Bari Chamber of Commerce. They are to be found in Archivio di Stato di Bari, Camera di Commercio, b. 5, fasc. "Produzione agraria e prezzi farinacei". The figures for Altamura in 1911, however, are missing.

11 Pompa, *Inchiesta sul latifondo: Agro di Foggia*, p.9.

12 D.A. Spada, "A proposito delle agitazioni agrarie", *Corriere delle Puglie*, 26 August 1907.

13 "Il primo urto", *Il Foglietto*, 24 April 1902.

14 "Le delizie della lotta di classe", *Bollettino Agricolo*, 30 April 1913, p.70. An earlier prophet of "ruin" as a result of unionization was M. Spera, "Le leghe dei contadini e la proprietà fondiaria in Puglia", *L'Agricoltore Pugliese*, 31 August 1906, pp.241–4.

15 Speech by Giuseppe Pavoncelli, n.d. (but probably 1902), Archivio Privato Pavoncelli, fondo Giuseppe Pavoncelli fu Federico.

16 D.A. Spada, "A proposito delle agitazioni agrarie", *Corriere delle Puglie*, 26 August 1907.

17 "Patrimonio della famiglia Pavoncelli al 31 dicembre del 1903", Archivio Privato Pavoncelli, fondo Gaetano Pavoncelli fu Giuseppe. Figures as in original; these in fact total 391.19 lire.

18 Speech by Giuseppe Pavoncelli, n.d., Archivio Privato Pavoncelli, fondo Giuseppe Pavoncelli fu Federico. Internal evidence suggests that the speech was given in 1902.

19 A catalogue of the immediate problems facing Apulian farmers in the early years of the new century is D.A. Spada, "A proposito delle agitazioni agrarie", *Corriere delle Puglie*, 26 August 1907.

20 The following account of the diversification of the Pavoncelli estate is based on the report drawn up by Giuseppe Pavoncelli, "Illustrazione di un latifondo del Tavoliere: L'azienda Pavoncelli di Cerignola", n.d., Archivio Privato Pavoncelli, fondo Giuseppe Pavoncelli fu Nicola, fasc. 9.

21 Text of speech by Giuseppe Pavoncelli, n.d. (but probably 1902), Archivio Privato Pavoncelli, fondo Giuseppe Pavoncelli fu Federico.

22 De Cesare, *Delle condizioni economiche e morali*, p.80.

23 For a study of the ideology of mezzadria in Tuscany, see my article "From Sharecropper to Proletarian: The Social Background to Fascism in Tuscany", in John A. Davis, ed., *Gramsci and Italy's Passive Revolution* (London, 1979).

24 Francesco Casardi, "Le delizie della lotta di classe", *Bollettino agricolo*, 30 April 1913.

25 For biographical information about Francesco Casardi, see "I candidati", *Corriere delle Puglie*, 8 May 1921.

26 Examples of the new enthusiasm for sharecropping on the part of Apulian landlords are: Francesco Casardi, "Ripopoliamo le campagne!", *L'Agricoltore Pugliese*, 30 April 1914, and "Contratto di fitto o contratto di mezzadria", *Bollettino Agricolo*, 1 July 1911; Vittorio Curato, "I patti colonici in Puglia", *L'Agricoltore Pugliese*, 20 and 21 March 1904; and M. Spera, "Le leghe dei contadini e la proprietà fondiaria in Puglia", *L'Agricoltore Pugliese*, 31 August 1906.

27 "Nella Puglia Nuova", *Avanti!*, 19 June 1908.

28 "Nelle tre Puglie", *Corriere delle Puglie*, 8 February 1915.

29 For a discussion of the various tactics adopted by employers, see V. Prosperi, "Le agitazioni agrarie e le ore di lavoro", *L'Agricoltore Pugliese*, 30 April 1915, pp.61–4; and *Inchiesta*, p.605.

30 Typical was the case of Foggia, where it was reported in 1903 that "Some landlords have exhausted the patience of our workers, sacking nearly all of the local peasants and hiring, for the mattocking of the vineyards, outsiders for low wages." "Nelle tre Puglie", *Corriere delle Puglie*, 25 April 1903.

31 "Le delizie della lotta di classe", *Bollettino Agricolo*, 30 April 1913, p.72; and "Continuando la lotta di classe", *Bollettino Agricolo*, 31 May 1913, pp.86–7.

32 "Lo sciopero agrario di Corato", *La Conquista*, 17 May 1908.

33 In an interview in 1903 the landlord and former mayor of Foggia, Ettore Valentini, discussed the strategy adopted by employers of using sheep for the purpose of containing wages. Cf. "Un'interessante intervista", *Corriere delle Puglie*, 30 March 1908.

34 "La granicoltura in Puglia", *L'Agricoltore Pugliese*, 15 October 1905, p.290.

35 "Il movimento agrario", *Avanti!*, 25 May 1908.

36 Fraccacreta, *Le forme del progresso economico*, pp.26–7.

37 Quoted by F. Turati in a speech to the Chamber of Deputies on 26 March 1903. *Atti del parlamento italiano*, Camera dei Deputati,

Legislatura XII, Discussioni, vol. VII, p.6933.

38 "Corriere di Cerignola", *Il Foglietto*, 6 October 1907; "Nelle tre Puglie", *Corriere delle Puglie*, 4 April 1906.

39 Letter of Camillo De Fabritiis to Ministero dell'Interno, Direzione Generale della Pubblica Sicurezza, 12 June 1919, Archivio Centrale dello Stato, PS (1919), b. 96, fasc. "Foggia", sottofasc. "Disoccupazione", n. 10085.

40 Interview at Minervino Murge, 20 September 1982.

41 "La vittoria socialista a Gravina", *La Conquista*, 23 July 1911.

42 "Nelle tre Puglie", *Corriere delle Puglie*, 17 July 1907.

43 *Inchiesta*, p.599. On the repeated attempts to bribe Canio Musacchio, cf. "La vittoria socialista a Gravina", *La Conquista*, 23 July 1911.

44 "Le scene di Ruvo", *Corriere delle Puglie*, 2 July 1907.

45 "La macchinazione contro la lega di Andria", *La Conquista*, 27 June 1909.

46 "Cronaco di partito e movimento operaio", *Avanti!* (Rome edition), 4 August 1907.

47 The events at Candela were described at length by F. Turati in a speech to the Chamber on 31 March 1903. *Atti del parlamento italiano*, Camera dei Deputati, Legislatura XII, Discussioni, vol. VIII, pp.6930–51.

48 Giuseppe De Falco, "Il proletariato nel paese degli eccidi cronici", *La Conquista*, 1 October 1911.

49 A full description of the events surrounding the strike is "Agitazione proletaria in Cerignola", *Il Pugliese*, 22 May 1904. The narrative here is based on this account.

50 *Ibid.*

51 *Ibid.*

52 *Ibid.*

53 Antonio Gramsci, *Quaderni del carcere* (Turin, 1975), vol. I, p.36.

54 Gaetano Salvemini, "Fu l'Italia prefascista una democrazia?", *Il Ponte*, VIII (1952), pp.178–9.

55 The files of the personnel of the Ministry of the Interior in Bari province are in Archivio di Stato di Bari, Gabinetto del Prefetto, seconda serie, Cat. II e III (Personale dell'amministrazione dell'interno).

56 Letter of Sottoprefetto di Barletta to Sig. Prefetto di Bari, 30 June 1916, Archivio di Stato di Bari, Gabinetto del Prefetto, seconda

serie, b. 289, fasc. 54 (Barbangelo Carmelo, commissario di P.S.), n. 875 Gabinetto.

57 Letter of Questore di Bari to Sig. Prefetto di Bari, 18 May 1921, Archivio di Stato di Bari, Gabinetto del Prefetto, seconda serie, b. 288, fasc. 11 (Ancona Donato, Commissario di P.S.), n. 364 Gabinetto.

58 The description of the state of the police in Foggia province by the public prosecutor Francesco De Fortunato is "L'inaugurazione dell'anno giuridico al Tribunale di Lucera", *Il Foglietto*, 10 January 1904.

59 Letter to Dott. Castelli, 20 January 1910, Archivio di Stato di Bari, Gabinetto del Prefetto, seconda serie, b. 287, fasc. 15 (Amari Benedetto, 1907–10).

60 Letter to Prefetto di Bari, 27 February 1914, Archivio Centrale dello Stato, PS (1914), b. 18, fasc. "Bari", sottofasc. "Andria", n. 147.

The prefect of Bari, Camillo De Fabritiis, adopted a similar language in explaining the slow development of producers' cooperation in large measure to "local ethnic conditions" and the "tardy evolution of the [working] class". Letter to S.E. il Presidente Consiglio Ministri, 6 July 1920, Archivio Centrale dello Stato, PS (1920), b. 77, fasc. "Bari: disoccupazione".

61 *Inchiesta*, p.606.

62 Letter of the Prefetto di Foggia to Ministero dell'Interno, Direzione Generale della Pubblica Sicurezza, 18 November 1913, Archivio Centrale dello Stato, PS (1913), b. 22, fasc. "Foggia". n. 1592.

63 On the methods of electoral abuse, see Gaetano Salvemini, "Fu l'Italia prefascista una democrazia?", *Il Ponte*, VIII (1952), pp.11–23; 166–81; and 281–97. Accounts of electoral violence were widely reported in the press during election campaigns. An example for the campaign of 1907 at Ruvo is "Le scene di Ruvo", *Corriere delle Puglie*, 2 July 1907. See also "Nelle tre Puglie", *Corriere delle Puglie*, 1 July 1907.

The most extensive official reports on abuses are to be found in the series of reports by the authorities on the elections of 1914. These reports are to be found in Archivio di Stato di Bari, Prefettura di Bari: Gabinetto fasc. 260, sottofasc. 7 (Elezioni generali amministrative). The account here is based primarily on these documents.

64 *Ibid.*

65 "Il commissario Prina in tribunale", *Corriere delle Puglie*, 9 and 10 November 1909.

66 A full discussion of the methods adopted by De Bellis is provided by Gaetano Salvemini, *Il ministro della mala vita* in *Opere*, vol. I (Milan, 1962), pp. 72–83.

67 The more authentic sentiments of his constituents were revealed rather more clearly by the aftermath of the election in Conversano. The announcement of De Bellis's success set off a massive riot that was put down by the infantry, who charged the crowd with fixed bayonets. The shouts of the crowd were indicative: "Down with De Bellis!", "Death to De Bellis!", and "shouts hostile to the government and to our institutions". "Una giornata di tumulti a Conversano", *Corriere delle Puglie*, 9 July 1908.

68 "Nuovi scandali", *Il Foglietto*, 1 September 1907.

69 For the regulations of the municipal guard at Cerignola see "Regolamento per le Guardie Municipali della Città di Cerignola", 5 November 1869, Archivio Comunale di Cerignola, cart. 120, fasc. 5.

70 Archivio Comunale di Cerignola, cat. 3 (Polizia Urbana e Rurale), cart. 118, fasc. "Stato nominativo degli individui componenti il corpo della guardia urbana in Cerignola – 1829".

71 Luigi Colonna, "Cenni monografici sull'agro altamurano", *La Puglia Agricola*, II (1879), p.4.

72 Commissario Prefettizio Palmieri, "Relazione d'inchiesta: S. Giovanni Rotondo, Amministrazione Comunale", 31 August 1907, Archivio di Stato di Foggia, Sottoprefettura di San Severo, fascio 458, fascicolo 11–3(1907).

73 "La verità sui fatti di Ruvo", *La Conquista*, 22 September 1907.

74 "Nelle tre Puglie", *Corriere delle Puglie*, 13 September and 26 November 1913.

75 Letter of Delegato di P.S. D'Alena to Sottoprefetto di Barletta, 24 February 1914, Archivio Centrale dello Stato, PS (1914), b. 18, fasc. "Bari", sottofasc. "Andria", n. 146.

76 Telegram of Prefetto di Bari to Ministero dell'Interno, 16 May 1914, Archivio Centrale dello Stato, PS (1914), b. 18, fasc. "Bari", sottofasc. "Canosa", n. 780.

77 "La mala vita diplomatica di Cerignola", *Il Randello*, 17 June 1906.

78 "Gli sciacalli di Cerignola", *Il Randello*, 13 September 1914.

79 "La verità sui fatti di Ruvo", *La Conquista*, 22 September 1907.
80 *Ibid.*
81 Pistillo, *Giuseppe Di Vittorio*, pp.80–2.
82 Francesco Ciccotti, "L'agitazione agraria nelle Puglie", *Avanti!*, 24 September 1907.
83 "L'agitazione agraria in provincia", *Corriere delle Puglie*, 19 September 1907.
84 "Il movimento agrario", *Avanti!*, 3 June 1908.
85 For accounts of the massacre at Gioia, see "La Tragedia del luglio a Gioia del Colle", *Puglia Rossa*, 2 July 1920 and 11 July 1920; and Alfredo Violante, "Le Tragiche giornate di Gioia del Colle", *Corriere delle Puglie*, 3 July 1920.
86 Rough draft of letter by the mayor of Cerignola, 25 January 1914, Archivio Comunale di Cerignola, Cat. 15 (Pubblica Sicurezza), cart. 344, fasc. "Scioperi effettuati nel 1914".
87 Lajolo, *Il volto umano di un rivoluzionario*, p.24.
88 *Ibid.*, pp.21–3.

8 The Great War

1 A social history of the war years in Italy has yet to be written, in good part because the necessary records for the reconstruction of life in Italy during the conflict – the archives of the armed forces and of the economic ministries – have never been opened to the public. My account here is greatly influenced by Piero Melograni, *Storia politica della grande guerra* (Bari, 1969).
2 The "relazione morale" by Giuseppe Musacchio is in "Tornata del 21 febbraio 1919", Archivio Comunale di Gravina, Deliberazioni del Consiglio Comunale, 1919.
3 "Tornata del 5 Settembre 1914", Archivio Comunale di Gravina, Deliberazioni della Giunta, 1914.
4 "Tornata del 7 novembre 1916", Archivio Comunale di Gravina, Deliberazioni della Giunta, 1916.
5 Giansiro Ferrata and Niccolo Gallo, eds., *2000 pagine di Gramsci* (Milan, 1964), vol. I, p.405.
6 Giuseppe Di Vittorio, "Intorno alla situazione di Cerignola", *Corriere delle Puglie*, 3 February 1922.
7 "Dalle Murge al mare", *Puglia Rossa*, 13 February 1921.

8 "Alle donne di Puglia", *Corriere delle Puglie*, 20 January 1918.

9 Letter of Tenente Generale Comandante del Corpo d'Armata to Sigg. Prefetti delle Provincie di Bari, Catanzaro, Cosenza, Lecce, Potenza, Reggio Calabria, 28 May 1918, Archivio di Stato di Bari, Gabinetto del Prefetto, seconda serie, b. 149, fasc. "Disertori".

10 Letter of Prefetto Camillo De Fabritiis to S.E. il Prof. Francesco Nitti, Presidente del Consiglio dei Ministri, 3 May 1920, Archivio Centrale dello Stato, PS (1920), b. 77, fasc. "Bari: disoccupazione".

11 "Il contributo meridionale alla guerra", *Corriere delle Puglie*, 5 September 1918.

12 For the text of the resolution voted by the Andria town council, see "Estratto del registro delle deliberazioni del consiglio comunale di Andria, Tornata del 9 agosto 1914", Archivio di Stato di Bari, Gabinetto del Prefetto di Bari, cart. 14, fasc. 3.

13 "I nemici, gli stranieri non son lungi, ma son qui", *Il Randello*, 17–18 April 1915.

14 Letter of Tenente Generale Comandante del Corpo d'Armata to Sigg. Prefetti delle Provincie di Bari, Catanzaro, Cosenza, Lecce, Potenza, Reggio Calabria, 28 May 1918, Archivio di Stato di Bari, Gabinetto del Prefetto, seconda serie, b. 149, fasc. "Disertori".

15 The list of promises, together with the names of those taking part at the meetings, is based on the following reports and open letters in the press: "Cronaca di Bari", *Corriere delle Puglie*, 4 February 1918; D.A. Spada, "La terra ai contadini!", *Corriere delle Puglie*, 10 February 1918; "Nelle tre Puglie", *Corriere delle Puglie*, 12 February 1918; Giovanni Colella, "Il problema della terra ai conta dini", *Corriere delle Puglie*, 23 February 1918; Luigi Vivarelli, "La terra ai contadini", *Corriere delle Puglie*, 26 February 1918; Sabino Fiorese, "Per la terra ai combattenti", *Corriere delle Puglie*, 28 February 1918; "Cronaca di Bari", *Corriere delle Puglie*, 10, 12, 13 March 1918; Diego Laudati, "A proposito della terra ai contadini", *Corriere delle Puglie*, 17 March 1918; "Per l'agricoltura e per le tariffe doganali", *Corriere delle Puglie*, 18 March 1918; and "Cronaca di Bari", *Corriere delle Puglie*, 2 April and 7 July 1918.

For the assurances given by the deputy Codacci-Pisanelli in the Chamber of Deputies, see *Atti del parlamento italiano*, Camera dei Deputati, Legislatura XXIV, Sessione 1913–19, vol. XVII, pp. 1847–8.

16 Giuseppe Di Vittorio, "Intorno alla situazione di Cerignola",

Corriere delle Puglie, 3 February 1922.
17 "Per i fatti di Andria", *Corriere delle Puglie*, 6 December 1919.

9 The Closed Shop

1 "Mano d'opera agricola e prigionieri", *Corriere delle Puglie*, 3 April 1919.
On the official demand by the Andria farm workers' league for an end to the use of prisoners, see letter of Sottoprefetto di Barletta to Sig. Prefetto di Bari, 8 April 1919, Archivio di Stato di Bari, Gabinetto del Prefetto di Bari, cart. 205, fasc. 67/1 (Andria: ordine pubblico), n. 455 Gabinetto.

2 Letter of Direttore della Cattedra di Agricoltura per la Provincia di Bari to Sig. Prefetto della Provincia di Bari, 26 September 1920, Archivio di Stato di Bari, Gabinetto del Prefetto di Bari, cart. 202, fasc. 39 (Gioia del Colle: invasione terreni), n. 1273.

3 Telegram of Prefetto di Bari to Ministero dell'Interno, 2 June 1920, Archivio di Stato di Bari, Gabinetto del Prefetto, cart. 188, fasc. "Mietitura: carteggio col Ministero", n. 10399.

4 An extensive report on unemployment in Bari province in 1920 is "Relazione della commissione governativa per la disoccupazione in provincia di Bari", Archivio Centrale dello Stato, PS (1920), b. 77, fasc. "Bari: disoccupazione".

5 "L'approvvigionamento granario", *Corriere delle Puglie*, 16 December 1919.

6 Speech of 2 August 1920, in *Atti del parlamento italiano: Camera dei Deputati*, Legislatura XXV, Sessione 1919–20, Discussioni, vol. V, pp. 4645 ff. The various abuses outlined above were carefully considered in this speech.
The sheer inability of the population of Lecce province to comprehend the bureaucratic complexities of the rationing system gave rise to a widespread unrest, as the prefect reported. Telegram of Prefetto di Lecce to Ministero dell'Interno, 8 July 1920, Archivio Centrale dello Stato, PS (1920), b. 88, fasc. "Lecce (agitazione agraria)", n. 84.

7 "Relazione della commissione governativa per la disoccupazione in provincia di Bari", Archivio Centrale dello Stato, PS (1920), b. 77, fasc. "Bari: disoccupazione", pp. 35–6.

8 On the national level, the term "Red Years" (*biennio rosso*) is nor-

mally used with reference to 1919 and 1920 alone. In Apulia, however, the revolutionary ferment lasted until the end of 1921.

9 For an account of the events at Nardò, see Report of Prefetto Limongelli to Ministero dell'Interno, Direzione Generale della Pubblica Sicurezza, Archivio Centrale dello Stato, PS (1920), b. 88, fasc. "Lecce (agitazione agraria)", n. 456.

10 Report of the Prefetto di Foggia to S.E. il Ministro dell'Interno (Gabinetto), 26 July 1919, Archivio Centrale dello Stato, PS (1919), b. 98, fasc. "Foggia", sottofasc. "Ordine pubblico", n. 2374.

11 Report of Prefetto di Bari to Ministero dell'Interno, 28 June 1919, Archivio Centrale dello Stato, PS (1920), b. 77, fasc. "Bari: agitazione agraria", n. 13089.

12 For a general account of the occupations in Bari province in 1919 and 1920, see "Relazione della commissione governativa per la disoccupazione in provincia di Bari", Archivio Centrale dello Stato, PS (1920), b. 77, fasc. "Bari: disoccupazione", pp.27–9.

13 Letter of Prefetto di Foggia Ferrara to Ministero dell'Interno. Ufficio Riservato P.S., 4 October 1919, Archivio Centrale dello Stato, PS (1919), b. 98, fasc. "Foggia", fasc. "Agitazione agraria", n. 1387/M/A.

14 "La lotta agraria a Spinazzola", *Puglia Rossa*, 12 September 1920.

15 Pierleone Abruzzese, "La Puglia nel dopo-guerra", *Corriere delle Puglie*, 9 February 1922. Abruzzese was an important landlord.

16 Telegram of Prefetto di Bari De Fabritiis to Ministero dell'Interno, 17 May 1920, Archivio Centrale dello Stato, PS (1920), b. 77, fasc. "Bari: disoccupazione", sottofasc. "Andria", n. 943.

17 Report of Spinetti to Ministero dell'Interno, Direzione Generale della Pubblica Sicurezza, 20 February 1920, Archivio Centrale dello Stato, PS (1920), b. 77, fasc. "Agitazione agraria" (1), n. 915.

18 Report of Prefetto di Bari Ferrara to Ministero dell'Interno, 29 March 1920, Archivio Centrale dello Stato, PS (1920), b. 77, fasc. "Bari e approvvigionamento", n. 728.

19 The demands of the provincial league federation in Bari province are considered in "Le richieste degli agrari e dei lavoratori del barese al prefetto", *Corriere delle Puglie*, 21 May 1920.

20 Report of Prefetto di Foggia to Ministero dell'Interno, Direzione Generale della Pubblica Sicurezza, 11 June 1920, Archivio Centrale dello Stato, PS (1920), b. 85, fasc. "Foggia (agitazione per uso civico di pesca)", n. 215.

21 Report of Prefetto di Bari to Ministero dell'Interno, Direzione Generale della Pubblica Sicurezza, 15 June 1920, Archivio Centrale dello Stato, PS (1920), b. 79, fasc. "Agitazione agraria" (1), n. 1086.

22 Telegram of Prefetto di Bari to Ministero dell'Interno, 1 June 1920, Archivio Centrale dello Stato, PS (1920), b. 77, fasc. "Agitazione agraria" (1), n. 949.

23 D.A. Spada, "Agricoltori e sindacalismo di classe", *Corriere delle Puglie*, 18 January 1920.

24 Letter of the Associazione degli Agricoltori di Spinazzola to S.E. il Presidente dei Ministri, 30 September 1920, Archivio Centrale dello Stato, PS (1920), b. 77, fasc. "Bari: disoccupazione".

25 Telegram to S.E. il Ministro dell'Interno, 6 May 1920, Archivio Centrale dello Stato, PS (1920), b. 85, fasc. "Foggia (agitazione per diritto civico di pesca)".

26 Letter of Avv. Francesco Addario Chieco, Presidente, Associazione Agricoltori di Corato, to Prefetto della Provincia di Bari, 28 June 1919, Archivio di Stato di Bari, Gabinetto del Prefetto di Bari, cart. 188, fasc. 2 (Mietitura).

27 Report of Prefetto di Bari to Ministero dell'Interno, 20 May 1920, Archivio Centrale dello Stato, PS (1920), b. 77, fasc. "Bari: disoccupazione", sottofasc. "Andria".

28 Report of Prefetto di Bari to Ministero dell'Interno: Ufficio Riservato P.S., 11 July 1920, Archivio Centrale dello Stato, PS (1920), b. 77, fasc. "Agitazione agraria" (1), n. 15738.

29 "Nelle tre Puglie", *Corriere delle Puglie*, 21 March 1920.

30 "Lo sciopero dei contadini proclamato in tutta la provincia", *Corriere delle Puglie*, 2 June 1920.

31 The text of the Bari agreement is "Concordato Generale", 3 November 1920, Archivio di Stato di Bari, Gabinetto del Prefetto di Bari, cart. 188, fasc. "Concordato per le tariffe agrarie".

32 The text of the Foggia agreement is "Tariffa per i lavori agricoli concordati fra gli agricoltori ed i contadini di Foggia", 24 May 1920, Archivio di Stato di Bari, Gabinetto del Prefetto di Bari, cart. 188, fasc. "Foggia: Condizioni dello spirito pubblico in provincia".

33 "Nelle tre Puglie", *Corriere delle Puglie*, 12 June 1919.

34 See, respectively, Letter of the Fascio della Democrazia, n.d., Archivio Centrale dello Stato, PS (1921), b. 67, fasc. "Foggia", sottofasc. "Seduta consiglio municipale"; and Resolution of the

Associazione Agraria di San Severo, 24 February 1921, Archivio Centrale dello Stato, PS (1921), b. 67, fasc. "Foggia", sottofasc. "Seduta consiglio municipale".

35 Letter of the Fascio della Democrazia, *op. cit.*

36 Resolution of the Associazione Agraria di San Severo, *op. cit.*

37 Report to Ill/mo. Sig. Gr. Uff. Avv. Giacomo Vigliani, Direttore Generale della Pubblica Sicurezza, Ministero dell'Interno, 26 July 1920, Archivio Centrale dello Stato, PS (1920) b. 77, fasc. "Bari: disoccupazione", n. 877.

38 "Ordine del giorno della Federazione Agraria di Cerignola", 19 May 1921, Archivio Centrale dello Stato, PS (1922), b. 67, fasc. "Foggia: agitazione agraria".

39 Telegram of Prefect of Bari to Ministero dell'Interno, 30 March 1920, Archivio Centrale dello Stato, PS (1920), b. 77, fasc. "Bari: disoccupazione", sottofasc. "Andria", n. 943.

40 Telegram to Ministero dell'Interno, Pubblica Sicurezza, 10 April 1920, Archivio Centrale dello Stato, PS (1920), b. 77, fasc. "Agitazione agraria" (1), n. 4319.

41 Letter to S.E. il Presidente Consiglio Ministri, 6 July 1920, Archivio Centrale dello Stato, PS (1920), b. 77, fasc. "Bari: disoccupazione".

42 Report of De Fabritiis to Ministero dell'Interno, 20 May 1920, Archivio Centrale dello Stato, PS (1920), b. 77, fasc. "Bari: disoccupazione", sottofasc. "Andria".

43 Report to S.E. il Presidente Consiglio Ministri, 23 November 1920, Archivio Centrale dello Stato, PS (1920), b. 77, fasc. "Bari: disoccupazione", n. 1924.

44 For the terms of the Visocchi Decree, cf. Valerio Castronovo, "La storia economica", in *Storia d'Italia*, vol. IV (1) (Turin, 1975), p.235.

45 The occupation of the factories has been much studied. An excellent brief account is Paolo Spriano, *L'occupazione delle fabbriche* (Turin, 1964).

46 Letter of Direttore, Associazione Agraria Cooperativa Andriese to Spett. Confederazione Generale degli Agricoltori Italiani, 30 April 1920, Archivio Centrale dello Stato, PS (1920), b. 77, fasc. "Agitazione agraria" (1).

47 Report to Ministero dell'Interno, Direzione Generale della Pubblica Sicurezza, 5 January 1921, Archivio Centrale dello Stato, PS (1922), b. 67, fasc. "Foggia (agitazione agraria)", n. 2.

10 Fascism

1 Report of Ispettore Generale di PS D'Orazi to l'on. Sig. Direttore Generale della Pubblica Sicurezza, 11 July 1922, Archivio Centrale dello Stato, PS (1922), b. 111, fasc. "Bari", sottofasc. "Andria".

2 Telegram of Prefetto Olivieri to Ministero dell'Interno, Direzione Generale della Pubblica Sicurezza, 5 July 1922, Archivio Centrale dello Stato, PS (1922), b. 111, fasc. "Bari", sottofasc. "Andria", n. 16388.

3 *Ibid.*, n. 16324.

4 A brief account of the rise of fascism in Cerignola is Giuseppe Di Vittorio, "Intorno alla situazione di Cerignola", *Corriere delle Puglie*, 3 February 1922.

5 A discussion of the origins of fascism at Minervino Murge is Report of Ispettore Generale di PS Secchi to l'on. Sig. Direttore Generale della Pubblica Sicurezza, 17 June 1921, Archivio Centrale dello Stato, PS (1921), b. 92, fasc. "Bari: fasci di combattimento" (2). On *limongellismo* cf. also "Dalle Murge al mare," *Puglia Rossa*, 7 November 1920.

6 On the leading role of the Spinazzola *fascio*, see Telegram of Prefetto Olivieri to Ministero dell'Interno, 11 March 1922, Archivio Centrale dello Stato, PS (1922), b. Bari, sottofasc. "Spinazzola", n. 609. The background and influence of Salvatore Addis are outlined in Telegram of Prefetto De Fabritiis to Ministero dell'Interno, 19 May 1921, Archivio Centrale dello Stato, PS (1921), b. 92, fasc. "Bari: fasci di combattimento" (2), n. 1125.

7 On the origins of fascism in the Po Valley, see Luigi Preti, *Le lotte agrarie nella valle padana* (Truin, 1955); Alessandro Roveri, *Le origini del fascismo a Ferrara, 1918–1921* (Milan, 1974); Paul Corner, *Fascism in Ferrara, 1915–1925* (Oxford, 1975); Anthony L. Cardoza, *Agrarian Elites and Fascism: The Province of Bologna, 1901–1926* (Princeton, 1982).

8 This alternative agrarian programme was explained in an interview by D.A. Spada, "Corriere dell'ultima ora", *Corriere delle Puglie*, 17 February 1921.

9 Letter of Prefetto Generale Raffaele De Vita to Sig. Com. Cesare Rossi, 20 October 1923, Archivio Centrale dello Stato PS (1923) b. 53, fasc. "Bari", sottofasc. "Agitazione agraria", n. 1812.

10 Letter of Direttore Generale della Pubblica Sicurezza to l'on.

Gabinetto, SS di Stato per l'Interno, 6 July 1922, Archivio Centrale dello Stato PS (1922), b. 111, fasc. "Bari", sottofasc. "Andria", b. 18404.

11 "La situazione politica della Capitanata", *Corriere delle Puglie*, 12 January 1922.

12 Report of Ispettore Generale di PS Secchi to l'on. Sig. Direttore Generale della Pubblica Sicurezza, 17 June 1921, Archivio Centrale dello Stato, PS (1921), b. 92, fasc. "Bari: fasci di combattimento" (2).

13 On the role of criminals at San Nicandro and at Bari, Barletta, and Spinazzola, see Report of Prefetto Pugliese to Ministero dell'Interno, Direttore Generale della Pubblica Sicurezza, 14 July 1922, and Telegram of Prefetto De Fabritiis to Ministero dell'Interno, 28 February 1921, Archivio Centrale dello Stato, PS (1922), b. 126, fasc. "Foggia", sottofasc. "S. Nicandro Garganico", n. 17259 and b. 92, fasc. "Bari: fasci di combattimento" (1), n. 6727. Cf. also "Dal bastone austriaco al bastone fascista", *Puglia Rossa*, 3 April 1921.

14 Letter of Sindaco di Corato to S.E. il Ministro dell'Interno, 7 June 1921, Archivio Centrale dello Stato, PS (1921), b. 92, fasc. "Bari: fasci di combattimento" (2).

15 Letter of Francesco Fato to CC dei fasci, 9 September 1921, Archivio Centrale dello Stato, Mostra della Rivoluzione Fascista, b. E, fasc. "Bari", cart. 2, n. 47.

16 Report of Ispettore Generale di PS Secchi to l'on. Sig. Direttore Generale della Pubblica Sicurezza, 17 June 1921, Archivio Centrale dello Stato, PS (1921), b. 92, fasc. "Bari: fasci di combattimento" (2). Cf. also Telegram of Prefetto De Fabritiis to Ministero dell'Interno, 28 February 1921, Archivio Centrale dello Stato, PS (1921), b. 92, fasc. "Bari: fasci di combattimento" (1), n. 6727.

17 Letter of Giordani to l'on. Direzione del PNF, June 1922, Archivio Centrale dello Stato, Mostra della Rivoluzione Fascista, b. E, fasc. "Bari", cart. 2, n. 100.

18 For the politics of the ANC in Apulia, cf. Simona Colarizi, *Dopoguerra e fascismo in Puglia (1919–1926)* (Bari, 1971), pp.15–26.

19 For analyses of fascism at S. Nicandro Garganico see Report of Ispettore Generale di PS D'Orazi to S.E. il Sottosegretario di Stato, Ministero dell'Interno, 28 August 1922, and Letter of Prefetto di Foggia to Ministero dell'Interno, Direzione Generale della Pubblica

Sicurezza, 17 February 1922, n. 591, Archivio Centrale dello Stato, PS (1922), b. 67, fasc. "Foggia: ordine pubblico".

20 On the major role of Dino Perrone Compagni in the organization of Apulian squadrism, see Telegram of Prefetto di Firenze Pericoli to Ministero dell'Interno, Direzione Generale della Pubblica Sicurezza, 13 September 1922), n. 3225 and Report of Prefetto di Foggia Pugliese to Ministero dell'Interno, Direzione Generale della Pubblica Sicurezza, 3 August 1922, n. 2837, in Archivio Centrale dello Stato, PS (1922), b. 126, fasc. "Foggia: San Nicandro Garganico".

21 On the events of Andria, see Archivio Centrale dello Stato, PS (1922), b. 111, fasc. "Bari", sottofasc. "Andria".

22 Report of Direttore Generale della Pubblica Sicurezza to l'on. Gabinetto di S.E. il Ministro dell'Interno, 14 October 1921, Archivio Centrale dello Stato, Ministero dell'Interno: Gabinetto Bonomi, b. 1, fasc. "Bari", n. 27459.

23 Telegram to Ministero dell'Interno, Direzione Generale della Pubblica Sicurezza, 23 May 1921, ACS, PS (1921), b. 92, fasc. "Bari: fasci di combattimento" (1), n. 19665.

24 Report to Sig. Direttore Generale della Pubblica Sicurezza, n.d., Archivio Centrale dello Stato, PS (1922), b. 126, fasc. "Foggia", sottofasc. "Cerignola".

25 "Concordato fra proprietari e lavoratori", 7 June 1922, Archivio Centrale dello Stato, PS (1922), b. 67, fasc. "Foggia, agitazione agraria".

26 Letter to Achille Starace, n.d. (but August 1922), Archivio Centrale dello Stato, MRF, b. D., fasc. "Andria", cart. 3, n. 110.

27 "I fatti di Toscana: lezioni da non dimenticare", *L'Ordine Nuovo*, 8 March 1921.

28 "Lo stato dei sindacati", *L'Ordine Nuovo*, 6 March 1921.

29 "Intorno alle gesta delle bande bianche", *Avanti!*, 6 March 1921.

30 On the events of the general strike of February 1921, see *Corriere delle Puglie*, 24 and 27 February 1921, and 1 March 1921. Cf. also Telegrams of Prefetto De Fabritiis to Ministero dell'Interno, Direzione Generale della Pubblica Sicurezza, 23 and 24 February 1921, Archivio Centrale dello Stato, PS (1921) fasc. "Bari: fasci di combattimento" (1), n. 512.

31 On the Bari uprising see Archivio Centrale dello Stato, PS (1923), b. 53, fasc. "Bari", sottofasc. "Sciopero generale politico".

32 Letter of Giuseppe Di Vittorio, 6 December 1921, Archivio Centrale dello Stato, PS (1921), b. 97, fasc. "Foggia", sottofasc. "Cerignola".

33 Telegram of Limongelli to Ministero dell'Interno, Direzione Generale della Pubblica Sicurezza, 13 December 1919, Archivio Centrale dello Stato, PS (1919), b. 100, fasc. "Lecce (agitazione agraria)", n. 18871.

34 Telegram of Corradini to S.E. Ministro Guerra, 29 May 1921, Archivio Centrale dello Stato, PS (1922), b. 67, fasc. "Foggia (agitazione agraria)", n. 12821. See also Letter of Prefetto di Foggia to S.E. Camillo Corradini, 27 May 1921, Archivio Centrale dello Stato, *ibid.*

35 Letter of De Fabritiis, 28 February 1921, Archivio Centrale dello Stato, PS (1921), b. 92, fasc. "Bari: fasci di combattimento" (2), n. 526.

36 Telegram of De Fabritiis to Ministero dell'Interno, 19 May 1921, *ibid.*, n. 1125.

37 The reports in the files of the Ministry of the Interior documenting the collusion of the authorities in Apulia with fascism are too numerous to be listed. Significance examples include:

Report of Ispettore Generale di PS Secchi to l'on. Sig. Direttore Generale della Pubblica Sicurezza, 17 June 1921, Archivio Centrale dello Stato, PS (1921), b. 92, fasc. "Bari: fasci di combattimento" (2).

Telegram of Ispettore Generale di PS Gaudino to Ministero dell'Interno, Direzione Generale della Pubblica Sicurezza, 25 February 1921, Archivio Centrale dello Stato, PS (1921), b. 92, fasc. "Bari: fasci di combattimento" (1), n. 6279.

Telegrams of Bonomi to Prefetto di Bari, 2 and 6 August 1921 Archivio Centrale dello Stato, Ministero dell'Interno, Gabinetto Bonomi, b. 1, fasc. "Bari".

Letter of Sottoprefetto di Barletta Di Sanza to Sig. Prefetto di Bari, 17 October 1921, Archivio di Stato di Bari, cart. 206, fasc. 70 (1921: Ordine pubblico, circondario di Barletta), sottofasc. 5 (Minervino), n. 556.

38 Telegram of Bonomi to Prefetto di Bari, 6 August 1921, Archivio Centrale dello Stato, PS (1921), b. 92, fasc. "Bari: fasci di combattimento" (2), n. 18527.

39 Cf. Telegrams to Ministero dell'Interno, Direzione Generale della

Pubblica Sicurezza, 6 January 1922 and 26 March 1922, Archivio Centrale dello Stato, PS (1922), b. 126, fasc. "Foggia", sottofasc. "Cerignola", n. 63 and n. 1151.

40 On the collusion between the police at Cerignola and fascism, see Report of Ispettore Generale di PS Secchi to Direttore Generale della Pubblica Sicurezza n.d., Archivio Centrale dello Stato, PS (1921), b. 97, fasc. "Foggia", and Telegram of Prefetto Pugliese to Ministero dell'Interno, Direzione Generale della Pubblica Sicurezza, 4 May 1922, Archivio Centrale dello Stato, PS (1922), b. 126, fasc. "Foggia", sottofasc. "Cerignola", b. 10181. Cf. also Colarizi, *Dopoguerra e fascismo*, pp.146–8.

41 Letter of 6 December 1921, Archivio Centrale dello Stato, PS (1921), b. 97, fasc. "Foggia", sottofasc. "Cerignola".

INDEX

Printed in the United States
64240LVS00002B/137